MW00529443

Thus Spoke Zarathustra
(Selections)

Also sprach Zarathustra
(Auswahl)

FRIEDRICH NIETZSCHE

A Dual-Language Book

Edited and Translated by
STANLEY APPELBAUM

DOVER PUBLICATIONS, INC.
Mineola, New York

Bibliographical Note

This Dover edition, first published in 2004, is a new selection of complete chapters from the German work originally published between 1883 and 1885 (see the Introduction for bibliographical details), together with a new English translation by Stanley Appelbaum, who also supplied the Introduction, the footnotes, and the summaries of the chapters not included.

International Standard Book Number: 0-486-43711-6

Manufactured in the United States of America
Dover Publications, Inc., 31 East 2nd Street, Mineola, N.Y. 11501

CONTENTS

iii

iv

Contents

Dritter Teil / Part Three

Vierter und letzter Teil / Fourth and Last Part

INTRODUCTION

Nietzsche's Life and Major Works

Nietzsche was born in 1844 in Röcken, near the larger town of Lützen, not far to the southwest of the great Saxon metropolis Leipzig. Röcken was in the Prussian province of Saxony, formerly the northern half of that kingdom, annexed by Prussia in 1815 because Saxony had abetted Napoleon. Nietzsche was born on October 15, the birthday of Friedrich Wilhelm IV, king of Prussia (reigned 1840–1861), after whom he was named. His father, a Lutheran pastor, died in 1849 after a protracted cerebral ailment (*possibly* caused by a fall); biographers differ as to the extent of Nietzsche's lifelong traumatic reaction to this experience.

In 1850 the family moved the short distance to Naumburg, which was to be the home that Nietzsche could return to for as long as his mother lived (until 1897). By 1856 he was already suffering sporadically from sore eyes and headaches. Between October 1858 and September 1864 he attended the prestigious secondary school at nearby Schulpforta, a seedbed for philologists (students of Latin and Greek, primarily). During these years the boy began to write poems, and definitively lost his religious faith.

From October 1864 to August 1865 he studied theology (nevertheless!) and philology at the University of Bonn. In February 1865, as he once confided to a close friend, he paid a visit to a brothel in the closest big city, Cologne; he reported the outing as completely innocuous, but it may have been there that he contracted syphilis, if that is indeed what eventually drove him mad and killed him. (Other theories are that his madness, or brain condition, was inherited, the cause of his headaches, etc.; or that he contracted some awful disease while tending sick soldiers in 1870.)

From late 1865 to the summer of 1867, he studied philology (only) at the University of Leipzig; in this period he discovered the extremely stimulating philosophy of Schopenhauer. A projected year's

military service, beginning in October 1867, was cut short by an accident due to clumsiness, and by May 1868 Nietzsche was off active duty, though he never stopped boasting of his old days in the artillery as a noble warrior. Before the year was over, back in Leipzig, he met one of the most influential men in his life, Wagner, whose disciple he soon became (besides his innovative stage ideas, Wagner also cultivated serious social thought).

In February 1869 Nietzsche was invited to teach the classics at the University of Basel (and at a top secondary school there); various prerequisites were waived for the brilliant student. Answering the call, he necessarily became a Swiss citizen. In May he paid his first visit to the Wagners' villa near Lucerne. When war broke out between France and Prussia in 1870, Nietzsche wanted to serve, but now, as a Swiss, he could only volunteer as a medic in the Prussian army. After just a few days' work he developed dysentery and diphtheria; on recovering (if he ever did fully), he resumed his professional duties in Basel.

Ill health plagued him; in February 1871 he was granted time off to cure indigestion and insomnia. Later that year he failed in his attempt to acquire a chair in philosophy as well as philology. From the early 1870s on, he toyed frequently with thoughts of marriage; he was never truly committed to the idea, and no woman ever seems to have desired him as a mate.

In 1872 he published his first major work, the long essay *Die Geburt der Tragödie* (The Birth of Tragedy), summarizing many of his concepts of the few previous years. Classical scholars were alienated by his revolutionary view of Greek culture (the unruly spirit represented by Dionysus partially restrained by the rationality represented by Apollo; Euripides and Socrates as the excessively rational destroyers of Greek tragedy, with its dependence on Dionysus), by the lack of scholarly apparatus and afflatus, and by what looked like a shameless plug for Wagner as restorer of the Greek music drama.

In 1873, ill, with sore eyes, he began the work, eventually consisting of four medium-length essays on a variety of subjects, that would be called *Unzeitgemäße Betrachtungen* (Inopportune Thoughts; aka Untimely Meditations; Unfashionable Observations). The first essay was published in August 1873; the second and third, in 1874; and the fourth (his last good word about Wagner), in 1876. In 1875 he became quite ill, and had to request a short leave from teaching in February 1876 and then a year's leave beginning in October. In between, during the summer, he had attended the first complete *Ring des Nibelungen* performances at Bayreuth, but his honeymoon with

Wagner, who had been using him as a tool and who was no longer behaving like an *Übermensch,* was over.

In 1877 the leave from teaching was extended to Easter of 1878. Nietzsche resided in spas and in sunny Italy, participating in an orgy of futile matchmaking in Sorrento. By 1878 he was relieved of his secondary-school duties in Basel. During that year he published *Menschliches, Allzumenschliches* (Human, All Too Human), in which he states that even the loftiest human ideas are not divinely inspired, but are sublimations of earthly drives. Like the later *Morgenröte* (Dawn; also translated by every equivalent for "dawn") and *Die fröhliche Wissenschaft* (The Cheerful Body of Knowledge; usually called The Gay Science), *Menschliches* is in the form of quite brief individual sections which Nietzsche called aphorisms. Late in 1878 he became very ill again, and friends who hadn't seen him for a while reported that he was greatly altered in temperament.

In 1879 he published two supplements to *Menschliches* and was finally pensioned off by the university. He then began a life of incessant wandering, usually to warm and/or isolated places: too many to be listed in an Introduction of this modest length. Just as an example, in 1880 alone he resided in Riva del Garda, Venice, Marienbad, Stresa, and Genoa. In the summer of 1881 he paid his first visit to the village of Sils-Maria in the Engadine, where he had his revelation about the "eternal return" (or "recurrence") in August (more of this below, in the next section). In that year he published *Morgenröte,* his first direct attack on conventional Christian morality (in this book, the "will to power" appears as just one among other human drives; it is not yet the leading one).

The year 1882 was a crucial one, not only in Nietzsche's life as a whole, but also as preparatory experience for *Zarathustra.* In that year he met Lou von Salomé (later in life, Lou Andreas-Salomé), a Russian-born pioneering female student (1861–1937) of extremely emancipated views. (Subsequently she wrote stories and essays, and became the mistress of the poet Rilke and a close associate of Freud.) After meeting her in Rome (where the gurgling fountains inspired the "Nachtlied" in *Zarathustra*), Nietzsche contemplated a trial marriage or even a ménage à trois in which they would be joined by a male friend of his who knew her first. He thought he was deeply in love and had found the only true soulmate and helpmate for him (she was aloof), but he gave her up after the violent reactions she aroused in his mother and his possessive sister (Elisabeth; later, Elisabeth Förster-Nietzsche; 1846–1935). His resentment is clearly mirrored in

Zarathustra: in its misogyny, in its plaints of betrayal, and in its condemnation of compassion, which can be seen as equivalent to his family's "benevolent" interference.

Also in 1882, he published the first four parts of *Die fröhliche Wissenschaft,* in which he appears as a prejudice-free pan-European, and in which he tentatively introduces Zarathustra as a character and the concept of the "eternal return" (see the next section, which is entirely devoted to *Zarathustra,* the work that occupied most of his time and attention from the beginning of 1883 through the first third of 1885).

In the summer of 1885, he dictated to secretaries much of the material that ended up in the volume *Jenseits von Gut und Böse* (Beyond Good and Evil), published in 1886 by C[onstantin] G[eorg] Naumann in Leipzig (though Nietzsche paid for it, as he had for Part Four of *Zarathustra*). *Jenseits* is a relatively more traditionally philosophical formulation of ideas enunciated without demonstration in *Zarathustra;* like Nietzsche's next complete work, it is also in more regular essay form, the aphorisms being tucked into the running text. (In 1885 Nietzsche also worked on a fifth part to *Die fröhliche Wissenschaft.*)

In Sils-Maria, in July 1887, Nietzsche wrote *Zur Genealogie der Moral* (On the Genealogy of Morals), his version of the historical development of morality. It was published by early November. His books didn't sell, and he remained virtually unknown (magnifying in his mind each review that wasn't totally damning and each letter from an individual adherent). Thus he was greatly encouraged in 1888 by significant public evaluations of his work by such authors, critics, philosophers, and lecturers as Carl Spitteler in Switzerland and Georg Brandes in Denmark (and personal congratulations from the novelist and playwright August Strindberg in Sweden, also mentally unbalanced).

In the spring of that year Nietzsche thought he had found the ideal place to live in: Turin. There he wrote his anti-Wagner treatise *Der Fall Wagner* (The Wagner Case—"case" being either judicial or medical), which was published later in the year. In Sils-Maria, in the summer, he wrote *Die Götzen-Dämmerung* (The Twilight of the Idols; the title is a lampoon on that of the last part of Wagner's *Ring*), which elaborates on the will to power (he received advance copies in November; it was published early the next year). He was also planning a major four-part work to be called *Der Wille zur Macht: Versuch einer Umwertung aller Werte* (The Will to Power: Essay on the

Revaluation of All Values); the completed volume *Antichrist* may have represented to him the first part of this large work, or possibly all of it that he finally wished to write.

In the fall of 1888, he returned to Turin (this was to be his last change of residence under his own control). He then wrote the peculiar, megalomaniac autobiography *Ecce homo* (not published until 1908) in an effort to stimulate sales for his forthcoming philosophic pieces. He also compiled a sort of dossier of his dealings with the titan of Bayreuth in *Nietzsche contra Wagner.*

On January 3 he suffered a nervous breakdown on the street in Turin, and never regained all his wits. He immediately dashed off a series of letters indicative of delusions of grandeur. (The perfect wording of these letters belies those biographers who find no hint of incipient insanity in *Ecce homo* and many 1888 personal letters, just because the syntax is rational.) Later came clinics in Basel and Jena. He was released into his mother's care in 1890. A victim of creeping paralysis, he became more and more detached from the world. Meanwhile, he was taken over (in every sense of the term) by his sister, a proto-Nazi who later welcomed Hitler's advent. She destroyed and falsified documents, published waste scraps, and oversaw editions to suit her purposes (the *Wille zur Macht* published under her aegis has been called both Nietzsche's greatest work and a worthless, if not dangerous, omnium gatherum). She set up a Nietzsche Archive in Naumburg in 1894, moving it in 1896 to Weimar, where she and her brother's living corpse moved in 1897. He died on August 25, 1900.

There will probably never be an end to the discussions, not only of the nature of his madness, but also of how soon it manifested itself. Was drug addiction part of his problem? (He insisted on doctoring himself.) Was his hermitlike isolation a cause of his madness, or a result of it? And so on.

Besides the works mentioned above, Nietzsche wrote many lyric poems, minor essays, lectures, and letters. He was also a good pianist, a music lover of sometimes erratic tastes, and an amateur composer of piano and choral works.

Also sprach Zarathustra

Each of some half-dozen works written by Nietzsche in the 1880s has been called his finest, but *Also sprach Zarathustra* remains the most widely popular, and seems to have been the author's own favorite. Its

subtitle, not often cited, in *Ein Buch für Alle und Keinen* (A Book for Everybody and Nobody).

Part One (not so labeled until the second part appeared) was written at Rapallo in January 1883. Nietzsche mailed the typesetter's manuscript to the publisher from Genoa on February 14, the day after Wagner died in Venice. The typesetting was done between March 31 and April 26, with ongoing proofreading (Nietzsche was in Genoa). The volume was published some time between the end of April and the beginning of June (accounts differ); by the latter date the author was in Rome. The publisher, located in Chemnitz, was E[rnst] Schmeitzner, who had taken over some of Nietzsche's earlier titles when their original publisher, E[rnst] W[ilhelm] Fritzsch of Leipzig, went bankrupt in 1878. (In turn, Fritzsch was to buy up old Nietzsche stock from Schmeitzner in 1886.)

Part Two was prepared during the spring and summer of 1883, largely at Sils-Maria in July. The setting copy was written out during the first half of that month, then mailed to Schmeitzner. Proofreading was done from the end of July to the end of August, and the volume was published shortly thereafter.

Part Three occupied Nietzsche between the late summer of 1883 and the very beginning of 1884, when he was in Nice. Proofs were ready by late February, and Schmeitzner published the volume in March. For the moment Nietzsche thought that *Zarathustra* was concluded, but circumstances brought about an unintended fourth part. While at Menton and Nice in the winter 1884–85, he conceived of a new three-volume work to be called *Mittag und Ewigkeit* (Noonday and Eternity), and, dissatisfied with sales of his previous books (though he was more to blame than any publisher), he decided to leave Schmeitzner. Failing to find any publisher even after he had reduced his pretensions to one further volume of *Zarathustra* (and even after agreeing to a title change to disguise the fact that it was a continuation volume), he himself reluctantly paid for a small printing of Part Four (40 or 45 copies), prepared by the Leipzig publisher C[onstantin] G[eorg] Naumann. The writing was completed in Nice, and he read proof in Venice in March and April. The volume appeared in mid-April of 1885.

Unsold sets of pages of Parts One through Three were bound into single volumes by Fritzsch in 1887, but the particularly blasphemous fourth part didn't reach a broader readership until 1892, when the first complete *Zarathustra* appeared as part of an ill-fated first collected-works edition halted by Nietzsche's sister.

In his often hard-to-swallow *Ecce homo* Nietzsche declared that the writing of each part of *Zarathustra* had taken him ten days. One modern editor considers this possible if the "writing" is taken to mean the assemblage into finished form of numerous preliminary jottings over much greater time periods: because *Zarathustra,* too, is essentially a collection of aphorisms and maxims, though here they are skillfully gathered into Gospel-like prophetic sermons and parable-like incidents within a very loose narrative framework per part.

The real Zarathustra (Zerdusht; Zoroaster), who probably lived around 600 B.C., reputedly formulated the dualistic principles of pre-Islamic Persian religion. (In Nietzsche's day he was generally thought to date back to the second pre-Christian millennium.) To Nietzsche, according to *Ecce homo,* Zarathustra was the first philosopher to make a metaphysics out of morality, with truth as the highest virtue; Nietzsche boasted that *he,* the "immoralist," had gone beyond that primitive stance, and that his fictional hero successfully combated the historical Zarathustra's error.

Nietzsche, an ardent admirer of Emerson (in German translation), seems to have been attracted to the figure of Zarathustra by the New Englander's writings. In Emerson's essay "History," Zarathustra is merely mentioned by name as an ancient religious legislator. But the essay "Character" (the third essay in the second, 1844, collection), in which Emerson proclaims his belief in the influence of great men, no two of whom were alike, contains this crucial passage:

"The most credible pictures are those of majestic men who prevailed at their entrance, and convinced the senses; as happened to the eastern magian who was sent to test the merits of Zertusht or Zoroaster. When the Yunani sage arrived at Balkh, the Persians tell us, Gushtasp appointed a day on which the Mobeds of every country should assemble, and a golden chair was placed for the Yunani sage. Then the beloved of Yezdam, the prophet Zertusht, advanced into the midst of the assembly. The Yunani sage, on seeing that chief, said, 'This form and this gait cannot lie, and nothing but truth can proceed from them.'"

Zarathustra's name appears frequently in Nietzsche's notes (autumn 1881) for *Die fröhliche Wissenschaft* (published 1882), but in the published work (at the time, containing only the first four parts), it appears only in the final aphorism (section 342), the wording of which Nietzsche took over virtually verbatim as the first subsection of "Zarathustras Vorrede" in *Also sprach Zarathustra.* (The preceding section of *Die fröhliche Wissenschaft,* no. 341, contains the earliest

published adumbration of the "eternal return" concept, which Nietzsche later reported as having come to him in a blinding flash on August 26, 1881 near Sils-Maria. The thought in section 341 is: "How would you react if you learned you would have to relive your entire life in exactly the same way?" In *Zarathustra* and later works, Nietzsche makes it clear that his ideal hero would be glad to! One suspects that this idea originally preceded, and even entailed, the very shaky metaphysical concept that the "eternal return" is inevitable because time is infinite in either direction (any stasis at any point would have wrecked the whole thing, philosophically), whereas the number of possible combinations of events, though large, must be finite (why??), and thus history must repeat itself again and again. At any rate, in *Ecce homo* Nietzsche considers the "eternal return" to be the greatest human idea ever conceived, and the writing of *Also sprach Zarathustra* to be the greatest human achievement of all time.

Eschewing formal, scholastic reasoning in general, *Zarathustra* is a dithyrambic prophecy and one of the most remarkable German-language works: a "symphony" for the language in the sense that Rimsky-Korsakov called his *Scheherazade* a composition for the orchestra rather than a piece of music that just happened to get scored for many instruments. Truly untranslatable in detail, the language of *Zarathustra* abounds in every kind of wordplay, new thoughts often being conjured up by the sound of contiguous ones; and there is an extremely intricate network of leitmotifs. There are numerous allusions (often parodistic) to the New Testament, Wagner, Goethe, Shakespeare, and others, and the political situation of Nietzsche's own time (e.g., Bismarck's heavy-handed creation of the German Empire) is very much in evidence in the background.

Works are obviously included in this Dover dual-language series primarily as pieces of world literature, but the *Zarathustra* chapters included here also reflect the most important philosophic concepts in the book, such as the "death of God" (i.e., the bankruptcy of traditional Christian morality), with the subsequent need for a new morality and of a more evolved humanity to administrate it (the *Übermensch*), and the "will to power" (which, Nietzsche stated in *Ecce homo*, was inspired in him by his chronic illness). The repeated notion of the "spontaneously rolling wheel" was derived from the 1675 *Cherubinischer Wandersmann* by "Angelus Silesius" (Johann Scheffler; 1624–1677). The donkey festival (the most scandalous incident in Part Four) was suggested by the medieval Feast of Fools held between Christmas and New Year's as a holdover from the ancient

Roman Saturnalia (same time of the year); this mock feast, instituted for clerics in the eleventh century in a vain attempt to channel at least *their* seasonal boisterousness, sometimes included (chiefly in France) a Festum Asinarium, in celebration of the outstanding donkeys in the Bible, at which parody hymns were sung. (The long chapter in Part Three, "Von alten und neuen Tafeln," which purportedly sprang to Nietzsche's mind *en bloc* during a long hike from Nice, is useful among other things, as a general summary of the main philosophical concepts in the whole book.)

Scholars disagree on the extent to which the Zarathustra in the book is to be equated with Nietzsche himself; after all, he is a fictional character, and even his creator once warned against too close an identification, but the attempt by some writers at drastic differentiation seems misguided, not only because so many of the philosophical standpoints are so readily explainable in terms of Nietzsche's personal experiences and reactions to them, but also because he shows no hesitation throughout the book in proclaiming his own real preferences in food, climate, pastimes, etc., as being those of Zarathustra (and, presumably, the only ones to be taken seriously).

Known only to a few kindred spirits until the very end of his life, Nietzsche's work rapidly became more widely appreciated by the 1890s. This is strikingly evidenced by the early use, made by three great composers, of texts and concepts from *Also sprach Zarathustra.* In 1896 Richard Strauss wrote his famous tone poem of that name (the opening motif of which became wildly popular after its use in Stanley Kubrick's 1968 film *2001: A Space Odyssey*), and Mahler set the "Trunknes Lied" in the fourth movement of his Third Symphony. In 1909 Delius compiled the text of *Eine Messe des Lebens* (A Mass of Life) from *Zarathustra*.

In literature, philosophy, psychology, and other fields Nietzsche's influence in the twentieth century was incalculable. Freud is said to have developed his theory of the ego from some passages in *Zarathustra*. The Surrealists and Existentialists looked up to Nietzsche, and with his skeptical and perspectivistic questioning of values he was a model for Postmodernist thinkers.

Of course, the twentieth-century group most closely associated with Nietzsche's ideas (largely because of his sister's machinations) was the Nazis, who battened on his "will to power," "superman," "master race," "thousand-year Reich," "degeneracy," rejection of compassion, and love of war. Obviously, they distorted many of his views (his superman was a supermoralist, not a superthug), but he cannot be

completely absolved from some of the brutal real-life consequences of his doctrines; for instance, his love of war has been explained away as meaning that "strife" or "contention" makes the world go round (in a pre-Socratic cosmological way), but his eagerness to serve in the Prussian army and his specific declarations in *Ecce homo* point to a genuine love of war in the most literal fashion.

The Nature of This Edition

The German text of *Zarathustra* in the present volume is based on that published prior to 1900 in the Großoktavausgabe (Large Octavo Edition) of Nietzsche's works published from 1894 onward by the above-mentioned firm of Naumann. The spelling and punctuation are discreetly adapted to the German usage of most of the twentieth century (e.g., *dies, Tier, Kamel* replacing the original *diess, Thier, Kameel*), but without altering and falsifying Nietzsche's very personal capitalization, compound forms, etc. A special feature of our German text is the use of italics instead of letter spacing to emphasize words; this not only saves space, but also avoids many uncertainties, particularly in very short words.

The limitation of volume length, requested by the publisher, made it necessary to include only about one third of the work, but the most famous (or notorious) key concepts appear here, with a great variety of moods and modes, and the full linguistic scope from the highflown near-biblical to the tinkly and scurrilous.

Included here are: from Part One (naturally emphasized as being the opening exposition), the Prologue and 10 of the 22 chapters; from Part Two (in which the daring statements of Part One are grounded a little more systematically), 7 of the 22 chapters; from Part Three (which, very diverse, ranges from the "eternal return" revelation to the scatology of "Vom Vorübergehen" and the broad summation of "Von alten und neuen Tafeln"), 6 of the 16 chapters (but one of those six is the longest chapter in the whole work); and from Part Four (which has the most thoroughgoing narrative framework, and takes place in one day), 5 of 20 chapters. Altogether, we have here the Prologue and 28 out of 80 chapters. The first and last chapters of each part are included, and each chapter is complete.

The omitted chapters are summarized in place to preserve continuity. The summaries (in English only) are intentionally very brief (since many chapters are long series of often noteworthy maxims, it's

The well

impossible to do justice to everything), but they attempt to provide the chief tenets, expressions, and/or leitmotifs contained in those chapters.

With regard to the new English translation to be found here, several remarks are in order. First of all, unlike some predecessors, it retains the short paragraphs (like Bible verses) of the German original. Second, among the varied goals that a translation of such a rich text can aim for, the primary one here has been literalness and unambiguous accuracy. Therefore:

(1) The language is not archaic; Nietzsche tinged his language with older forms very occasionally, but basically did not use an older stage of German, so that an imitation of the King James Bible in English is uncalled for. In fact, where Nietzsche actually becomes very colloquial, the present translation is especially faithful to his intentions.

(2) Ambiguous language has been scrupulously avoided. For instance, we never merely use the verb "lies" where there could be confusion between the meanings "is located" and "tells untruths," and where earlier translations have "I will" (which can readily be taken as a mere future) or "I hate reading idlers," we have "It is my will" and "I hate idlers who read," respectively.

(3) No attempt (such attempts are quixotic and can't be carried through) has been made to use a single English word for a single German word throughout (*Geist,* for example, simply has too many English equivalents based on context and feeling). For another thing, *Zarathustra* is too far from being a Scholastic piece of rigorous demonstration for such an attempt to be desirable even a priori.

(4) With only a couple of exceptions, no attempt (such attempts are often clumsy and confusing) has been made to duplicate German wordplays in English "equivalents." A few outstanding examples of Nietzsche's word-wizardry are analyzed in footnotes; luckily, in this dual-language edition, the reader has the original German before his eyes and can detect what the author is doing phonologically.

(5) This translation *does* attempt to avoid an excessive adherence to the German language in word formation and syntax; some predecessors have even relied on false cognates and have even failed to recognize idioms in places.

Nietzsche's terminology is very special, and a few remarks are in order about how it has been rendered here:

Übermensch: Among previous renderings, "superman" (very good in its day) now has indelible associations with the special powers possessed by natives of Krypton (and with the Nazis), while "overman"

suggests (if it suggests anything) some kind of supervisor or Big Brother. As a prefix, *über-* regularly suggests "excess, going beyond" (while it's *ober-* that indicates "upper, situated above"), and the present translation, striving for precision and clarity, renders *Übermensch* as "more-than-man."

Überwinden: Not content to use "overcome" each and every time, we here often use "surpass" and, especially, "supersede," depending on context.

Untergang: "Going under" (besides suggesting drowning or being given an anesthetic) is simply too primitive and hyperetymological. The word means "sunset" and, figuratively, "ruin, downfall, perishing." In this translation, the rendering changes with context, and even "descent" is sometimes used. In the crucial first section of "Zarathustra's Prologue," the rendering "sunset" is perfectly natural, because Zarathustra is descending from his mountains to enlighten mankind, just as the sun visits the "nether world" when it isn't visible to us.

Hinterweltler: I have never seen a real explanation of this cranky coinage. The word is virtually a homonym of *Hinterwäldler,* which is itself a deliberate German calque ("loan translation") from the English "backwoodsman," with the same meaning but with the special connotation of an uncouth bumpkin. It seemed only natural to render the word with the equally peculiar "backworldsman." Of course, this doesn't immediately suggest the sense in which Nietzsche uses it—a believer in heaven and hell, of worlds "behind" this one—but neither does the German word! The statement that it is an equivalent of "metaphysician" is pure bunk from every point of view. (The *hinter-* element of the word comes into its own with a vengeance in the chapter "Von alten und neuen Tafeln" in Part Three.)

Other special terms have either been discussed earlier in this Introduction; or will be taken up in footnotes to the translation.

Thus Spoke Zarathustra
(Selections)

Also sprach Zarathustra
(Auswahl)

ERSTER TEIL

Zarathustras Vorrede

1.

Als Zarathustra dreißig Jahre alt war, verließ er seine Heimat und den See seiner Heimat und ging in das Gebirge. Hier genoß er seines Geistes und seiner Einsamkeit und wurde dessen zehn Jahre nicht müde. Endlich aber verwandelte sich sein Herz, – und eines Morgens stand er mit der Morgenröte auf, trat vor die Sonne hin und sprach zu ihr also:

»Du großes Gestirn! Was wäre dein Glück, wenn du nicht Die hättest, welchen du leuchtest!

Zehn Jahre kamst du hier herauf zu meiner Höhle: du würdest deines Lichtes und dieses Weges satt geworden sein, ohne mich, meinen Adler und meine Schlange.

Aber wir warteten deiner an jedem Morgen, nahmen dir deinen Überfluß ab und segneten dich dafür.

Siehe! Ich bin meiner Weisheit überdrüssig, wie die Biene, die des Honigs zuviel gesammelt hat, ich bedarf der Hände, die sich ausstrecken.

Ich möchte verschenken und austeilen, bis die Weisen unter den Menschen wieder einmal ihrer Torheit und die Armen wieder einmal ihres Reichtums froh geworden sind.

Dazu muß ich in die Tiefe steigen: wie du des Abends tust, wenn du hinter das Meer gehst und noch der Unterwelt Licht bringst, du überreiches Gestirn!

Ich muß, gleich dir, *untergehen,* wie die Menschen es nennen, zu denen ich hinab will.

So segne mich denn, du ruhiges Auge, das ohne Neid auch ein allzu großes Glück sehen kann!

PART ONE

Zarathustra's Prologue

1.

When Zarathustra was thirty years old,[1] he left his homeland and the lake of his homeland and went into the mountains. Here he enjoyed his intellect and his solitude and didn't grow tired of it for ten years. But finally his heart changed, and one morning he arose with the dawn, stepped out before the sun, and addressed it thus:

"You great star! How happy would you be if you didn't have beings to shine on?

"For ten years you have come up here to my cave: you would have grown weary of your light and this path without me, my eagle, and my serpent.

"But we were waiting for you every morning, relieving you of your surplus and blessing you for it.

"See! I am tired of my wisdom, like bees that have gathered too much honey; I have need of hands stretching out toward me.

"I want to give of myself and share myself until the wise among men are once more happy in their folly, and the poor once more happy in their wealth.

"For that, I must descend to the lowlands, just as you do in the evening when you disappear behind the sea and then bring light to the nether world, you most abundant star!

"Like you, I must 'set,' as the people call it to whom I wish to go down.

"So then, bless me, you tranquil eye, which can look upon even excessive happiness without envy!

---

1. Like Jesus at the beginning of his ministry.

3

Segne den Becher, welcher überfließen will, daß das Wasser golden
aus ihm fließe und überallhin den Abglanz deiner Wonne trage!

Siehe! Dieser Becher will wieder leer werden, und Zarathustra will
wieder Mensch werden.«

– Also begann Zarathustras Untergang.

2.

Zarathustra stieg allein das Gebirge abwärts und Niemand begegnete
ihm. Als er aber in die Wälder kam, stand auf einmal ein Greis vor
ihm, der seine heilige Hütte verlassen hatte, um Wurzeln im Walde
zu suchen. Und also sprach der Greis zu Zarathustra:

»Nicht fremd ist mir dieser Wandrer: vor manchem Jahre ging er
hier vorbei. Zarathustra hieß er; aber er hat sich verwandelt.

Damals trugst du deine Asche zu Berge: willst du heute dein Feuer
in die Täler tragen? Fürchtest du nicht des Brandstifters Strafen?

Ja, ich erkenne Zarathustra. Rein ist sein Auge, und an seinem
Munde birgt sich kein Ekel. Geht er nicht daher wie ein Tänzer?

Verwandelt ist Zarathustra, zum Kind ward Zarathustra, ein
Erwachter ist Zarathustra; was willst du nun bei den Schlafenden?

Wie im Meere lebtest du in der Einsamkeit, und das Meer trug
dich. Wehe, du willst ans Land steigen? Wehe, du willst deinen Leib
wieder selber schleppen?«

Zarathustra antwortete: »Ich liebe die Menschen.«

»Warum«, sagte der Heilige, »ging ich doch in den Wald und die
Einöde? War es nicht, weil ich die Menschen allzusehr liebte?

Jetzt liebe ich Gott: die Menschen liebe ich nicht. Der Mensch ist
mir eine zu unvollkommene Sache. Liebe zum Menschen würde
mich umbringen.«

Zarathustra antwortete: »Was sprach ich von Liebe! Ich bringe den
Menschen ein Geschenk.«

»Gib ihnen Nichts«, sagte der Heilige. »Nimm ihnen lieber Etwas
ab und trage es mit ihnen – das wird ihnen am wohlsten tun: wenn es
dir wohltut!

Und willst du ihnen geben, so gib nicht mehr als ein Almosen, und
laß sie noch darum betteln!«

»Nein«, antwortete Zarathustra, »ich gebe kein Almosen. Dazu bin
ich nicht arm genug.«

"Bless the cup that wishes to run over, so that the water flows from it in a golden hue and bears the reflection of your bliss everywhere!

"See! This cup wishes to become empty again, and Zarathustra wishes to become human again."

Such was the beginning of Zarathustra's "setting."

2.

Zarathustra descended from the mountains alone, meeting no one. But when he entered the forests, all at once an aged man stood before him; he had left his holy cabin to seek roots in the forest. And the old man spoke to Zarathustra thus:

"This wayfarer is no stranger to me; many years ago he passed this way. His name was Zarathustra, but he has changed.

"At that time you were carrying your ashes uphill: do you wish today to carry your fire to the valleys? Don't you fear the punishments accorded to arsonists?

"Yes, I recognize Zarathustra. His eyes are pure, and no disgust is concealed in his lips. Does he not proceed like a dancer?

"Zarathustra is changed, Zarathustra has become a child, Zarathustra is an 'awakened one';[2] what do you wish to do now among the sleepers?

"You dwelt in solitude as if in the sea, and the sea carried you. Woe! You want to go ashore? Woe! You want to drag around your body again under your own power?"

Zarathustra replied: "I love mankind."

"Why," asked the holy man, "did I go into the forest and the lonely wilderness? Wasn't it because I loved mankind too well?

"Now I love God: I don't love mankind. For me, man is something too imperfect. Love for mankind would destroy me."

Zarathustra replied: "Why did I speak of love?! I am bringing mankind a gift."

"Give them nothing," said the holy man. "Instead, take something from them and help them carry it—that will do them the most good: if it does you good!

"And if you want to give them something, give merely alms, and let them beg for it, too!"

"No," replied Zarathustra , "I am no almsgiver. I'm not poor enough for that."

---

2. Like the Buddha.

Der Heilige lachte über Zarathustra und sprach also: »So sieh zu, daß sie deine Schätze annehmen! Sie sind mißtrauisch gegen die Einsiedler und glauben nicht, daß wir kommen, um zu schenken.

Unsre Schritte klingen ihnen zu einsam durch die Gassen. Und wie wenn sie nachts in ihren Betten einen Mann gehen hören, lange bevor die Sonne aufsteht, so fragen sie sich wohl: wohin will der Dieb?

Gehe nicht zu den Menschen und bleibe im Walde! Gehe lieber noch zu den Tieren! Warum willst du nicht sein wie ich – ein Bär unter Bären, ein Vogel unter Vögeln?«

»Und was macht der Heilige im Wald?« fragte Zarathustra.

Der Heilige antwortete: »Ich mache Lieder und singe sie, und wenn ich Lieder mache, lache, weine und brumme ich: also lobe ich Gott.

Mit Singen, Weinen, Lachen und Brummen lobe ich den Gott, der mein Gott ist. Doch was bringst du uns zum Geschenke?«

Als Zarathustra diese Worte gehört hatte, grüßte er den Heiligen und sprach: »Was hätte ich euch zu geben! Aber laßt mich schnell davon, daß ich euch Nichts nehme!« – Und so trennten sie sich voneinander, der Greis und der Mann, lachend, gleichwie zwei Knaben lachen.

Als Zarathustra aber allein war, sprach er also zu seinem Herzen: »Sollte es denn möglich sein! Dieser alte Heilige hat in seinem Walde noch Nichts davon gehört, daß *Gott tot* ist!« –

3.

Als Zarathustra in die nächste Stadt kam, die an den Wäldern lag, fand er daselbst viel Volk versammelt auf dem Markte: denn es war verheißen worden, daß man einen Seiltänzer sehen sollte. Und Zarathustra sprach also zum Volke:

Ich lehre euch den Übermenschen. Der Mensch ist Etwas, das überwunden werden soll. Was habt ihr getan, ihn zu überwinden?

Alle Wesen bisher schufen Etwas über sich hinaus: und ihr wollt die Ebbe dieser großen Flut sein und lieber noch zum Tiere zurückgehn, als den Menschen überwinden?

Was ist der Affe für den Menschen? Ein Gelächter oder eine schmerzliche Scham. Und ebendas soll der Mensch für den Übermenschen sein: ein Gelächter oder eine schmerzliche Scham.

Ihr habt den Weg vom Wurme zum Menschen gemacht, und Vieles ist in euch noch Wurm. Einst wart ihr Affen, und auch jetzt noch ist der Mensch mehr Affe, als irgendein Affe.

The holy man laughed at Zarathustra and said: "In that case, see to it that they accept your treasures! They are suspicious of hermits and they don't believe that we come to give gifts.

"Our footsteps in the streets sound too lonely to them. And when they are in bed at night and hear a man walking long before sunrise, they surely wonder: 'Where is the thief heading?'

"Don't go to mankind, but remain in the forest! It's better to go to the animals! Why don't you want to be like me—a bear among bears, a bird among birds?"

"And what does the holy man do in the forest?" Zarathustra asked.

The holy man replied: "I compose songs and sing them, and when I compose songs, I laugh, weep, and drone: in that fashion I praise God.

"With singing, weeping, laughing, and droning I praise the god who is my God. But what do you bring us as a gift?"

After hearing those words, Zarathustra took leave of the holy man, saying: "What could I give you?! But let me depart quickly before I take something from you!" And so they separated, the aged one and the mature man, laughing as two boys laugh.

But when Zarathustra was alone, he addressed his heart thus: "Can it really be possible? This old holy man in his forest still hasn't received any notice that *God is dead!*"

3.

When Zarathustra arrived in the nearest city, situated on the edge of the woods, he found a great throng assembled there in the marketplace: for they had been promised they would see a tightrope walker. And Zarathustra addressed the townspeople as follows:

"*I teach you about the more-than-man.* Man is something that must be superseded. What have you done to supersede him?

"Up till now all beings have created something beyond themselves: and do you want to be the ebb to this great flood tide, would you rather revert to animality than supersede man?

"What is an ape to people? A source of laughter or of painful shame. And man will be just that to the more-than-man: a source of laughter or a painful shame.

"You have come all the way from worm to man, and there is still much of the worm in you. Once you were apes, and even now man is still more of an ape than any ape is.

Wer aber der Weiseste von euch ist, der ist auch nur ein Zwiespalt und Zwitter von Pflanze und von Gespenst. Aber heiße ich euch zu Gespenstern oder Pflanzen werden?

Seht, ich lehre euch den Übermenschen!

Der Übermensch ist der Sinn der Erde. Euer Wille sage: der Übermensch *sei* der Sinn der Erde!

Ich schwöre euch, meine Brüder, *bleibt der Erde treu* und glaubt Denen nicht, welche euch von überirdischen Hoffnungen reden! Giftmischer sind es, ob sie es wissen oder nicht.

Verächter des Lebens sind es, Absterbende und selber Vergiftete, deren die Erde müde ist: so mögen sie dahinfahren!

Einst war der Frevel an Gott der größte Frevel, aber Gott starb, und damit starben auch diese Frevelhaften. An der Erde zu freveln ist jetzt das Furchtbarste, und die Eingeweide des Unerforschlichen höher zu achten, als den Sinn der Erde!

Einst blickte die Seele verächtlich auf den Leib: und damals war diese Verachtung das Höchste: – sie wollte ihn mager, gräßlich, verhungert. So dachte sie ihm und der Erde zu entschlüpfen.

Oh diese Seele war selber noch mager, gräßlich und verhungert: und Grausamkeit war die Wollust dieser Seele!

Aber auch ihr noch, meine Brüder, sprecht mir: was kündet euer Leib von eurer Seele? Ist eure Seele nicht Armut und Schmutz und ein erbärmliches Behagen?

Wahrlich, ein schmutziger Strom ist der Mensch. Man muß schon ein Meer sein, um einen schmutzigen Strom aufnehmen zu können, ohne unrein zu werden.

Seht, ich lehre euch den Übermenschen: der ist dies Meer, in ihm kann eure große Verachtung untergehn.

Was ist das Größte, das ihr erleben könnt? Das ist die Stunde der großen Verachtung. Die Stunde, in der euch auch euer Glück zum Ekel wird und ebenso eure Vernunft und eure Tugend.

Die Stunde, wo ihr sagt: »Was liegt an meinem Glücke! Es ist Armut und Schmutz und ein erbärmliches Behagen. Aber mein Glück sollte das Dasein selber rechtfertigen!«

Die Stunde, wo ihr sagt: »Was liegt an meiner Vernunft! Begehrt sie nach Wissen wie der Löwe nach seiner Nahrung? Sie ist Armut und Schmutz und ein erbärmliches Behagen!«

Die Stunde, wo ihr sagt: »Was liegt an meiner Tugend! Noch hat sie mich nicht rasen gemacht. Wie müde bin ich meines Guten und meines Bösen! Alles das ist Armut und Schmutz und ein erbärmliches Behagen!«

"For even the wisest among you is merely a dichotomy and hybrid of plant and ghost. But am I asking you to become ghosts or plants?

"Behold, I am teaching you about the more-than-man!

"The more-than-man is the meaning of the earth. Let your will say: 'The more-than-man *shall* be the meaning of the earth!'

"I conjure you, my brothers: *remain true to the earth* and don't believe those who speak to you of superterrestrial hopes! They are poisoners, whether they know it or not.

"They are despisers of life, themselves slowly dying of poison, and the earth is tired of them: then let them pass on!

"Once, blasphemy against God was the greatest blasphemy, but God has died, and therewith those blasphemers have died, too. The most terrible thing now is to blaspheme against the earth and to esteem the bowels of the unknowable more highly than the meaning of the earth!

"Once, the soul looked upon the body with contempt; and at that time this contempt was the highest value: the soul wanted the body to be gaunt, abominable, emaciated. In that way the soul thought it could escape the body and the earth.

"Oh, this soul was still gaunt, abominable, and emaciated itself: and cruelty was this soul's lust!

"But you, too, my brothers, tell me: what does your body report about your soul? Isn't your soul poverty and filth and a pathetic contentment?

"Truly, man is a filthy stream. One must be a sea if one is to receive a filthy stream without becoming impure.

"See, I teach you about the more-than-man: he is that sea, in him your great contempt can be immersed.

"What is the greatest thing you can experience? It is the hour of the great contempt. The hour in which even your happiness turns to disgust, along with your reasoning powers and your virtue.

"The hour when you say: 'What is there to my happiness? It's poverty and filth and a pathetic contentment. But my happiness ought to justify existence itself!'

"The hour when you say: 'What is there to my reason? Does it yearn for knowledge as the lion yearns for its food? It's poverty and filth and a pathetic contentment!'

"The hour when you say: 'What is there to my virtue? It has never yet made me frenzied. How tired I am of my good and my evil! It's all poverty and filth and a pathetic contentment!'

Die Stunde, wo ihr sagt: »Was liegt an meiner Gerechtigkeit! Ich
sehe nicht, daß ich Glut und Kohle wäre. Aber der Gerechte ist Glut
und Kohle!«

Die Stunde, wo ihr sagt: »Was liegt an meinem Mitleiden! Ist nicht
Mitleid das Kreuz, an das Der genagelt wird, der die Menschen liebt?
Aber mein Mitleiden ist keine Kreuzigung.«

Spracht ihr schon so? Schriet ihr schon so? Ach, daß ich euch schon
so schreien gehört hätte!

Nicht eure Sünde – eure Genügsamkeit schreit gen Himmel, euer
Geiz selbst in eurer Sünde schreit gen Himmel!

Wo ist doch der Blitz, der euch mit seiner Zunge lecke? Wo ist der
Wahnsinn, mit dem ihr geimpft werden müßtet?

Seht, ich lehre euch den Übermenschen: der ist dieser Blitz, der ist
dieser Wahnsinn! –

Als Zarathustra so gesprochen hatte, schrie Einer aus dem Volke:
»Wir hörten nun genug von dem Seiltänzer; nun laßt uns ihn auch
sehen!« Und alles Volk lachte über Zarathustra. Der Seiltänzer
aber, welcher glaubte, daß das Wort ihm gälte, machte sich an sein
Werk.

4.

Zarathustra aber sahe das Volk an und wunderte sich. Dann sprach er
also:

Der Mensch ist ein Seil, geknüpft zwischen Tier und Übermensch,
– ein Seil über einem Abgrunde.

Ein gefährliches Hinüber, ein gefährliches Auf-dem-Wege, ein gefährliches Zurückblicken, ein gefährliches Schaudern und Stehenbleiben.

Was groß ist am Menschen, das ist, daß er eine Brücke und kein
Zweck ist: was geliebt werden kann am Menschen, das ist, daß er ein
Übergang und ein *Untergang* ist.

Ich liebe Die, welche nicht zu leben wissen, es sei denn als Untergehende, denn es sind die Hinübergehenden.

Ich liebe die großen Verachtenden, weil sie die großen Verehrenden sind und Pfeile der Sehnsucht nach dem andern Ufer.

Ich liebe Die, welche nicht erst hinter den Sternen einen Grund
suchen, unterzugehen und Opfer zu sein: sondern die sich der Erde
opfern, daß die Erde einst des Übermenschen werde.

Ich liebe Den, welcher lebt, damit er erkenne, und welcher erkennen will, damit einst der Übermensch lebe. Und so will er seinen
Untergang.

"The hour when you say: 'What is there to my justice? I don't see where I've become fire and a live coal. But the just man is fire and a live coal!'

"The hour when you say: 'What is there to my compassion? Isn't compassion the cross to which the lover of mankind is nailed? But my compassion is no crucifixion.'

"Have you ever said this? Have you ever shouted this? Oh, if I had ever heard you shout this!

"It is not your sin, but your self-satisfaction, that cries to heaven, your niggardliness even in sinning cries to heaven!

"Where is the lightning that will lick you with its tongue? Where is the madness with which you need to be inoculated?

"See, I am teaching you about the more-than-man: he is that lightning, he is that madness!"

After Zarathustra had spoken thus, someone in the throng shouted: "By now we've heard enough of the tightrope walker; now let's see him, too!" And all the townspeople laughed at Zarathustra. But the tightrope walker, who thought that the remark was meant for him, prepared to perform his act.

4.

But Zarathustra looked at the people in surprise. Then he said:

"Man is a rope stretched between the animal and the more-than-man—a rope over an abyss.

"A dangerous crossing, dangerous while on the way, dangerous when looking back, dangerous when trembling and coming to a halt.

"That which is great in man is that he is a bridge and not a final purpose: that which is lovable in man is that he is a *transition* and a *sunset*.

"I love those who don't know how to live except when setting like the sun, for they are those who cross over.

"I love those who despise greatly, for they are those who revere greatly, arrows of longing for the farther shore.

"I love those who don't begin by seeking beyond the stars for a reason to set and be a sacrificial victim, but who sacrifice themselves to the earth, so that the earth may some day belong to the more-than-man.

"I love the man who lives to gain knowledge and wishes to gain knowledge so that the more-than-man can live one day. For that reason he wishes to set.

Ich liebe Den, welcher arbeitet und erfindet, daß er dem Übermenschen das Haus baue und zu ihm Erde, Tier und Pflanze vorbereite: denn so will er seinen Untergang.

Ich liebe Den, welcher seine Tugend liebt: denn Tugend ist Wille zum Untergang und ein Pfeil der Sehnsucht.

Ich liebe Den, welcher nicht einen Tropfen Geist für sich zurückbehält, sondern ganz der Geist seiner Tugend sein will: so schreitet er als Geist über die Brücke.

Ich liebe Den, welcher aus seiner Tugend seinen Hang und sein Verhängnis macht: so will er um seiner Tugend willen noch leben und nicht mehr leben.

Ich liebe Den, welcher nicht zu viele Tugenden haben will. Eine Tugend ist mehr Tugend als zwei, weil sie mehr Knoten ist, an den sich das Verhängnis hängt.

Ich liebe Den, dessen Seele sich verschwendet, der nicht Dank haben will und nicht zurückgibt: denn er schenkt immer und will sich nicht bewahren.

Ich liebe Den, welcher sich schämt, wenn der Würfel zu seinem Glücke fällt und der dann fragt: bin ich denn ein falscher Spieler? – denn er will zugrunde gehen.

Ich liebe Den, welcher goldne Worte seinen Taten vorauswirft und immer noch mehr hält, als er verspricht: denn er will seinen Untergang.

Ich liebe Den, welcher die Zukünftigen rechtfertigt und die Vergangenen erlöst: denn er will an den Gegenwärtigen zugrunde gehen.

Ich liebe Den, welcher seinen Gott züchtigt, weil er seinen Gott liebt: denn er muß am Zorne seines Gottes zugrunde gehen.

Ich liebe Den, dessen Seele tief ist auch in der Verwundung und der an einem kleinen Erlebnisse zugrunde gehen kann: so geht er gerne über die Brücke.

Ich liebe Den, dessen Seele übervoll ist, so daß er sich selber vergißt, und alle Dinge in ihm sind: so werden alle Dinge sein Untergang.

Ich liebe Den, der freien Geistes und freien Herzens ist: so ist sein Kopf nur das Eingeweide seines Herzens, sein Herz aber treibt ihn zum Untergang.

Ich liebe alle Die, welche wie schwere Tropfen sind, einzeln fallend aus der dunklen Wolke, die über den Menschen hängt: sie verkündigen, daß der Blitz kommt, und gehn als Verkündiger zugrunde.

Seht, ich bin ein Verkündiger des Blitzes und ein schwerer Tropfen aus der Wolke: dieser Blitz aber heißt *Übermensch*. –

"I love the man who works and invents so that he can build the more-than-man's house and prepare earth, animals, and plants for him: for thus he wishes to set.

"I love the man who loves his virtue: for virtue is the will to set and an arrow of longing.

"I love the man who doesn't hold back one drop of spirit for himself, but wishes to be entirely the spirit of his virtue: thus he strides as a spirit across the bridge.

"I love the man who makes his virtue his inclination and his calamity: thus, for the sake of his virtue, he wants to go on living and to cease living.

"I love the man who doesn't want to have too many virtues. One virtue is more virtue than two, because it is a larger knot for calamity to suspend itself from.

"I love the man whose soul expends itself, who asks for no thanks and gives nothing back: for he makes presents always and doesn't want to preserve himself.

"I love the man who feels ashamed when the dice fall to his advantage and who then asks: 'Have I cheated, then?' For he wishes to be ruined.

"I love the man who flings out golden works before he acts and always performs more than he has promised: for he wishes to set.

"I love the man who justifies those in the future and redeems those in the past: for he wishes to be destroyed by those in the present.

"I love the man who chastises his god because he loves his god: for he must be destroyed by the wrath of his god.

"I love the man whose soul is deep even when wounded and who can be destroyed by a minor experience: thus he is glad to cross the bridge.

"I love the man whose soul is flowing over, so that he forgets about himself and all things are in him: thus all things become his sunset.

"I love the man who is free in spirit and heart: thus his head is only the entrails of his heart, while his heart urges him to set.

"I love all those who are like heavy drops falling separately from the dark cloud that hangs over mankind: they herald the coming of the lightning, and as heralds they are destroyed.

"See, I am a herald of the lightning and a heavy drop from the cloud: and this lightning is called *more-than-man*."

5.

Als Zarathustra diese Worte gesprochen hatte, sahe er wieder das Volk an und schwieg. »Da stehen sie«, sprach er zu seinem Herzen, »da lachen sie: sie verstehen mich nicht, ich bin nicht der Mund für diese Ohren.

Muß man ihnen erst die Ohren zerschlagen, daß sie lernen, mit den Augen hören? Muß man rasseln gleich Pauken und Bußpredigern? Oder glauben sie nur dem Stammelnden?

Sie haben Etwas, worauf sie stolz sind. Wie nennen sie es doch, was sie stolz macht? Bildung nennen sie's, es zeichnet sie aus vor den Ziegenhirten.

Drum hören sie ungern von sich das Wort ›Verachtung‹. So will ich denn zu ihrem Stolze reden.

So will ich ihnen vom Verächtlichsten sprechen: das aber ist der *letzte Mensch*.«

Und also sprach Zarathustra zum Volke:

Es ist an der Zeit, daß der Mensch sich sein Ziel stecke. Es ist an der Zeit, daß der Mensch den Keim seiner höchsten Hoffnung pflanze.

Noch ist sein Boden dazu reich genug. Aber dieser Boden wird einst arm und zahm sein, und kein hoher Baum wird mehr aus ihm wachsen können.

Wehe! Es kommt die Zeit, wo der Mensch nicht mehr den Pfeil seiner Sehnsucht über den Menschen hinaus wirft, und die Sehne seines Bogens verlernt hat, zu schwirren!

Ich sage euch: man muß noch Chaos in sich haben, um einen tanzenden Stern gebären zu können. Ich sage euch: ihr habt noch Chaos in euch.

Wehe! Es kommt die Zeit, wo der Mensch keinen Stern mehr gebären wird. Wehe! Es kommt die Zeit des verächtlichsten Menschen, der sich selber nicht mehr verachten kann.

Seht! Ich zeige euch den *letzten Menschen*.

»Was ist Liebe? Was ist Schöpfung? Was ist Sehnsucht? Was ist Stern?« – so fragt der letzte Mensch und blinzelt.

Die Erde ist dann klein geworden, und auf ihr hüpft der letzte Mensch, der Alles klein macht. Sein Geschlecht ist unaustilgbar wie der Erdfloh; der letzte Mensch lebt am längsten.

»Wir haben das Glück erfunden« – sagen die letzten Menschen und blinzeln.

5.

After Zarathustra spoke these words, he looked at the populace again and fell silent. "There they stand," he said to his heart, "there they laugh: they don't understand me; I'm not the lips for these ears.

"Must they first have their ears smashed so they learn to hear with their eyes? Must one rumble like drums and preachers of penitence? Or do they believe only one who stammers?

"They have something they're proud of. But what do they call the thing that makes them proud? They call it culture, it distinguishes them from goatherds.

"Therefore they don't like to hear the word 'contempt' applied to themselves. And so I shall address their pride.

"And so I shall speak to them of that which is most contemptible, and that is the *last man*."[3]

And Zarathustra addressed the populace thus:

"It's high time for man to set a goal for himself. It's high time for man to plant the seed of his loftiest hope.

"His soul is still rich enough for it. But some day this soul will become poor and tame, and no tall tree will be able to grow from it any more.

"Woe! The time is coming when man will no longer shoot the arrow of his longing out over other men, and the string of his bow has forgotten how to whir!

"I say to you: one must still have chaos within oneself if one is to be able to give birth to a dancing star. I say to you: you still have chaos within yourselves.

"Woe! The time is coming when man will no longer be able to give birth to a star. Woe! The time of the most contemptible man is coming, one who can no longer despise himself.

"See! I show you the *last man*.

"'What is love? What is creation? What is longing? What is star?' The last man asks this and blinks.

"The earth has become small then, and on it hops the last man, who makes everything small. His race is as hard to exterminate as the flea beetle; the last man has the greatest longevity.

"'We have invented happiness,' the last men say, and blink.

---

3. *Der letzte Mensch* denotes "the last (final) human being" and connotes "the lowest of men."

Sie haben die Gegenden verlassen, wo es hart war zu leben: denn man braucht Wärme. Man liebt noch den Nachbar und reibt sich an ihm: denn man braucht Wärme.

Krankwerden und Mißtrauen-Haben gilt ihnen sündhaft: man geht achtsam einher. Ein Tor, der noch über Steine oder Menschen stolpert!

Ein wenig Gift ab und zu: das macht angenehme Träume. Und viel Gift zuletzt, zu einem angenehmen Sterben.

Man arbeitet noch, denn Arbeit ist eine Unterhaltung. Aber man sorgt, daß die Unterhaltung nicht angreife.

Man wird nicht mehr arm und reich: Beides ist zu beschwerlich. Wer will noch regieren? Wer noch gehorchen? Beides ist zu beschwerlich.

Kein Hirt und Eine Herde! Jeder will das gleiche, Jeder ist gleich: wer anders fühlt, geht freiwillig ins Irrenhaus.

»Ehemals war alle Welt irre« sagen die Feinsten und blinzeln.

Man ist klug und weiß Alles, was geschehn ist: so hat man kein Ende zu spotten. Man zankt sich noch, aber man versöhnt sich bald – sonst verdirbt es den Magen.

Man hat sein Lüstchen für den Tag und sein Lüstchen für die Nacht: aber man ehrt die Gesundheit.

»Wir haben das Glück erfunden« – sagen die letzten Menschen und blinzeln. –

Und hier endete die erste Rede Zarathustras, welche man auch »die Vorrede« heißt: denn an dieser Stelle unterbrach ihn das Geschrei und die Lust der Menge. »Gib uns diesen letzten Menschen, oh Zarathustra«, – so riefen sie – »mache uns zu diesen letzten Menschen! So schenken wir dir den Übermenschen!« Und alles Volk jubelte und schnalzte mit der Zunge, Zarathustra aber wurde traurig und sagte zu seinem Herzen:

»Sie verstehen mich nicht: ich bin nicht der Mund für diese Ohren.

Zu lange wohl lebte ich im Gebirge, zu viel horchte ich auf Bäche und Bäume: nun rede ich ihnen gleich den Ziegenhirten.

Unbewegt ist meine Seele und hell wie das Gebirge am Vormittag. Aber sie meinen, ich sei kalt und ein Spötter in furchtbaren Späßen.

Und nun blicken sie mich an und lachen: und indem sie lachen, hassen sie mich noch. Es ist Eis in ihrem Lachen.«

6.

Da aber geschah Etwas, das jeden Mund stumm und jedes Auge starr machte. Inzwischen nämlich hatte der Seiltänzer sein Werk begonnen:

"They have left the regions where life was difficult, for they need warmth. They still love their neighbors and rub up against them, for they need warmth.

"To fall ill or show mistrust they count as sinful: they go about cautiously. Only a fool would still stumble over stones or people!

"A little narcotic now and then: it gives pleasant dreams. And finally a lot of drugs, for a pleasant death.

"They still work, because work is a pastime. But they make sure that the pastime doesn't strain them.

"People no longer become poor or rich: it's equally exhausting. Who still wishes to govern? Who still wants to obey? It's equally exhausting.

"No shepherd and one flock! Everyone wants the same thing, everyone is equal: whoever thinks differently goes to the madhouse voluntarily.

"'In the past the whole world was insane,' the most cultured one say, and blink.

"They are clever and know all that has ever happened; thus, there's no end to their mockery. They still have disputes, but settle them quickly—otherwise it upsets their stomach.

"They have a special little pleasure by day and another one by night, but they look out for their health.

"'We have invented happiness,' the last men say, and blink."

And here ended Zarathustra's first oration, which is also known as "the prologue"—because at this point he was interrupted by the joyful shouts of the multitude. "Give us this last man, O Zarathustra!" they called. "Make us this last man! And you can keep your more-than-man!" And all the townspeople hallooed and clicked their tongues; but Zarathustra became sad and said to his heart:

"They don't understand me: I'm not the lips for these ears.

"I have probably lived in the mountains too long, I have listened too much to brooks and trees: now I speak to them as to goatherds.

"My soul is as steadfast and bright as the mountains in the morning. But they think I'm cold, a mocker with frightening jokes.

"And now they look at me and laugh: and while they laugh they still hate me. There is ice in their laughter."

6.

But then something occurred which made every mouth mute and every eye rigid. For, meanwhile, the tightrope walker had begun his

er war aus einer kleinen Tür hinausgetreten und ging über das Seil, welches zwischen zwei Türmen gespannt war, also, daß er über dem Markt und dem Volke hing. Als er eben in der Mitte seines Weges war, öffnete sich die kleine Tür noch einmal, und ein bunter Gesell, einem Possenreißer gleich, sprang heraus und ging mit schnellen Schritten dem Ersten nach. »Vorwärts, Lahmfuß«, rief seine fürchterliche Stimme, »vorwärts Faultier, Schleichhändler, Bleichgesicht! Daß ich dich nicht mit meiner Ferse kitzle! Was treibst du hier zwischen Türmen? In den Turm gehörst du, einsperren sollte man dich, einem Bessern, als du bist, sperrst du die freie Bahn!« – Und mit jedem Worte kam er ihm näher und näher: als er aber nur noch einen Schritt hinter ihm war, da geschah das Erschreckliche, das jeden Mund stumm und jedes Auge starr machte: – er stieß ein Geschrei aus wie ein Teufel und sprang über Den hinweg, der ihm im Wege war. Dieser aber, als er so seinen Nebenbuhler siegen sah, verlor dabei den Kopf und das Seil; er warf seine Stange weg und schoß schneller als diese, wie ein Wirbel von Armen und Beinen, in die Tiefe. Der Markt und das Volk glich dem Meere, wenn der Sturm hineinfährt: Alles floh auseinander und übereinander, und am meisten dort, wo der Körper niederschlagen mußte.

Zarathustra aber blieb stehen, und gerade neben ihn fiel der Körper hin, übel zugerichtet und zerbrochen, aber noch nicht tot. Nach einer Weile kam dem Zerschmetterten das Bewußtsein zurück, und er sah Zarathustra neben sich knien. »Was machst du da?« sagte er endlich, »ich wußte es lange, daß mir der Teufel ein Bein stellen werde. Nun schleppt er mich zur Hölle: willst du's ihm wehren?«

»Bei meiner Ehre, Freund«, antwortete Zarathustra, »das gibt es Alles nicht, wovon du sprichst: es gibt keinen Teufel und keine Hölle. Deine Seele wird noch schneller tot sein als dein Leib: fürchte nun Nichts mehr!«

Der Mann blickte mißtrauisch auf. »Wenn du die Wahrheit sprichst«, sagte er dann, »so verliere ich Nichts, wenn ich das Leben verliere. Ich bin nicht viel mehr als ein Tier, das man tanzen gelehrt hat, durch Schläge und schmale Bissen.«

»Nicht doch«, sprach Zarathustra; »du hast aus der Gefahr deinen Beruf gemacht, daran ist Nichts zu verachten. Nun gehst du an deinem Beruf zugrunde: dafür will ich dich mit meinen Händen begraben.«

Als Zarathustra dies gesagt hatte, antwortete der Sterbende nicht mehr; aber er bewegte die Hand, wie als ob er die Hand Zarathustras zum Dank suche. –

performance: he had come out of a small door and was walking on the rope that was strung between two towers, so that he was suspended above the market and the populace. When he had just reached the halfway point of his trajectory, the small door opened again, and a fellow in motley, like a clown, leaped out and followed the first man with rapid steps. "Get a move on, slowpoke," his terrifying voice called; "get a move on, sloth, creeper,[4] pastyface! Or else I'll tickle you with my heels! What are you doing here between towers? You ought to be locked up in a tower, you should be thrown into jail for blocking the way of someone better than you!" And with each word he came closer and closer to him; when he was only a pace behind him, the frightful thing happened which made every mouth mute and every eye rigid: he uttered a cry like a devil and jumped over the man who was in his way. And when that man saw the victory of his rival, he lost his head and his footing on the rope; he dropped his pole and, even faster than it, in a flurry of arms and legs, he plummeted downward. The marketplace and the populace resembled the sea when a storm assails it: They all separated in confusion, especially those standing where the body had to land.

But Zarathustra remained where he was, and the body fell right next to him, badly injured and shattered, but not yet dead. After a while the broken man regained consciousness, and he saw Zarathustra kneeling beside him. "What are you doing here?" he finally said. "I've known for some time that the devil would trip me up. Now he's dragging me to hell: are you going to stop him?"

"On my honor, friend," Zarathustra replied, "none of what you're talking about exists: there is no devil and no hell. Your soul will be dead even sooner than your body: have no more fear of anything!"

The man looked up suspiciously. "If you're telling the truth," he then said, "I'm losing nothing by losing life. I'm not much more than an animal that has been taught to dance by being beaten and fed on scanty fare."

"Not so," said Zarathustra, "you have made a profession out of danger, that's nothing to be despised. Now you're being destroyed by your profession: as a recompense I shall bury you with my own hands."

After Zarathustra had said this, the dying man made no further response; but he moved his hand as if seeking Zarathustra's hand in gratitude.

---

4. *Schleichhändler* usually denotes "smuggler," someone who traffics (*händelt*) in a sneaky, slinky way (*schleicht*).

7.

Inzwischen kam der Abend, und der Markt barg sich in Dunkelheit: da verlief sich das Volk, denn selbst Neugierde und Schrecken werden müde. Zarathustra aber saß neben dem Toten auf der Erde und war in Gedanken versunken: so vergaß er die Zeit. Endlich aber wurde es Nacht, und ein kalter Wind blies über den Einsamen. Da erhob sich Zarathustra und sagte zu seinem Herzen:

»Wahrlich, einen schönen Fischfang tat heute Zarathustra! Keinen Menschen fing er, wohl aber einen Leichnam.

Unheimlich ist das menschliche Dasein und immer noch ohne Sinn: ein Possenreißer kann ihm zum Verhängnis werden.

Ich will die Menschen den Sinn ihres Seins lehren: welcher ist der Übermensch, der Blitz aus der dunklen Wolke Mensch.

Aber noch bin ich ihnen ferne, und mein Sinn redet nicht zu ihren Sinnen. Eine Mitte bin ich noch den Menschen zwischen einem Narren und einem Leichnam.

Dunkel ist die Nacht, dunkel sind die Wege Zarathustras. Komm, du kalter und steifer Gefährte! Ich trage dich dorthin, wo ich dich mit meinen Händen begrabe.«

8.

Als Zarathustra dies zu seinem Herzen gesagt hatte, lud er den Leichnam auf seinen Rücken und machte sich auf den Weg. Und noch nicht war er hundert Schritte gegangen, da schlich ein Mensch an ihn heran und flüsterte ihm ins Ohr – und siehe! Der, welcher redete, war der Possenreißer vom Turme. »Geh weg von dieser Stadt, oh Zarathustra«, sprach er; »es hassen dich hier zu Viele. Es hassen dich die Guten und Gerechten, und sie nennen dich ihren Feind und Verächter; es hassen dich die Gläubigen des rechten Glaubens, und sie nennen dich die Gefahr der Menge. Dein Glück war es, daß man über dich lachte: und wahrlich, du redest gleich einem Possenreißer. Dein Glück war es, daß du dich dem toten Hunde geselltest: als du dich so erniedrigtest, hast du dich selber für heute errettet. Geh aber fort aus dieser Stadt – oder morgen springe ich über dich hinweg, ein Lebendiger über einen Toten.« Und als er dies gesagt hatte, verschwand der Mensch; Zarathustra aber ging weiter durch die dunklen Gassen.

Am Tore der Stadt begegneten ihm die Totengräber: sie leuchteten ihm mit der Fackel ins Gesicht, erkannten Zarathustra und spotteten

7.

Meanwhile, evening came, and the marketplace was hidden in darkness: then the people dispersed, because even curiosity and terror grow weary. But Zarathustra sat on the ground next to the dead man, lost in thought: thus, he forgot about the time. But finally night fell, and a cold wind blew over the solitary man. Then Zarathustra arose and said to his heart:

"Truly, Zarathustra has made a fine haul of fish today! He didn't catch a person, but a corpse.

"Human existence is uncanny and still always meaningless: a clown can become its calamity.

"I wish to teach mankind the meaning of its existence, which is the more-than-man, the lightning from the dark cloud man.

"But I am still remote from them, and my meaning fails to address their senses. For man I am still something in between a fool and a corpse.

"Dark is the night, dark are Zarathustra's paths. Come, you cold, stiff companion! I'll carry you to the place where I'll bury you with my own hands."

8.

After Zarathustra said this to his heart, he loaded the corpse on his back and set out. And he had not yet gone a hundred paces when a man sidled up to him and whispered in his ear—and behold! the man speaking was the clown from the tower. "Leave this city, O Zarathustra," he said; "too many people here hate you. You are hated by the good and the just, who call you their enemy and despiser; you are hated by those who believe in the true faith, who call you a menace to society. You were lucky that you were laughed at; and actually you do talk like a clown. You were lucky to have associated yourself with the dead dog; by stooping that low, you saved yourself for today. But leave this city—or else tomorrow I'll jump over *you*, a living man over a dead man." And saying that, the fellow vanished; but Zarathustra walked on through the dark streets.

At the city gate he came across the gravediggers; they shone their torch in his face, recognized Zarathustra, and had a good laugh at his

sehr über ihn. »Zarathustra trägt den toten Hund davon: brav, daß Zarathustra zum Totengräber wurde! Denn unsere Hände sind zu reinlich für diesen Braten. Will Zarathustra wohl dem Teufel seinen Bissen stehlen? Nun wohlan! Und gut Glück zur Mahlzeit! Wenn nur nicht der Teufel ein besserer Dieb ist als Zarathustra! – er stiehlt sie Beide, er frißt sie Beide!« Und sie lachten miteinander und steckten die Köpfe zusammen.

Zarathustra sagte dazu kein Wort und ging seines Weges. Als er zwei Stunden gegangen war, an Wäldern und Sümpfen vorbei, da hatte er zu viel das hungrige Geheul der Wölfe gehört, und ihm selber kam der Hunger. So blieb er an einem einsamen Hause stehn, in dem ein Licht brannte.

»Der Hunger überfällt mich«, sagte Zarathustra, »wie ein Räuber. In Wäldern und Sümpfen überfällt mich mein Hunger, und in tiefer Nacht.

Wunderliche Launen hat mein Hunger. Oft kommt er mir erst nach der Mahlzeit, und heute kam er den ganzen Tag nicht: wo weilte er doch?«

Und damit schlug Zarathustra an das Tor des Hauses. Ein alter Mann erschien; er trug das Licht und fragte: »Wer kommt zu mir und zu meinem schlimmen Schlafe?«

»Ein Lebendiger und ein Toter«, sagte Zarathustra. »Gebt mir zu essen und zu trinken, ich vergaß es am Tage. Der, welcher den Hungrigen speiset, erquickt seine eigene Seele: so spricht die Weisheit.«

Der Alte ging fort, kam aber gleich zurück und bot Zarathustra Brot und Wein. »Eine böse Gegend ist's für Hungernde«, sagte er; »darum wohne ich hier. Tier und Mensch kommen zu mir, dem Einsiedler. Aber heiße auch deinen Gefährten essen und trinken, er ist müder als du.« Zarathustra antwortete: »Tot ist mein Gefährte, ich werde ihn schwerlich dazu überreden.« »Das geht mich nichts an«, sagte der Alte mürrisch; »wer an meinem Haus anklopft, muß auch nehmen, was ich ihm biete. Eßt und gehabt euch wohl!« –

Darauf ging Zarathustra wieder zwei Stunden und vertraute dem Wege und dem Lichte der Sterne: denn er war ein gewohnter Nachtgänger und liebte es, allem Schlafenden ins Gesicht zu sehn. Als aber der Morgen graute, fand sich Zarathustra in einem tiefen Walde, und kein Weg zeigte sich ihm mehr. Da legte er den Toten in einen hohlen Baum sich zu Häupten – denn er wollte ihn vor den Wölfen schützen – und sich selber auf den Boden und das Moos. Und alsbald schlief er ein, müden Leibes, aber mit einer unbewegten Seele.

expense. "Zarathustra is carrying away the dead dog: good for Zarathustra for becoming a gravedigger! For our hands are too clean for such a morsel. Does Zarathustra possibly want to rob the devil of his snack? All right, then! And hearty appetite! That is, unless the devil is a better thief than Zarathustra! He'll steal them both, he'll devour them both!" And they laughed together and put their heads together.

Zarathustra said no word to this, but proceeded on his way. After walking for two hours, past forests and swamps, he had heard too much of the wolves' hungry howling, and he grew hungry, too. So he stopped at a lonely house in which a candle was burning.

"Hunger is assailing me," said Zarathustra, "like a highway robber. In forests and swamps my hunger assails me, and in the dead of night.

"My appetite has strange caprices. Often it doesn't come to me until after meals, and today it didn't come all day: where could it have been keeping itself?"

And therewith Zarathustra knocked at the house door. An old man appeared, carrying the candle, and asked: "Who is coming to me and to my insomnia?"

"A living man and a dead one," said Zarathustra. "Give me food and drink; I forgot about it during the day. The man who feeds the hungry refreshes his own soul: so says wisdom."

The old man went away, but returned at once and offered Zarathustra bread and wine. "This is a bad neighborhood for the hungry," he said; "that's why I live here. Animals and people come to me, the hermit. But tell your companion to eat and drink, too; he's wearier than you." Zarathustra replied: "My companion is dead, I can hardly talk him into it." "That doesn't concern me," the old man said sullenly; "whoever knocks at my door must take what I offer him. Eat, both of you, and good-bye!"

After that, Zarathustra walked for another two hours, relying on the path and the starlight: for he was used to walking at night and loved to look all sleeping things in the face. But when day broke, Zarathustra found himself in a dense forest, and no path was any longer to be seen. Then he placed the dead man in a hollow tree next to his own head—for he wanted to protect him from the wolves—and lay down on the mossy ground. And he fell asleep at once, weary of body but steadfast of soul.

9.

Lange schlief Zarathustra, und nicht nur die Morgenröte ging über sein Antlitz, sondern auch der Vormittag. Endlich aber tat sein Auge sich auf: verwundert sah Zarathustra in den Wald und die Stille, verwundert sah er in sich hinein. Dann erhob er sich schnell, wie ein Seefahrer, der mit Einem Male Land sieht, und jauchzte: denn er sah eine neue Wahrheit. Und also redete er dann zu seinem Herzen:

Ein Licht ging mir auf: Gefährten brauche ich, und lebendige – nicht tote Gefährten und Leichname, die ich mit mir trage, wohin ich will.

Sondern lebendige Gefährten brauche ich, die mir folgen, weil sie sich selber folgen wollen – und dorthin, wo ich will.

Ein Licht ging mir auf: nicht zum Volke rede Zarathustra, sondern zu Gefährten ! Nicht soll Zarathustra einer Herde Hirt und Hund werden!

Viele wegzulocken von der Herde – dazu kam ich. Zürnen soll mir Volk und Herde: Räuber will Zarathustra den Hirten heißen.

Hirten sage ich, aber sie nennen sich die Guten und Gerechten. Hirten sage ich: aber sie nennen sich die Gläubigen des rechten Glaubens.

Siehe die Guten und Gerechten! Wen hassen sie am meisten? Den, der zerbricht ihre Tafeln der Werte, den Brecher, den Verbrecher: – das aber ist der Schaffende.

Siehe die Gläubigen aller Glauben! Wen hassen sie am meisten? Den, der zerbricht ihre Tafeln der Werte, den Brecher, den Verbrecher: – das aber ist der Schaffende.

Gefährten sucht der Schaffende und nicht Leichname, und auch nicht Herden und Gläubige. Die Mitschaffenden sucht der Schaffende, Die, welche neue Werte auf neue Tafeln schreiben.

Gefährten sucht der Schaffende, und Miterntende: denn Alles steht bei ihm reif zur Ernte. Aber ihm fehlen die hundert Sicheln: so rauft er Ähren aus und ist ärgerlich.

Gefährten sucht der Schaffende, und solche, die ihre Sicheln zu wetzen wissen. Vernichter wird man sie heißen und Verächter des Guten und Bösen. Aber die Erntenden sind es und die Feiernden.

Mitschaffende sucht Zarathustra, Miterntende und Mitfeiernde sucht Zarathustra: was hat er mit Herden und Hirten und Leichnamen zu schaffen!

Und du, mein erster Gefährte, gehab dich wohl! Gut begrub ich dich in deinem hohlen Baume, gut barg ich dich vor den Wölfen.

9.

Zarathustra slept a long time, and not only the dawn passed across his face, but also the morning. But finally his eyes opened: in surprise Zarathustra gazed into the forest and the silence, in surprise he gazed into himself. Then he arose quickly, like a mariner who has suddenly caught sight of land, and he rejoiced: for he saw a new truth. And then he addressed his heart as follows:

"A light has dawned on me: I need companions, living ones—not dead companions and corpses that I can carry with me wherever I want.

"But I need living companions who will follow *me* because they want to follow *themselves*—and to any place that I wish.

"A light has dawned on me: Zarathustra is not to talk to the populace, but to companions! Zarathustra is not to become the shepherd and dog of a flock!

"To lure many away from the flock—that is why I have come. Let the populace and flock be angry with me: Zarathustra wants to be called a robber by the shepherds.

"I say 'shepherds,' but they call themselves 'the good and the just.' I say 'shepherds,' but they call themselves 'the believers in the true faith.'

"Behold the good and the just! Whom do they hate most? The man who shatters the stone tablets of their values, the breaker, the lawbreaker: but that is the creative man.

"Behold the believers in all faiths! Whom do they hate most? The man who shatters the stone tablets of their values, the breaker, the lawbreaker: but that is the creative man.

"The creative man seeks companions, not corpses or flocks and believers. The creative man seeks co-creators who inscribe new values on new tablets.

"The creative man seeks companions and fellow reapers: for everything in him is ripe for harvesting. But he lacks the hundred sickles, so he plucks out stalks of grain in vexation.

"The creative man seeks companions, of the sort who know how to hone their sickles. They will be called annihilators and despisers of good and evil. But they are the reapers and the celebrants.

"Zarathustra seeks co-creators; Zarathustra seeks fellow reapers, and fellow celebrants; what has he to do with flocks and shepherds and corpses?!

"And you, my first companion, farewell! I have buried you properly in this hollow tree, I have protected you safely from the wolves.

Aber ich scheide von dir, die Zeit ist um. Zwischen Morgenröte und Morgenröte kam mir eine neue Wahrheit.

Nicht Hirt soll ich sein, nicht Totengräber. Nicht reden einmal will ich wieder mit dem Volke; zum letzten Male sprach ich zu einem Toten.

Den Schaffenden, den Erntenden, den Feiernden will ich mich zugesellen: den Regenbogen will ich ihnen zeigen und alle die Treppen des Übermenschen.

Den Einsiedlern werde ich mein Lied singen und den Zweisiedlern: und wer noch Ohren hat für Unerhörtes, dem will ich sein Herz schwermachen mit meinem Glücke.

Zu meinem Ziele will ich, ich gehe meinen Gang; über die Zögernden und Saumseligen werde ich hinwegspringen. Also sei mein Gang ihr Untergang!

10.

Dies hatte Zarathustra zu seinem Herzen gesprochen, als die Sonne im Mittag stand: da blickte er fragend in die Höhe – denn er hörte über sich den scharfen Ruf eines Vogels. Und siehe! Ein Adler zog in weiten Kreisen durch die Luft, und an ihm hing eine Schlange, nicht einer Beute gleich, sondern einer Freundin: denn sie hielt sich um seinen Hals geringelt.

»Es sind meine Tiere!« sagte Zarathustra und freute sich von Herzen.

»Das stolzeste Tier unter der Sonne und das klügste Tier unter der Sonne – sie sind ausgezogen auf Kundschaft.

Erkunden wollen sie, ob Zarathustra noch lebe. Wahrlich, lebe ich noch?

Gefährlicher fand ich's unter Menschen als unter Tieren, gefährliche Wege geht Zarathustra. Mögen mich meine Tiere führen!«

Als Zarathustra dies gesagt hatte, gedachte er der Worte des Heiligen im Walde, seufzte und sprach also zu seinem Herzen:

»Möchte ich klüger sein! Möchte ich klug von Grund aus sein, gleich meiner Schlange!

Aber Unmögliches bitte ich da: so bitte ich denn meinen Stolz, daß er immer mit meiner Klugheit gehe!

Und wenn mich einst meine Klugheit verläßt: – ach, sie liebt es davonzufliegen! – möge mein Stolz dann noch mit meiner Torheit fliegen!«

– Also begann Zarathustras Untergang.

"But I depart from you, the time has come. Between dawn and dawn a new truth has come to me.

"I am not to be a shepherd or a gravedigger. I won't even speak to the populace again; I have spoken to a dead man for the last time.

"I want to associate with the creative, with reapers and celebrants. I will show them the rainbow and all the steps leading to the more-than-man.

"I shall sing my song to hermits living alone or in pairs: and whoever still has ears for the unheard-of, his heart I shall make heavy with my happiness.

"I wish to proceed toward my goal, I go my own way; I shall leap over the hesitant and the sluggish. Thus let my way be their way to ruin!"

10.

Zarathustra had said this to his heart, when the sun reached the zenith: then he looked upward questioningly, for he heard above him the shrill cry of a bird. And behold! An eagle was describing wide circles in the air, and from it there hung a serpent, not as if it were its prey, but as a friend; for it had coiled itself around the eagle's neck.

"Those are my animals!" said Zarathustra, and rejoiced in his heart.

"The proudest creature beneath the sun and the wisest beneath the sun—they have gone out reconnoitering.

"They want to find out whether Zarathustra is still alive. Truly, am I still alive?

"I found life more dangerous among people than among animals; Zarathustra is treading dangerous paths. May my animals guide me!"

After Zarathustra said this, he recalled the words of the holy man in the forest; he sighed and addressed his heart as follows:

"I wish I were wiser! I wish I were thoroughly wise, like my serpent!

"But that is an impossible request: and so I ask my pride to accompany my wisdom everywhere!

"And if my wisdom ever abandons me (alas, it likes to fly away!), may my pride continue to fly along with my folly!"

Thus began Zarathustra's sunset descent.

Von den drei Verwandlungen

Drei Verwandlungen nenne ich euch des Geistes: wie der Geist zum Kamele wird, und zum Löwen das Kamel, und zum Kinde zuletzt der Löwe.

Vieles Schwere gibt es dem Geiste, dem starken, tragsamen Geiste, dem Ehrfurcht innewohnt: nach dem Schweren und Schwersten verlangt seine Stärke.

Was ist schwer? so fragt der tragsame Geist, so kniet er nieder, dem Kamele gleich, und will gut beladen sein.

Was ist das Schwerste, ihr Helden? so fragt der tragsame Geist, daß ich es auf mich nehme und meiner Stärke froh werde.

Ist es nicht das: sich erniedrigen, um seinem Hochmut wehe zu tun? Seine Torheit leuchten lassen, um seiner Weisheit zu spotten?

Oder ist es das: von unserer Sache scheiden, wenn sie ihren Sieg feiert? Auf hohe Berge steigen, um den Versucher zu versuchen?

Oder ist es das: sich von Eicheln und Gras der Erkenntnis nähren und um der Wahrheit willen an der Seele Hunger leiden?

Oder ist es das: krank sein und die Tröster heimschicken und mit Tauben Freundschaft schließen, die niemals hören, was du willst?

Oder ist es das: in schmutziges Wasser steigen, wenn es das Wasser der Wahrheit ist, und kalte Frösche und heiße Kröten nicht von sich weisen?

Oder ist es das: Die lieben, die uns verachten, und dem Gespenste die Hand reichen, wenn es uns fürchten machen will?

Alles dies Schwerste nimmt der tragsame Geist auf sich: dem Kamele gleich, das beladen in die Wüste eilt, also eilt er in seine Wüste.

Aber in der einsamsten Wüste geschieht die zweite Verwandlung: zum Löwen wird hier der Geist, Freiheit will er sich erbeuten und Herr sein in seiner eignen Wüste.

Seinen letzten Herrn sucht er sich hier: feind will er ihm werden und seinem letzten Gotte, um Sieg will er mit dem großen Drachen ringen.

Welches ist der große Drache, den der Geist nicht mehr Herr und Gott heißen mag? »Du-sollst« heißt der große Drache. Aber der Geist des Löwen sagt »ich will«.

»Du-sollst« liegt ihm am Wege, goldfunkelnd, ein Schuppentier, und auf jeder Schuppe glänzt golden »Du-sollst!«

Of the Three Transformations[5]

I name to you three transformations of the spirit: how the spirit becomes a camel, how the camel becomes a lion, and how the lion finally becomes a child.

There is much that is heavy for the spirit, for the strong, burden-bearing spirit in which respect dwells: its strength longs for the heavy and the most heavy.

"What is heavy?" asks the burden-bearing spirit, as it kneels down like a camel, asking to be well laden.

"What is most heavy, O heroes?" asks the burden-bearing spirit. "Let me take it upon myself and be happy in my strength."

Isn't it: to humble oneself, in order to wound one's arrogance? To let one's folly shine forth, in order to mock one's wisdom?

Or is it this—to walk away from our cause when it celebrates its victory? To climb high mountains, in order to tempt the tempter?

Or is it this—to feed on the acorns and grass of knowledge and endure hunger of the soul for the sake of truth?

Or is it this—to be ill and send home those who comfort you, and to make friends with the deaf, who never hear what you ask for?

Or is it this—to wade into dirty water when it's the water of truth and not brush aside cold frogs and hot toads?

Or is it this—to love those who despise us and to hold out our hand to the ghost when it wishes to frighten us?

All these most heavy things the burden-bearing spirit takes upon itself: Like the camel that hastens into the desert with its load, it hastens into its own desert.

But in the remotest part of the desert the second transformation takes place: here the spirit becomes a lion; it wants freedom as its quarry, it wants to be lord of its own desert.

It seeks out its final master here, it wants to become hostile to him and to his last god; it wants to contend for victory with the great dragon.

What is the great dragon that the spirit no longer wishes to call lord and god? The great dragon is called "Thou shalt." But the spirit of the lion says: "It is my will."

"Thou shalt" obstructs his path, sparkling with gold, a scaly animal, on each of whose scales gleam in gold the words "Thou shalt!"

5. The chapters in Part One following the Prologue have a general heading in the original full text: "Zarathustra's Orations." Henceforth, no quotation marks are used in this translation when the entire chapter is a speech by Zarathustra.

Tausendjährige Werte glänzen an diesen Schuppen, und also spricht
der mächtigste aller Drachen: »aller Wert der Dinge – der glänzt an mir.«
»Aller Wert ward schon geschaffen, und aller geschaffene Wert –
das bin ich. Wahrlich, es soll kein ›Ich will‹ mehr geben!« Also spricht
der Drache.

Meine Brüder, wozu bedarf es des Löwen im Geiste? Was genügt
nicht das lastbare Tier, das entsagt und ehrfürchtig ist?

Neue Werte schaffen – das vermag auch der Löwe noch nicht: aber
Freiheit sich schaffen zu neuem Schaffen – das vermag die Macht
des Löwen.

Freiheit sich schaffen und ein heiliges Nein auch vor der Pflicht:
dazu, meine Brüder, bedarf es des Löwen.

Recht sich nehmen zu neuen Werten – das ist das furchtbarste
Nehmen für einen tragsamen und ehrfürchtigen Geist. Wahrlich, ein
Rauben ist es ihm und eines raubenden Tieres Sache.

Als sein Heiligstes liebte er einst das »Du-sollst«: nun muß er Wahn
und Willkür auch noch im Heiligsten finden, daß er sich Freiheit
raube von seiner Liebe: des Löwen bedarf es zu diesem Raube.

Aber sagt, meine Brüder, was vermag noch das Kind, das auch der
Löwe nicht vermochte? Was muß der raubende Löwe auch noch zum
Kinde werden?

Unschuld ist das Kind und Vergessen, ein Neubeginnen, ein Spiel,
ein aus sich rollendes Rad, eine erste Bewegung, ein heiliges Ja-Sagen.

Ja, zum Spiele des Schaffens, meine Brüder, bedarf es eines heiligen Ja-Sagens: *seinen* Willen will nun der Geist, *seine* Welt gewinnt
sich der Weltverlorene.

Drei Verwandlungen nannte ich euch des Geistes: wie der Geist
zum Kamele ward, und zum Löwen das Kamel, und der Löwe zuletzt
zum Kinde. –

Also sprach Zarathustra. Und damals weilte er in der Stadt, welche
genannt wird: die bunte Kuh.

Age-old values gleam on those scales, and so that mightiest of all dragons says: "All the value of things gleams on me."

"All value has already been created, and I am all created value. Truly, there must no longer be any 'It is my will.'" Thus speaks the dragon.

My brothers, why is the lion in the spirit needed? Why is the self-abnegating, respectful beast of burden not sufficient?

To create new values—not even the lion can do that yet. But the lion's power *is* able to gain freedom for new creativity.

To gain freedom and a sacred refusal even of duty: for that, my brothers, the lion is needed.

To claim the right to new values—that is the most terrifying claim for a burden-bearing, respectful spirit. Truly, for such a spirit it is predation and the business of a predatory animal.

It once loved the "Thou shalt" as its most sacred possession; now it must find delusion and arbitrariness even in that most sacred thing, in order to gain freedom from that love; for this predatory gain it needs the lion.

But tell me, my brothers, what can the child do that the lion was unable to do? Why must the predatory lion still become a child?

The child is innocence and forgetting, a new beginning, a game, a spontaneously rolling wheel, a prime motion, a sacred yea-saying.

Yes, for the game of creation, my brothers, a sacred yea-saying is necessary: the spirit now wishes to have its own will, the man lost to the world obtains his own world.

I have named to you three transformations of the spirit: how the spirit became a camel; the camel, a lion; and finally the lion, a child.

Thus spoke Zarathustra. And at that time he resided in the city called the Spotted Cow.

VON DEN LEHRSTUHLEN DER TUGEND (Of the Professorships of Virtue): Zarathustra audits the lectures of a sage who praises sleep as the highest goal; one must be virtuous, law-abiding, and unexceptional in order to sleep well. Zarathustra realizes that this is what professorial wisdom amounts to.

Von den Hinterweltlern

Einst warf auch Zarathustra seinen Wahn jenseits des Menschen, gleich allen Hinterweltlern. Eines leidenden und zerquälten Gottes Werk schien mir da die Welt.

Traum schien mir da die Welt, und Dichtung eines Gottes; farbiger Rauch vor den Augen eines göttlich Unzufriednen.

Gut und böse und Lust und Leid und Ich und Du – farbiger Rauch dünkte mich's vor schöpferischen Augen. Wegsehn wollte der Schöpfer von sich, – da schuf er die Welt.

Trunkne Lust ist's dem Leidenden, wegzusehn von seinem Leiden und sich zu verlieren. Trunkne Lust und Selbst-sich-Verlieren dünkte mich einst die Welt.

Diese Welt, die ewig unvollkommene, eines ewigen Widerspruches Abbild und unvollkommnes Abbild – eine trunkne Lust ihrem unvollkommnen Schöpfer: – also dünkte mich einst die Welt.

Also warf auch ich einst meinen Wahn jenseits des Menschen, gleich allen Hinterweltlern. Jenseits des Menschen in Wahrheit?

Ach, ihr Brüder, dieser Gott, den ich schuf, war Menschen-Werk und -Wahnsinn, gleich allen Göttern!

Mensch war er, und nur ein armes Stück Mensch und Ich: aus der eigenen Asche und Glut kam es mir, dieses Gespenst, und wahrlich! Nicht kam es mir von Jenseits!

Was geschah, meine Brüder? Ich überwand mich, den Leidenden, ich trug meine eigne Asche zu Berge, eine hellere Flamme erfand ich mir. Und siehe! Da wich das Gespenst von mir!

Leiden wäre es mir jetzt und Qual dem Genesenen, solche Gespenster zu glauben: Leiden wäre es mir jetzt und Erniedrigung. Also rede ich zu den Hinterweltlern.

Leiden war's und Unvermögen – das schuf alle Hinterwelten; und jener kurze Wahnsinn des Glücks, den nur der Leidendste erfährt.

Müdigkeit, die mit Einem Sprunge zum Letzten will, mit einem Todessprunge, eine arme unwissende Müdigkeit, die nicht einmal mehr wollen will: die schuf alle Götter und Hinterwelten.

Glaubt es mir, meine Brüder! Der Leib war's, der am Leibe verzweifelte, – der tastete mit den Fingern des betörten Geistes an die letzten Wände.

Of the Backworldsmen[6]

Once Zarathustra, too, cast his delusion beyond mankind, as every backworldsman does. At that time the world appeared to me as the work of a suffering God who was tortured to death.

At that time the world appeared to me as a dream, and the poem of some god; colorful smoke in the eyes of one divinely dissatisfied.

Good and bad and pleasure and pain and I and thou—it all seemed to me like colorful smoke in creative eyes. The Creator wanted to look away from himself—and so he created the world.

It's an intoxicating pleasure for a sufferer to look away from his pain and to lose himself. Intoxicating pleasure and losing of self is what the world once seemed to me.

This world, eternally imperfect, the image—and an imperfect image—of an eternal contradiction—an intoxicating pleasure for its imperfect creator—that's what the world once seemed to me.

And so I, too, once cast my delusion beyond mankind, as every backworldsman does. Beyond mankind, really?

Ah, my brothers, this god that I created was the work and madness of human beings, as all gods are!

He was human, and merely a poor specimen of a man, and myself: this ghost came to me from my own ashes and fire, and truly! It didn't come to me from beyond!

What happened, my brothers? I overcame myself, the sufferer, I carried my own ashes uphill, I invented a brighter flame for myself. And see! Then the ghost departed from me!

Now, as I recover, it would be suffering and torture to me to believe in such ghosts: now it would be suffering and humiliation to me. Thus I speak to the backworldsmen.

It was suffering and incapacity that created all "back worlds," and that brief insanity of happiness experienced only by the greatest sufferer.

Weariness that wants to attain finality at one leap, with one salto mortale; a wretched, ignorant weariness that no longer even wants to exert its will: that's what created all gods and "back worlds."

Believe me, brothers! It was the body, despairing of the body, that ran the fingers of its numbed intellect along the walls of finality.

---

6. See the analysis of the word *Hinterweltler* in the Introduction.

Glaubt es mir, meine Brüder! Der Leib war's, der an der Erde verzweifelte, – der hörte den Bauch des Seins zu sich reden.

Und da wollte er mit dem Kopfe durch die letzten Wände, und nicht nur mit dem Kopfe, – hinüber zu »jener Welt«.

Aber »jene Welt« ist gut verborgen vor dem Menschen, jene entmenschte unmenschliche Welt, die ein himmlisches Nichts ist; und der Bauch des Seins redet gar nicht zum Menschen, es sei denn als Mensch.

Wahrlich, schwer zu beweisen ist alles Sein und schwer zum Reden zu bringen. Sagt mir, ihr Brüder, ist nicht das Wunderlichste aller Dinge noch am besten bewiesen?

Ja, dies Ich und des Ichs Widerspruch und Wirrsal redet noch am redlichsten von seinem Sein, dieses schaffende, wollende, wertende Ich, welches das Maß und der Wert der Dinge ist.

Und dies redlichste Sein, das Ich – das redet vom Leibe, und es will noch den Leib, selbst wenn es dichtet und schwärmt und mit zerbrochnen Flügeln flattert.

Immer redlicher lernt es reden, das Ich: und je mehr es lernt, um so mehr findet es Worte und Ehren für Leib und Erde.

Einen neuen Stolz lehrte mich mein Ich, den lehre ich die Menschen: nicht mehr den Kopf in den Sand der himmlischen Dinge zu stecken, sondern frei ihn zu tragen, einen Erden-Kopf, der der Erde Sinn schafft!

Einen neuen Willen lehre ich die Menschen: diesen Weg wollen, den blindlings der Mensch gegangen, und gut ihn heißen und nicht mehr von ihm beiseite schleichen, gleich den Kranken und Absterbenden!

Kranke und Absterbende waren es, die verachteten Leib und Erde und erfanden das Himmlische und die erlösenden Blutstropfen: aber auch noch diese süßen und düstern Gifte nahmen sie von Leib und Erde!

Ihrem Elende wollten sie entlaufen, und die Sterne waren ihnen zu weit. Da seufzten sie: »Oh daß es doch himmlische Wege gäbe, sich in ein andres Sein und Glück zu schleichen!« – da erfanden sie sich ihre Schliche und blutigen Tränklein!

Ihrem Leibe und dieser Erde nun entrückt wähnten sie sich, diese Undankbaren. Doch wem dankten sie ihrer Entrückung Krampf und Wonne? Ihrem Leibe und dieser Erde.

Milde ist Zarathustra den Kranken. Wahrlich, er zürnt nicht ihren Arten des Trostes und Undanks. Mögen sie Genesende werden und Überwindende und einen höheren Leib sich schaffen!

Nicht auch zürnt Zarathustra dem Genesenden, wenn er zärtlich nach seinem Wahne blickt und mitternachts um das Grab seines

Believe me, brothers! It was the body, despairing of the earth, that heard the belly of existence talking to it.[7]

And then it wanted to thrust its head—and not only its head— through the walls of finality, to attain the "other world."

But the "other world" is well concealed from man, that dehumanized, inhuman world which is a heavenly nothing; and the belly of existence doesn't talk to man, except as another man.

Truly, all existence is hard to prove and it's hard to make it speak. Tell me, brothers, isn't the strangest of all things the most clearly proved one?

Yes, this "I," and the "I's" contradiction and confusion, speaks most honestly about its existence: this creative "I" which exerts its will and establishes values, which is the measure and value of things.

And this most honest existence, the "I," speaks about the body, and still wants the body, even when it writes poems, fantasizes, and flutters with shattered wings.

The "I" learns to speak more honestly all the time; and the more it learns, the more it finds words and honors for the body and the earth.

My "I" taught me a new pride, which I teach to mankind: no longer to bury one's head in the sand of heavenly things, but to carry it freely—a terrestrial head that creates a meaning for the earth!

I teach mankind a new will: to want this path which man has blindly followed, to approve of it, and no longer to slink away from it, as the sick and slowly dying do!

It was sick and slowly dying people who despised body and earth, and invented deity and redeeming drops of blood: but even these sweet, gloomy poisons they derived from body and earth!

They wanted to escape their misery, and the stars were too far away for them. So they sighed: "Oh, if only there were heavenly paths by which to sneak into another, happier existence!" Then they invented their wiles and their little blood-potions!

They now thought they were removed from their body and this earth, those ungrateful men. But to what did they owe the blissful spasms of their release? To their body and this earth.

Zarathustra is gentle with the sick. Truly, he isn't angry with their types of consolation and ingratitude. Let them convalesce, overcome, and create a higher body for themselves!

Nor is Zarathustra angry with convalescents when they gaze tenderly at their delusion and slink around the grave of their god at mid-

---

7. *Bauchredner* ("belly speaker") is the German word for "ventriloquist."

Gottes schleicht: aber Krankheit und kranker Leib bleiben mir auch seine Tränen noch.

Vieles krankhafte Volk gab es immer unter Denen, welche dichten und gottsüchtig sind; wütend hassen sie den Erkennenden und jene jüngste der Tugenden, welche heißt: Redlichkeit.

Rückwärts blicken sie immer nach dunklen Zeiten: da freilich war Wahn und Glaube ein ander Ding; Raserei der Vernunft war Gottähnlichkeit, und Zweifel Sünde.

Allzugut kenne ich diese Gottähnlichen: sie wollen, daß an sie geglaubt werde, und Zweifel Sünde sei. Allzugut weiß ich auch, woran sie selber am besten glauben.

Wahrlich nicht an Hinterwelten und erlösende Blutstropfen: sondern an den Leib glauben auch sie am besten, und ihr eigner Leib ist ihnen ihr Ding an sich.

Aber ein krankhaftes Ding ist er ihnen: und gerne möchten sie aus der Haut fahren. Darum horchen sie nach den Predigern des Todes und predigen selber Hinterwelten.

Hört mir lieber, meine Brüder, auf die Stimme des gesunden Leibes: eine redlichere und reinere Stimme ist dies.

Redlicher redet und reiner der gesunde Leib, der vollkommne und rechtwinklige: und er redet vom Sinn der Erde. –

Also sprach Zarathustra.

Von den Freuden- und Leidenschaften

Mein Bruder, wenn du eine Tugend hast, und es deine Tugend ist, so hast du sie mit Niemandem gemeinsam.

Freilich, du willst sie bei Namen nennen und liebkosen; du willst sie am Ohre zupfen und Kurzweil mit ihr treiben.

Und siehe! Nun hast du ihren Namen mit dem Volke gemeinsam und bist Volk und Herde geworden mit deiner Tugend!

Besser tätest du, zu sagen: »unaussprechbar ist und namenlos, was meiner Seele Qual und Süße macht und auch noch der Hunger meiner Eingeweide ist.«

night: but even their tears still remain sickness and a sick body in my eyes.

There have always been many sickly people among those who write poetry and are God-addicts; they hate with a fury the man with knowledge and that most recent of virtues called honesty.

They always look back to dark ages: yes, then delusion and faith were something else; the frenzy of reason was "being like God," and doubt was "sin."

I know these godlike people all too well: they want to be believed in, they want doubt to be sin. I also know only too well what they themselves believe in most.

Truly, not in "back worlds" and redeeming drops of blood! It's in the body that they, too, believe most, and their own body is their "transcendental object."

But it's a sickly object to them, and they'd like to slip out of their skin. That's why they listen to preachers of death, and why they themselves preach of "back worlds."

Rather than that, brothers, I'd have you listen to the voice of the healthy body: it is a more honest, purer voice.

The healthy body, perfect and foursquare, speaks more honestly and purely: and it speaks of the meaning of the earth.

Thus spoke Zarathustra.

VON DEN VERÄCHTERN DES LEIBES (Of Those Who Despise the Body): "Soul" is merely a term for something bodily. The senses and the mind are the tools and playthings of the self, which is equivalent to the body. Those who despise the body no longer have the power to go beyond themselves, though they desire to; they are envious.

Of Joyful and Painful Passions

My brother, if you have a virtue, and it is your virtue, you don't have it in common with anyone else.

Of course, you want to call it by name and caress it; you want to tug its ear and have fun with it.

And behold! Now you share its name with the populace, and you've become rabble and herd, with your virtue!

You would have done better to say: "It is inexpressible and nameless, that which forms the torment and sweetness of my soul and which is also the hunger of my bowels."

Deine Tugend sei zu hoch für die Vertraulichkeit der Namen: und mußt du von ihr reden, so schäme dich nicht, von ihr zu stammeln.

So sprich und stammle: »Das ist *mein* Gutes, das liebe ich, so gefällt es mir ganz, so allein will *ich* das Gute.

Nicht will ich es als eines Gottes Gesetz, nicht will ich es als eine Menschen-Satzung und -Notdurft: kein Wegweiser sei es mir für Über-Erden und Paradiese.

Eine irdische Tugend ist es, die ich liebe: wenig Klugheit ist darin, und am wenigsten die Vernunft aller.

Aber dieser Vogel baute bei mir sich das Nest: darum liebe und herze ich ihn, – nun sitzt er bei mir auf seinen goldnen Eiern.«

So sollst du stammeln und deine Tugend loben.

Einst hattest du Leidenschaften und nanntest sie böse. Aber jetzt hast du nur noch deine Tugenden: die wuchsen aus deinen Leidenschaften.

Du legtest dein höchstes Ziel diesen Leidenschaften ans Herz: da wurden sie deine Tugenden und Freudenschaften.

Und ob du aus dem Geschlechte der Jähzornigen wärest oder aus dem der Wollüstigen oder der Glaubens-Wütigen oder der Rachsüchtigen:

Am Ende wurden alle deine Leidenschaften zu Tugenden und alle deine Teufel zu Engeln.

Einst hattest du wilde Hunde in deinem Keller: aber am Ende verwandelten sie sich zu Vögeln und lieblichen Sängerinnen.

Aus deinen Giften brautest du dir deinen Balsam; deine Kuh Trübsal melktest du, – nun trinkst du die süße Milch ihres Euters.

Und nichts Böses wächst mehr fürderhin aus dir, es sei denn das Böse, das aus dem Kampfe deiner Tugenden wächst.

Mein Bruder, wenn du Glück hast, so hast du Eine Tugend und nicht mehr: so gehst du leichter über die Brücke.

Auszeichnend ist es, viele Tugenden zu haben, aber ein schweres Los; und Mancher ging in die Wüste und tötete sich, weil er müde war, Schlacht und Schlachtfeld von Tugenden zu sein.

Mein Bruder, ist Krieg und Schlacht böse? Aber notwendig ist dies Böse, notwendig ist der Neid und das Mißtrauen und die Verleumdung unter deinen Tugenden.

Siehe, wie jede deiner Tugenden begehrlich ist nach dem Höchsten: sie will deinen ganzen Geist, daß er *ihr* Herold sei, sie will deine ganze Kraft in Zorn, Haß und Liebe.

Eifersüchtig ist jede Tugend auf die andre, und ein furchtbares Ding ist Eifersucht. Auch Tugenden können an der Eifersucht zugrunde gehn.

Wen die Flamme der Eifersucht umringt, der wendet zuletzt, gleich dem Skorpione, gegen sich selber den vergifteten Stachel.

Let your virtue be too lofty for the intimacy of namegiving; and, if you must speak of it, don't be ashamed to stammer when you do so.

And so, speak and stammer: "This is *my* good, I love it; in this way it pleases me altogether, only in this way do *I* want the good.

"I don't want it as a law dictated by some god, I don't want it as a human ordinance or necessary action; it mustn't be a guide to superior earths and paradises.

"It's an earthly virtue that I love: it contains little wisdom; much less, reason common to everyone.

"But this bird built its nest with me: that's why I love and caress it— now, with me, it is sitting on its golden eggs."

Thus should you stammer in praise of your virtue.

Once you had passions and called them evil. But now you have only your virtues: they grew from your passions.

You warmly commended your loftiest goal to those passions: then they became your virtues and joys.

And whether you were of the race of the wrathful or that of the lustful or faith-rabid or vengeful:

Finally all your passions became virtues, and all your devils became angels.

Once you had wild dogs in your basement: but they finally turned into birds and lovely singing girls.

From your poisons you concocted your balm; you milked your cow Tribulation—now you drink the sweet milk of her udder.

And in the future no more evil will grow from you, except for that evil which grows from the clash of your virtues.

My brother, if you're lucky, you have one virtue and no more; in that way you will be lighter when crossing the bridge.

It's a mark of distinction to have many virtues, but it's a hard lot; and many a man has gone to the desert and killed himself because he was tired of being a battle and battlefield of virtues.

My brother, are war and battle evil? Yet this evil is necessary; envy, distrust, and slander among your virtues are necessary.

See how each of your virtues is desirous of the highest goal; it claims your entire mind to be *its* herald, it claims all your strength in anger, hate, and love.

Each virtue is jealous of the others, and jealousy is a terrible thing. Even virtues can be destroyed by jealousy.

The man encircled by the flame of jealousy finally, like the scorpion, turns his poisonous sting against himself.

Ach, mein Bruder, sahst du noch nie eine Tugend sich selber verleumden und erstechen?

Der Mensch ist Etwas, das überwunden werden muß: und darum sollst du deine Tugenden lieben –: denn du wirst an ihnen zugrunde gehn. –

Also sprach Zarathustra.

Vom Lesen und Schreiben

Von allem Geschriebenen liebe ich nur Das, was einer mit seinem Blute schreibt. Schreibe mit Blut: und du wirst erfahren, daß Blut Geist ist.

Es ist nicht leicht möglich, fremdes Blut zu verstehen: ich hasse die lesenden Müßiggänger.

Wer den Leser kennt, der tut Nichts mehr für den Leser. Noch ein Jahrhundert Leser – und der Geist selber wird stinken.

Daß Jedermann lesen lernen darf, verdirbt auf die Dauer nicht allein das Schreiben, sondern auch das Denken.

Einst war der Geist Gott, dann wurde er zum Menschen, und jetzt wird er gar noch Pöbel.

Wer in Blut und Sprüchen schreibt, der will nicht gelesen, sondern auswendig gelernt werden.

Im Gebirge ist der nächste Weg von Gipfel zu Gipfel: aber dazu mußt du lange Beine haben. Sprüche sollen Gipfel sein: und Die, zu denen gesprochen wird, Große und Hochwüchsige.

Die Luft dünn und rein, die Gefahr nahe und der Geist voll einer fröhlichen Bosheit: so paßt es gut zueinander.

Ich will Kobolde um mich haben, denn ich bin mutig. Mut, der die Gespenster verscheucht, schafft sich selber Kobolde – der Mut will lachen.

Ich empfinde nicht mehr mit euch: diese Wolke, die ich unter mir sehe, diese Schwärze und Schwere, über die ich lache, – gerade das ist eure Gewitterwolke.

Ihr seht nach Oben, wenn ihr nach Erhebung verlangt. Und ich sehe hinab, weil ich erhoben bin.

Wer von euch kann zugleich lachen und erhoben sein?

Ah, my brother, have you never seen a virtue slandering itself and stabbing itself to death?

Man is something that must be superseded: and therefore you should love your virtues—because you will be destroyed by them.

Thus spoke Zarathustra.

VOM BLEICHEN VERBRECHER (Of the Pale Criminal): The man who killed while committing a burglary is a sick man, unable to overcome himself: his true goal was the murder. But the smug judges who condemn him to death out of revenge are even more loathsome, with none of his divine madness.

Of Reading and Writing

Of all written matter I love only that which a man writes with his own blood. Write with blood, and you will learn that blood is mind or spirit.

It isn't very easy to understand someone else's blood: I hate idlers who read.

Whoever knows the reader does no more for the reader's benefit. Another century of readers—and the mind itself will stink.

The fact that everyone is allowed to learn to read will eventually corrupt not only writing, but also thinking.

Once the spirit was God, then it became man, and now it's even becoming rabble.

The man who writes maxims in blood wishes, not to be read, but to be learnt by heart.

In the mountains, the shortest path is from peak to peak, but for that you've got to have long legs. Maxims should be peaks, and those to whom they're addressed should be great men, tall in stature.

The air thin and clear, the danger near at hand, and the mind full of a merry malice: those things go well together.

I want to have goblins around me, for I am courageous. Courage that scares away ghosts creates its own goblins—courage wants to laugh.

I no longer share your feelings: this cloud I see below me, this blackness and heaviness that I laugh at—for you it's a storm cloud.

You look upward when you yearn for uplift. And I look downward, because I am exalted.

Who among you can laugh and be exalted at the same time?

Wer auf den höchsten Bergen steigt, der lacht über alle Trauer-Spiele und Trauer-Ernste.

Mutig, unbekümmert, spöttisch, gewalttätig – so will uns die Weisheit: sie ist ein Weib und liebt immer nur einen Kriegsmann.

Ihr sagt mir: »das Leben ist schwer zu tragen.« Aber wozu hättet ihr vormittags euren Stolz und abends eure Ergebung?

Das Leben ist schwer zu tragen: aber so tut mir doch nicht so zärtlich! Wir sind allesamt hübsche lastbare Esel und Eselinnen.

Was haben wir gemein mit der Rosenknospe, welche zittert, weil ihr ein Tropfen Tau auf dem Leibe liegt?

Es ist wahr: wir lieben das Leben, nicht, weil wir ans Leben, sondern weil wir ans Lieben gewöhnt sind.

Es ist immer etwas Wahnsinn in der Liebe. Es ist aber immer auch etwas Vernunft im Wahnsinn.

Und auch mir, der ich dem Leben gut bin, scheinen Schmetterlinge und Seifenblasen und was ihrer Art unter Menschen ist, am meisten vom Glücke zu wissen.

Diese leichten, törichten, zierlichen, beweglichen Seelchen flattern zu sehen – das verführt Zarathustra zu Tränen und Liedern.

Ich würde nur an einen Gott glauben, der zu tanzen verstünde.

Und als ich meinen Teufel sah, da fand ich ihn ernst, gründlich, tief, feierlich: es war der Geist der Schwere – durch ihn fallen alle Dinge.

Nicht durch Zorn, sondern durch Lachen tötet man. Auf, laßt uns den Geist der Schwere töten!

Ich habe gehen gelernt: seitdem lasse ich mich laufen. Ich habe fliegen gelernt: seitdem will ich nicht erst gestoßen sein, um von der Stelle zu kommen.

Jetzt bin ich leicht, jetzt fliege ich, jetzt sehe ich mich unter mir, jetzt tanzt ein Gott durch mich.

Also sprach Zarathustra.

Whoever climbs the highest mountains laughs at all tragic plays and tragic realities.

Brave, free of worries, mocking, violent—that's how Wisdom would have us be: she's a woman and always loves only a warrior.

You say to me: "Life is hard to bear." But for what purpose do you have your morning pride and your evening dedication?

Life is hard to bear: but, in that case, please don't be so delicate! We are all nice load-bearing donkeys, male and female.

What have we in common with the rosebud, which trembles because a dewdrop lies on its body?

It's true: we love life, not because we're accustomed to life, but because we're accustomed to love.

There is always some element of madness in love. But there is always some reason in madness, too.

And to me as well, since I am fond of life, butterflies and soap bubbles and people of that same type seem to know the most about happiness.

To watch the fluttering of these light, foolish, pretty, agile little souls entices Zarathustra into weeping and singing.

I would only believe in a god if he knew how to dance.

And when I saw my devil, I found him serious, thorough, profound, solemn: it was the spirit of gravity,[8] through which all things fall.

People kill not by anger but by laughter. Come, let's kill the spirit of gravity!

I have learned how to walk: ever since, I have let myself run. I have learned how to fly: ever since, I don't need a push to start moving.

Now I am light, now I fly, now I see myself below me, now a god dances through me.

Thus spoke Zarathustra.

VOM BAUM AM BERGE (Of the Tree on the Mountain): As the unseen wind shakes the tree, we are tormented by invisible hands; like the tree, our roots seek the dark "evil" of the earth, though we strive upward into the solitary cold. We yearn for a bolt of lightning to make an end of us, until we are truly free, cleansed, and heroic.

---

8. In both senses: ponderous earnestness, and the physical force associated with Newton.

Von den Predigern des Todes

Es gibt Prediger des Todes: und die Erde ist voll von Solchen, denen Abkehr gepredigt werden muß vom Leben.

Voll ist die Erde von Überflüssigen, verdorben ist das Leben durch die Viel-zu-Vielen. Möge man sie mit dem »ewigen Leben« aus diesem Leben weglocken!

»Gelbe«: so nennt man die Prediger des Todes, oder »Schwarze«. Aber ich will sie euch noch in andern Farben zeigen.

Da sind die Fürchterlichen, welche in sich das Raubtier herumtragen und keine Wahl haben, es sei denn Lüste oder Selbstzerfleischung. Und auch ihre Lüste sind noch Selbstzerfleischung.

Sie sind noch nicht einmal Mensch geworden, diese Fürchterlichen: mögen sie Abkehr predigen vom Leben und selber dahinfahren!

Da sind die Schwindsüchtigen der Seele: kaum sind sie geboren, so fangen sie schon an zu sterben und sehnen sich nach Lehren der Müdigkeit und Entsagung.

Sie wollen gerne tot sein, und wir sollten ihren Willen gutheißen! Hüten wir uns, diese Toten zu erwecken und diese lebendigen Särge zu versehren!

Ihnen begegnet ein Kranker oder ein Greis oder ein Leichnam; und gleich sagen sie »das Leben ist widerlegt!«

Aber nur sie sind widerlegt und ihr Auge, welches nur das Eine Gesicht sieht am Dasein.

Eingehüllt in dicke Schwermut und begierig auf die kleinen Zufälle, welche den Tod bringen: so warten sie und beißen die Zähne aufeinander.

Oder aber: sie greifen nach Zuckerwerk und spotten ihrer Kinderei dabei: sie hängen an ihrem Strohhalm Leben und spotten, daß sie noch an einem Strohhalm hängen.

Ihre Weisheit lautet: »Ein Tor, der leben bleibt, aber so sehr sind wir die Toren! Und das eben ist das Törichste am Leben!« –

»Das Leben ist nur Leiden« – so sagen Andre und lügen nicht: so sorgt doch, daß *ihr* aufhört! So sorgt doch, daß das Leben aufhört, welches nur Leiden ist!

Und also laute die Lehre eurer Tugend »du sollst dich selber töten! Du sollst dich selber davonstehlen!« –

Of the Preachers of Death

There are preachers of death, and the earth is full of men to whom turning away from life must be preached.

The earth is full of superfluous people; life has been corrupted by the far-too-many. I hope that their "eternal life" lures them out of *this* life!

"Yellow robes": that's what the preachers of death are called, or else "black robes." But I want to show them to you in yet other colors.

First there are the frightful ones, who carry around the predatory beast within themselves and have no other choice but pleasures or self-laceration. And even their pleasures are still self-laceration.

As yet they haven't even become human, these frightful ones: let them preach a turning away from life and let them pass away themselves!

Then there are the consumptives-in-the-soul: scarcely born, they already begin to die, and they yearn for doctrines of weariness and renunciation.

They would like to be dead, and we ought to approve their wishes! Let's be careful not to awaken these dead men or to damage these living coffins!

They meet a sick man or an old man or a corpse,[9] and immediately they say: "Life is refuted!"

But only they are refuted, and their eyes, which see only one face of existence.

Cloaked in dense melancholy and desirous of the minor incidents that bring death, they wait and gnash their teeth.

Or else: they reach for candy and, at the same time, laugh at their childishness: they clutch their straw, life, and they laugh at their still clutching a straw.

Their wisdom states: "Only a fool stays alive, but we are just such fools! And that, precisely, is the most foolish thing about life!"

"Life is merely suffering," say others, and they aren't lying. In that case, take steps for *yourself* to cease! Take steps for life to cease, if it is merely suffering!

And let the doctrine of your virtue state: "Thou shalt kill thyself! Thou shalt steal away!"

---

9. A reference to the legend of the Buddha's gradual "awakening" to the grim truth of earthly life.

»Wollust ist Sünde« – so sagen die Einen, welche den Tod predigen – »laßt uns beiseite gehn und keine Kinder zeugen!«

»Gebären ist mühsam« – sagen die Andren – »Wozu noch gebären? Man gebiert nur Unglückliche!« Und auch sie sind Prediger des Todes.

»Mitleid tut not« – so sagen die Dritten. »Nehmt hin, was ich habe! Nehmt hin, was ich bin! Um so weniger bindet mich das Leben!«

Wären sie Mitleidige von Grund aus, so würden sie ihren Nächsten das Leben verleiden. Böse sein – das wäre ihre rechte Güte.

Aber sie wollen loskommen vom Leben: was schiert es sie, daß sie Andre mit ihren Ketten und Geschenken noch fester binden! –

Und auch ihr, denen das Leben wilde Arbeit und Unruhe ist; seid ihr nicht sehr müde des Lebens? Seid ihr nicht sehr reif für die Predigt des Todes?

Ihr Alle, denen die wilde Arbeit lieb ist und das Schnelle, Neue, Fremde, – ihr ertragt euch schlecht, euer Fleiß ist Flucht und Wille, sich selber zu vergessen.

Wenn ihr mehr an das Leben glaubtet, würdet ihr weniger euch dem Augenblicke hinwerfen. Aber ihr habt zum Warten nicht Inhalt genug in euch – und selbst zur Faulheit nicht!

Überall ertönt die Stimme Derer, welche den Tod predigen: und die Erde ist voll von Solchen, welchen der Tod gepredigt werden muß.

Oder »das ewige Leben«: das gilt mir gleich, – wofern sie nur schnell dahinfahren!

Also sprach Zarathustra.

Vom Krieg und Kriegsvolke

Von unsern besten Feinden wollen wir nicht geschont sein, und auch von Denen nicht, welche wir von Grund aus lieben. So laßt mich denn euch die Wahrheit sagen!

Meine Brüder im Kriege! Ich liebe euch von Grund aus, ich bin und war Euresgleichen. Und ich bin auch euer bester Feind. So laßt mich denn euch die Wahrheit sagen!

Ich weiß um den Haß und Neid eures Herzens. Ihr seid nicht groß genug, um Haß und Neid nicht zu kennen. So seid denn groß genug, euch ihrer nicht zu schämen!

Und wenn ihr nicht Heilige der Erkenntnis sein könnt, so seid mir wenigstens deren Kriegsmänner. Das sind die Gefährten und Vorläufer solcher Heiligkeit.

"Lust is sin," say some who preach death; "let us withdraw and beget no children!"

"Giving birth is laborious," say a second group. "Why keep on bearing children? We only give birth to unfortunates!" And they, too, are preachers of death.

"Compassion is needed," say a third group. "Take all that I have! Take all that I am! I will be tied to life so much the less!"

If they were thoroughgoing compassionaters, they would make their neighbors' life miserable. To be evil would be their proper goodness.

But they want to be freed from life: what do they care if they bind others even more tightly with their chains and gifts?!

And you, too, you for whom life is rugged labor and disquiet, aren't you very tired of life? Aren't you very ripe for the sermon of death?

All of you who love rugged labor and all that is swift, new, unfamiliar—you find it hard to put up with yourselves, your industriousness is escape and the will to forget yourselves.

If you believed more in life, you wouldn't sacrifice yourself to the passing moment so much. But you don't have enough inner substance for waiting—or even for laziness!

Everywhere resounds the voice of those who preach death, and the earth is full of those to whom death must be preached.

Or call it "eternal life"; it's all the same to me, as long as they pass on quickly!

Thus spoke Zarathustra.

Of War and Warriors

We don't want to be spared by our greatest enemies, or even by those whom we love deeply. And so, let me tell you the truth!

My brothers in war! I love you deeply, I am and was one of you. And I'm also your greatest enemy. And so, let me tell you the truth!

I know about the hate and envy in your heart. You aren't big enough to be free of hate and envy. So be big enough not to be ashamed of them!

And if you can't be saints of knowledge, at least be its warriors! These are the companions and forerunners of such sainthood.

Ich sehe viel Soldaten: möchte ich viel Kriegsmänner sehen! »Einform« nennt man's, was sie tragen: möge es nicht Ein-form sein, was sie damit verstecken!

Ihr sollt mir Solche sein, deren Auge immer nach einem Feinde sucht – nach *eurem* Feinde. Und bei Einigen von euch gibt es einen Haß auf den ersten Blick.

Euren Feind sollt ihr suchen, euren Krieg sollt ihr führen, und für eure Gedanken! Und wenn euer Gedanke unterliegt, so soll eure Redlichkeit darüber noch Triumph rufen!

Ihr sollt den Frieden lieben als Mittel zu neuen Kriegen. Und den kurzen Frieden mehr als den langen.

Euch rate ich nicht zur Arbeit, sondern zum Kampfe. Euch rate ich nicht zum Frieden, sondern zum Siege. Eure Arbeit sei ein Kampf, euer Friede sei ein Sieg!

Man kann nur schweigen und stillsitzen, wenn man Pfeil und Bogen hat: sonst schwätzt und zankt man. Euer Friede sei ein Sieg!

Ihr sagt, die gute Sache sei es, die sogar den Krieg heilige? Ich sage euch: der gute Krieg ist es, der jede Sache heiligt.

Der Krieg und der Mut haben mehr große Dinge getan, als die Nächstenliebe. Nicht euer Mitleiden, sondern eure Tapferkeit rettete bisher die Verunglückten.

Was ist gut? fragt ihr. Tapfer sein ist gut. Laßt die kleinen Mädchen reden: »gut sein ist, was hübsch zugleich und rührend ist.«

Man nennt euch herzlos: aber euer Herz ist ächt, und ich liebe die Scham eurer Herzlichkeit. Ihr schämt euch eurer Flut, und Andre schämen sich ihrer Ebbe.

Ihr seid häßlich? Nun wohlan, meine Brüder! So nehmt das Erhabne um euch, den Mantel des Häßlichen!

Und wenn eure Seele groß wird, so wird sie übermütig, und in eurer Erhabenheit ist Bosheit. Ich kenne euch.

In der Bosheit begegnet sich der Übermütige mit dem Schwächlinge. Aber sie mißverstehen einander. Ich kenne euch.

Ihr dürft nur Feinde haben, die zu hassen sind, aber nicht Feinde zum Verachten. Ihr müßt stolz auf euern Feind sein: dann sind die Erfolge eures Feindes auch eure Erfolge.

Auflehnung – das ist die Vornehmheit am Sklaven. Eure Vornehmheit sei Gehorsam! Euer Befehlen selber sei ein Gehorchen!

Einem guten Kriegsmanne klingt »du sollst« angenehmer als »ich will«. Und Alles, was euch lieb ist, sollt ihr euch erst noch befehlen lassen.

Eure Liebe zum Leben sei Liebe zu eurer höchsten Hoffnung: und eure höchste Hoffnung sei der höchste Gedanke des Lebens!

I see many soldiers; I'd like to see many warriors! Their clothing is called a uniform. Let that which is hidden under it *not* be uniform!

I'd like you to be men whose eyes always seek a foe—*your* foe. And some of you harbor hatred at first sight.

You must seek your foe, you must wage your war, and do so for your own ideas! And if your cause loses, your uprightness must still proclaim triumph at it!

You must love peace as a means to new wars. And a brief peace more than a long one.

I advise you, not to work, but to fight. I advise you to seek not peace, but victory. Let your work be a battle, let your peace be a victory!

One can be silent and in repose only when one has a bow and arrow: otherwise one chatters and quarrels. Let your peace be a victory!

You say that it's the just cause that even sanctifies war? I say to you: it's a good war that sanctifies every cause.

War and courage have performed more great actions than Christian charity has. It is not your compassion, but your bravery, that has rescued the unfortunate hitherto.

"What is good?" you ask. Being brave is good. Let little girls say: "Being good is what is pretty and touching at the same time."

You are called heartless, but your heart is in the right place, and I love the modesty of your cordiality. You are ashamed of your floodtide, whereas others are ashamed of their ebbtide.

You're ugly? All right, then, my brothers! In that case, wrap yourself in loftiness, the mantle of the ugly!

And when your soul becomes great, it becomes boisterous, and in your loftiness there is malice. I know you.

In malice, the boisterous man joins up with the weakling. But they misunderstand each other. I know you.

You should only have enemies to hate, not enemies to despise. You must be proud of your enemy: then your enemy's successes are also your successes.

Rebellion is the slave's way of being aristocratic. Let your aristocracy be obedience! Let even your giving orders be an act of obedience!

To a good warrior, "you must" sounds more pleasant than "I want." And everything that is dear to you, you should accept only when you have received orders to do so.

Let your love of life be love of your highest hopes; and let your highest hopes be the highest idea in life!

Euren höchsten Gedanken aber sollt ihr euch von mir befehlen lassen
– und er lautet: der Mensch ist Etwas, das überwunden werden soll.
So lebt euer Leben des Gehorsams und des Krieges! Was liegt am
Lang-Leben! Welcher Krieger will geschont sein!
Ich schone euch nicht, ich liebe euch von Grund aus, meine Brüder
im Kriege! –

Also sprach Zarathustra.

Vom neuen Götzen

Irgendwo gibt es noch Völker und Herden, doch nicht bei uns, meine
Brüder: da gibt es Staaten.
Staat? Was ist das? Wohlan! Jetzt tut mir die Ohren auf, denn jetzt
sage ich euch mein Wort vom Tode der Völker.
Staat heißt das kälteste aller kalten Ungeheuer. Kalt lügt es auch; und
diese Lüge kriecht aus seinem Munde:»Ich, der Staat, bin das Volk.«
Lüge ist's! Schaffende waren es, die schufen die Völker und hängten
einen Glauben und eine Liebe über sie hin: also dienten sie dem Leben.
Vernichter sind es, die stellen Fallen auf für Viele und heißen sie
Staat: sie hängen ein Schwert und hundert Begierden über sie hin.
Wo es noch Volk gibt, da versteht es den Staat nicht und haßt ihn
als bösen Blick und Sünde an Sitten und Rechten.
Dieses Zeichen gebe ich euch: jedes Volk spricht seine Zunge des
Guten und Bösen: die versteht der Nachbar nicht. Seine Sprache er-
fand es sich in Sitten und Rechten.
Aber der Staat lügt in allen Zungen des Guten und Bösen; und was
er auch redet, er lügt – und was er auch hat, gestohlen hat er's.
Falsch ist Alles in ihm; mit gestohlenen Zähnen beißt er, der
Bissige. Falsch sind selbst seine Eingeweide.
Sprachverwirrung des Guten und Bösen: dieses Zeichen gebe ich
euch als Zeichen des Staates. Wahrlich, den Willen zum Tode deutet
dieses Zeichen! Wahrlich, es winkt den Predigern des Todes!
Viel zu Viele werden geboren: für die Überflüssigen ward der Staat
erfunden!
Seht mir doch, wie er sie an sich lockt, die Viel-zu-Vielen! Wie er
sie schlingt und kaut und wiederkäut!
»Auf der Erde ist nichts Größeres als ich: der ordnende Finger bin
ich Gottes« – also brüllt das Untier. Und nicht nur Langgeohrte und
Kurzgeäugte sinken auf die Knie!

But you should receive your highest idea under orders from me, and it is as follows: "Man is something that must be superseded."

And so, live your life of obedience and war! What is there to long life? What warrior wishes to be spared?

I don't spare you, I love you deeply, my brothers in war!

Thus spoke Zarathustra.

Of the New Idol

Somewhere there are still peoples and herds, but not among us, my brothers: here there are states.

State? What is that? All right! Now open your ears, for now I shall tell you my thoughts on the death of peoples.

State is the name for the coldest of all cold monsters. It tells cool lies, too; and this lie crawls out of its mouth: "I, the state, am the people."

It's a lie! It was creative men who created nations and gave them a faith and love to look up to: in that way they were serving life.

It is annihilators who set traps for many and call them "state": they give them a sword and a hundred desires to look up to.

Where there is still a people, it doesn't understand the state, but hates it as an evil eye and a sin against customs and rights.

I give you this sign: every nation speaks its own language of good and evil, which its neighbor doesn't understand. It invented its own language of customs and rights.

But the state tells lies in every language of good and evil; and whatever it says is a lie, and whatever it has, it stole.

Everything about it is false; it bites with stolen teeth, that vicious dog. Even its entrails are false.

Confusion of tongues with regard to good and evil: I give you this sign as the sign of the state. Truly, this sign indicates the will to death! Truly, it beckons to the preachers of death!

Far too many are born: the state was invented for the superfluous!

Just see how it lures them, the far-too-many! How it swallows them, chews them, and then even ruminates!

"There is nothing greater on earth than I; I am God's governing finger," the horrible beast bellows. And not only the long-eared and the shortsighted fall to their knees!

Ach, auch in euch, ihr großen Seelen, raunt er seine düsteren Lügen! Ach, er errät die reichen Herzen, die gerne sich verschwenden!

Ja, auch euch errät er, ihr Besieger des alten Gottes! Müde wurdet ihr im Kampfe, und nun dient eure Müdigkeit noch dem neuen Götzen!

Helden und Ehrenhafte möchte er um sich aufstellen, der neue Götze! Gerne sonnt er sich im Sonnenschein guter Gewissen – das kalte Untier!

Alles will er *euch* geben, wenn ihr ihn anbetet, der neue Götze: also kauft er sich den Glanz eurer Tugend und den Blick eurer stolzen Augen.

Ködern will er mit euch die Viel-zu-Vielen! Ja, ein Höllenkunststück ward da erfunden, ein Pferd des Todes, klirrend im Putz göttlicher Ehren!

Ja, ein Sterben für Viele ward da erfunden, das sich selber als Leben preist: wahrlich, ein Herzensdienst allen Predigern des Todes!

Staat nenne ich's, wo Alle Gifttrinker sind, Gute und Schlimme: Staat, wo Alle sich selber verlieren, Gute und Schlimme: Staat, wo der langsame Selbstmord aller – »das Leben« heißt.

Seht mir doch diese Überflüssigen! Sie stehlen sich die Werke der Erfinder und die Schätze der Weisen: Bildung nennen sie ihren Diebstahl – und Alles wird ihnen zu Krankheit und Ungemach!

Seht mir doch diese Überflüssigen! Krank sind sie immer, sie erbrechen ihre Galle und nennen es Zeitung. Sie verschlingen einander und können sich nicht einmal verdauen.

Seht mir doch diese Überflüssigen! Reichtümer erwerben sie und werden ärmer damit. Macht wollen sie, und zuerst das Brecheisen der Macht, viel Geld, – diese Unvermögenden!

Seht sie klettern, diese geschwinden Affen! Sie klettern übereinander hinweg und zerren sich also in den Schlamm und die Tiefe.

Hin zum Throne wollen sie Alle: ihr Wahnsinn ist es – als ob das Glück auf dem Throne säße! Oft sitzt der Schlamm auf dem Thron – und oft auch der Thron auf dem Schlamme.

Wahnsinnige sind sie mir Alle und kletternde Affen und Überheiße. Übel riecht mir ihr Götze, das kalte Untier: übel riechen sie mir alle zusammen, diese Götzendiener.

Meine Brüder, wollt ihr denn ersticken im Dunste ihrer Mäuler und Begierden! Lieber zerbrecht doch die Fenster und springt ins Freie!

Geht doch dem schlechten Geruche aus dem Wege! Geht fort von der Götzendienerei der Überflüssigen!

Alas, even to you, great souls, it whispers its somber lies! Alas, it detects the generous hearts that are glad to expend themselves!

Yes, it even detects you, conquerors of the old god! You grew weary in battle, and now your weariness serves the new idol!

It wants to station heroes and honorable men around itself, this new idol! It likes to bask in the sunshine of good consciences—the cold monster!

It wants to give *you* everything if you worship it, the new idol; in that way it purchases the glory of your virtue and the gaze of your proud eyes.

It wants to lure you, with the far-too-many as bait! Yes, a hellish trick was there devised, a horse of death, jingling in the adornment of divine honors!

Yes, a death for many was there devised, one that praises itself as being life: truly, a cordial service to all preachers of death!

I call that "state" in which everyone drinks poison, the good and the bad; "state," in which everyone loses himself, the good and the bad; "state," in which the slow suicide of everyone is termed "life."

Just look at these superfluous people! They usurp the efforts of the inventors and the treasures of the sages: they call their theft "culture"—and for them everything turns into sickness and adversity!

Just look at these superfluous people! They're always sick, they vomit their gall and call it "a newspaper." They gulp one another down and can't even digest one another.

Just look at these superfluous people! They amass wealth while growing poorer. They want power, and first the jimmy to break their way into power: a lot of money—these incapable, penniless ones!

Watch them climb, these nimble apes! They climb over one another and thus pull one another into the mire and the depths.

They all went to reach the throne: it's their mania—as if happiness sat on the throne! Often mire sits on the throne—and, likewise, the throne is often situated in the mire.

To me they're all madmen, climbing apes, and overheated. Their idol, that cold monster, stinks in my nostrils; all of them smell bad to me, these idol-servers.

My brothers, do you really want to choke in the vapor of their mouths and desires? Instead, demolish the windows and jump outdoors!

Avoid the bad smell! Abandon the idol-worship of the superfluous!

Geht doch dem schlechten Geruche aus dem Wege! Geht fort von dem Dampfe dieser Menschenopfer!

Frei steht großen Seelen auch jetzt noch die Erde. Leer sind noch viele Sitze für Einsame und Zweisame, um die der Geruch stiller Meere weht.

Frei steht noch großen Seelen ein freies Leben. Wahrlich, wer wenig besitzt, wird um so weniger besessen: gelobt sei die kleine Armut!

Dort, wo der Staat aufhört, da beginnt erst der Mensch, der nicht überflüssig ist: da beginnt das Lied des Notwendigen, die einmalige und unersetzliche Weise.

Dort, wo der Staat *aufhört*, – so seht mir doch hin, meine Brüder! Seht ihr ihn nicht, den Regenbogen und die Brücken des Übermenschen? –

Also sprach Zarathustra.

Von den Fliegen des Marktes

Fliehe, mein Freund, in deine Einsamkeit! Ich sehe dich betäubt vom Lärme der großen Männer und zerstochen von den Stacheln der kleinen.

Würdig wissen Wald und Fels mit dir zu schweigen. Gleiche wieder dem Baume, den du liebst, dem breitästigen: still und aufhorchend hängt er über dem Meere.

Wo die Einsamkeit aufhört, da beginnt der Markt; und wo der Markt beginnt, da beginnt auch der Lärm der großen Schauspieler und das Geschwirr der giftigen Fliegen.

In der Welt taugen die besten Dinge noch Nichts, ohne Einen, der sie erst aufführt: große Männer heißt das Volk diese Aufführer.

Wenig begreift das Volk das Große, das ist: das Schaffende. Aber Sinne hat es für alle Aufführer und Schauspieler großer Sachen.

Um die Erfinder von neuen Werten dreht sich die Welt: – unsichtbar dreht sie sich. Doch um die Schauspieler dreht sich das Volk und der Ruhm: so ist es »der Welt Lauf«.

Geist hat der Schauspieler, doch wenig Gewissen des Geistes. Immer glaubt er an Das, womit er am stärksten glauben macht – glauben an *sich* macht!

Morgen hat er einen neuen Glauben und übermorgen einen neueren. Rasche Sinne hat er, gleich dem Volke, und veränderliche Witterungen.

Avoid the bad smell! Abandon the steam of these human sacrifices!

The earth still lies open to great souls even now. There are still many empty chairs for individuals or couples where the smell of calm seas still wafts.

A free life still lies open to great souls. Truly, the man with few possessions is himself possessed by so much less: praised be humble poverty!

Where the state ends, there the unsuperfluous man begins: there, the song of the necessary begins, that unique, irreplaceable melody.

Where the state *ends*—just look over there, my brothers! Don't you see them, the rainbow and the bridges to the more-than-man?

Thus spoke Zarathustra.

Of the Flies in the Marketplace

Escape, my friend, into your solitude! I see you deafened by the noise of the big men and badly wounded by the stings of the little men.

Forest and crag know how to share your silence in a dignified manner. Resemble once more the tree you used to love, the broad-boughed one: silently hearkening, it projects above the sea.

Where solitude ends, the marketplace begins; and where the market begins, so does the noise of the big actors and the whirring of the poisonous flies.

In the world the best things still are worthless without someone to present them: the populace calls these presenters and performers "great men."

The populace has little comprehension of greatness—that is, creativity. But it's receptive to all performers and actors of great causes.

The world revolves around the inventors of new values—it turns imperceptibly. But the populace and fame revolve around the actors: that's why it's "the way of the world."

The actor has intellect, but not much intellectual conscience. He always believes that with which he generates the strongest belief—the belief in himself!

Tomorrow he has a new belief, and the day after tomorrow a newer one. He has quick senses, as the populace does, and changeable weather patterns.

Umwerfen – das heißt ihm: beweisen. Toll machen – das heißt ihm: überzeugen. Und Blut gilt ihm als aller Gründe bester.

Eine Wahrheit, die nur in feine Ohren schlüpft, nennt er Lüge und Nichts. Wahrlich, er glaubt nur an Götter, die großen Lärm in der Welt machen!

Voll von feierlichen Possenreißern ist der Markt – und das Volk rühmt sich seiner großen Männer! Das sind ihm die Herrn der Stunde.

Aber die Stunde drängt sie: so drängen sie dich. Und auch von dir wollen sie Ja oder Nein. Wehe, du willst zwischen Für und Wider deinen Stuhl setzen?

Dieser Unbedingten und Drängenden halber sei ohne Eifersucht, du Liebhaber der Wahrheit! Niemals noch hängte sich die Wahrheit an den Arm eines Unbedingten.

Dieser Plötzlichen halber gehe zurück in deine Sicherheit: nur auf dem Markt wird man mit Ja? oder Nein? überfallen.

Langsam ist das Erleben allen tiefen Brunnen: lange müssen sie warten, bis sie wissen, *was* in ihre Tiefe fiel.

Abseits vom Markte und Ruhme begibt sich alles Große: abseits vom Markte und Ruhme wohnten von je die Erfinder neuer Werte.

Fliehe, mein Freund, in deine Einsamkeit: ich sehe dich von giftigen Fliegen zerstochen. Fliehe dorthin, wo rauhe, starke Luft weht!

Fliehe in deine Einsamkeit! Du lebtest den Kleinen und Erbärmlichen zu nahe. Fliehe vor ihrer unsichtbaren Rache! Gegen dich sind sie Nichts als Rache.

Hebe nicht mehr den Arm gegen sie! Unzählbar sind sie, und es ist nicht dein Los, Fliegenwedel zu sein.

Unzählbar sind diese Kleinen und Erbärmlichen; und manchem stolzen Baue gereichten schon Regentropfen und Unkraut zum Untergange.

Du bist kein Stein, aber schon wurdest du hohl von vielen Tropfen. Zerbrechen und zerbersten wirst du mir noch von vielen Tropfen.

Ermüdet sehe ich dich durch giftige Fliegen, blutig geritzt sehe ich dich an hundert Stellen; und dein Stolz will nicht einmal zürnen.

Blut möchten sie von dir in aller Unschuld, Blut begehren ihre blutlosen Seelen – und sie stechen daher in aller Unschuld.

Aber du Tiefer, du leidest zu tief, auch an kleinen Wunden; und ehe du dich noch geheilt hast, kroch dir der gleiche Giftwurm über die Hand.

Zu stolz bist du mir dafür, diese Naschhaften zu töten. Hüte dich aber, daß es nicht dein Verhängnis werde, all ihr giftiges Unrecht zu tragen!

Sie summen um dich auch mit ihrem Lobe: Zudringlichkeit ist ihr Loben. Sie wollen die Nähe deiner Haut und deines Blutes.

To him, to overturn is to "prove." To him, driving someone crazy means "convincing" him. And to him, blood is the best of all reasons.

A truth that can only slip into delicate ears, he calls a "lie" and "nothing." Truly, he believes only in gods that create a big stir in the world!

The marketplace is full of solemn clowns—and the populace is proud of its great men! For it, they are the masters of the hour.

But the hour presses in upon them, and so they press in upon you. And from you, too, they demand a yes or a no. Alas, do you want to place your chair between pro and con?

Be without jealousy of these absolutists and insistent people, you lover of truth! Never yet has truth taken the arm of an absolutist.

Because of these hasty people, return to your safety: only in the marketplace is one assailed by "Yes or no?"

For all deep springs, experience is slow: they must wait a long time before they know *what* fell into their depths.

All great things occur far from the market and fame; the inventors of new values have always dwelt far from the market and fame.

Escape, my friend, into your solitude: I see you badly wounded by poisonous flies. Escape to where rough, strong winds blow!

Escape into your solitude! You were living too close to small, pathetic people. Escape their invisible revenge! Toward you they feel nothing but revenge.

No longer raise your arm against them! They're innumerable, and it's not your role to be a fly whisk.

Innumerable are these small, pathetic people; and many a proud building has already been destroyed by raindrops and weeds.

You're not a stone, but you've already been hollowed out by all those drops. You may yet shatter and burst from all those drops.

I see you worn out by poisonous flies, I see you scratched bloody in a hundred places; and your pride even refuses to grow angry.

They want blood from you in all innocence, their bloodless souls crave blood—and they bite away in all innocence.

But you, a man of deep feeling, suffer too deeply, even from small wounds; and even before you have healed, the same poisonous worm has crawled over your hand.

I find you too proud to kill these greedy feeders. But take care lest it become your calamity to endure all their poisonous injustice!

They buzz around you even with their praise: their way of praising is pushiness. They want the proximity of your skin and your blood.

Sie schmeicheln dir wie einem Gotte oder Teufel; sie winseln vor dir wie vor einem Gotte oder Teufel. Was macht es! Schmeichler sind es und Winsler, und nicht mehr.

Auch geben sie sich dir oft als Liebenswürdige. Aber das war immer die Klugheit der Feigen. Ja, die Feigen sind klug!

Sie denken viel über dich mit ihrer engen Seele – bedenklich bist du ihnen stets! Alles, was viel bedacht wird, wird bedenklich.

Sie bestrafen dich für alle deine Tugenden. Sie verzeihen dir von Grund aus nur – deine Fehlgriffe.

Weil du milde bist und gerechten Sinnes, sagst du:»unschuldig sind sie an ihrem kleinen Dasein.« Aber ihre enge Seele denkt: »Schuld ist alles große Dasein.«

Auch wenn du ihnen milde bist, fühlen sie sich noch von dir verachtet; und sie geben dir deine Wohltat zurück mit versteckten Wehtaten.

Dein wortloser Stolz geht immer wider ihren Geschmack; sie frohlocken, wenn du einmal bescheiden genug bist, eitel zu sein.

Das, was wir an einem Menschen erkennen, das entzünden wir an ihm auch. Also hüte dich vor den Kleinen!

Vor dir fühlen sie sich klein, und ihre Niedrigkeit glimmt und glüht gegen dich in unsichtbarer Rache.

Merktest du nicht, wie oft sie stumm wurden, wenn du zu ihnen tratest, und wie ihre Kraft von ihnen ging, wie der Rauch von einem erlöschenden Feuer?

Ja, mein Freund, das böse Gewissen bist du deinen Nächsten: denn sie sind deiner unwert. Also hassen sie dich und möchten gerne an deinem Blute saugen.

Deine Nächsten werden immer giftige Fliegen sein; Das, was groß an dir ist, – das selber muß sie giftiger machen und immer fliegenhafter.

Fliehe, mein Freund, in deine Einsamkeit und dorthin, wo eine rauhe, starke Luft weht. Nicht ist es dein Los, Fliegenwedel zu sein. –

Also sprach Zarathustra.

VON KEUSCHHEIT (Of Chastity): Most people are slaves to morbid lust, which is unpalatable. But Zarathustra doesn't preach the deadening of the senses; the chaste tend to be secretly resentful. Chastity is acceptable when it comes to one naturally. / VOM FREUNDE (Of Friends): Hermits need a worthy friend, one who is also a potential enemy. One mustn't bare oneself entirely. Friends should incite each other to sur-

They flatter you as if you were a god or devil; they whine before you as if before a god or devil. What does it matter? They're flatterers and whiners, and nothing else.

Also, they frequently pass themselves off to you as being amiable. But that has always been the shrewdness of cowards. Yes, cowards are shrewd!

They think a lot about you in their narrow souls—you're always a matter of concern to them! Everything that is thought about a lot becomes a cause of concern.

They punish you for all your virtues. The only thing they forgive you for completely is—your mistakes.

Because you're gentle and fairminded, you say: "They're not to blame for their petty existence." But their narrow soul thinks: "All great existence is blameworthy."

Even when you're gentle with them, they still feel that you despise them; and they repay your beneficence with hidden acts of enmity.

Your taciturn pride always goes against their grain; they rejoice when at times you are modest enough to be vain.

What we recognize in a person, we also incite him to. So be on your guard against small folk!

In your presence they feel small, and their lowliness smolders and flares up against you in invisible revenge.

Haven't you noticed how often they have fallen silent when you came up to them, and how their strength deserted them, like smoke from a dying fire?

Yes, my friend, you are your fellow men's bad conscience, because they're unworthy of you. And so they hate you and would gladly suck your blood.

Your fellow men will always be poisonous flies; what is great in you—that very thing has to make them more poisonous and ever more flylike.

Escape, my friend, into your solitude, to where rough, strong winds blow. It isn't your role to be a fly whisk.

Thus spoke Zarathustra.

---

pass themselves and become more-than-man. Women are not yet capable of friendship, only of love, because they have always been either slaves or tyrants. / VOM TAUSEND UND EINEM ZIELE (Of 1,001 Goals): Nations are individuated by differing opinions on what is good or bad. Each nation's set of rules (for self-surpassment)—rules that are self-invented (not divinely inspired)—is the voice of its will to power. Creators

must demolish old values; individuals spell the downfall of the herd. Mankind still lacks its ultimate goal. / VON DER NÄCHSTENLIEBE (Of Christian Charity): Love for one's neighbor is self-hate disguised. Love for future goals is loftier. People should derive their contentment from themselves or from true friends. / VOM WEGE DES SCHAFFENDEN (Of

Von alten und jungen Weiblein

»Was schleichst du so scheu durch die Dämmerung, Zarathustra? Und was birgst du behutsam unter deinem Mantel?«

»Ist es ein Schatz, der dir geschenkt? Oder ein Kind, das dir geboren wurde? Oder gehst du jetzt selber auf den Wegen der Diebe, du Freund der Bösen?« –

Wahrlich, mein Bruder! sprach Zarathustra, es ist ein Schatz, der mir geschenkt wurde: eine kleine Wahrheit ist's, die ich trage.

Aber sie ist ungebärdig wie ein junges Kind; und wenn ich ihr nicht den Mund halte, so schreit sie überlaut.

Als ich heute allein meines Weges ging, zur Stunde, wo die Sonne sinkt, begegnete mir ein altes Weiblein und redete also zu meiner Seele:

»Vieles sprach Zarathustra auch zu uns Weibern, doch nie sprach er uns über das Weib.«

Und ich entgegnete ihr: »über das Weib soll man nur zu Männern reden.«

»Rede auch zu mir vom Weibe«, sprach sie; »ich bin alt genug, um es gleich wieder zu vergessen.«

Und ich willfahrte dem alten Weiblein und sprach also zu ihm:

Alles am Weibe ist ein Rätsel, und Alles am Weibe hat Eine Lösung: sie heißt Schwangerschaft.

Der Mann ist für das Weib ein Mittel: der Zweck ist immer das Kind. Aber was ist das Weib für den Mann?

Zweierlei will der ächte Mann: Gefahr und Spiel. Deshalb will er das Weib, als das gefährlichste Spielzeug.

Der Mann soll zum Kriege erzogen werden, und das Weib zur Erholung des Kriegers: alles Andre ist Torheit.

Allzu süße Früchte – die mag der Krieger nicht. Darum mag er das Weib; bitter ist auch noch das süßeste Weib.

Besser als ein Mann versteht das Weib die Kinder, aber der Mann ist kindlicher als das Weib.

Im ächten Manne ist ein Kind versteckt: das will spielen. Auf, ihr Frauen, so entdeckt mir doch das Kind im Manne!

the Creative Man's Path): One shouldn't regret abandoning the herd, but should do so only if truly capable of it, and not out of ambition. Freedom should be sought only for a lofty purpose. One should be sure of oneself and unafraid of solitude, derision, or self-discovery.

Of Females Old and Young

"Why are you stealing about in the twilight so timidly, Zarathustra? And what are you hiding carefully under your cloak?

"Is it a treasure you have been given? Or a child that has been born to you? Or are you yourself now treading the path of thieves, you friend of the wicked?"

"Truly, my brother!" said Zarathustra. "It is a treasure I have been given: what I'm carrying is a small truth.

"But it's unruly as a young child; and if I don't hold its mouth closed, it yells too loudly.

"Today, when I was going my way alone, at the hour of sunset, I met a little old lady who addressed my soul as follows:

"'Zarathustra has spoken of many things to us women, as well, but he has never spoken to us about woman.'

"And I countered: 'Woman should be discussed only with men.'

"'Speak to me of woman, also,' she said; 'I'm old enough to forget it again right away.'

"And I obliged the little old lady and spoke to her thus:

"'Everything about woman is a riddle, and everything about woman has a solution: it's called pregnancy.

"'For a woman, a man is a means; the end is always the child. But what is a woman for a man?

"'Real men want two things: danger and play. And so they want woman, who is the most dangerous plaything.

"'Man ought to be educated for war, and woman to be the warrior's relaxation: anything else is folly.

"'Fruits that are too sweet the warrior dislikes. And so he likes woman; even the sweetest woman is bitter.

"'Women understand children better than men do, but men are more childlike than women.

"'Within every real man a child is concealed; it wants to play. Come, ladies, discover the child in man!

Ein Spielzeug sei das Weib, rein und fein, dem Edelsteine gleich, bestrahlt von den Tugenden einer Welt, welche noch nicht da ist.

Der Strahl eines Sternes glänze in eurer Liebe! Eure Hoffnung heiße: »möge ich den Übermenschen gebären!«

In eurer Liebe sei Tapferkeit! Mit eurer Liebe sollt ihr auf Den losgehn, der euch Furcht einflößt.

In eurer Liebe sei eure Ehre! Wenig versteht sich sonst das Weib auf Ehre. Aber dies sei eure Ehre, immer mehr zu lieben, als ihr geliebt werdet, und nie die Zweiten zu sein.

Der Mann fürchte sich vor dem Weibe, wenn es liebt: da bringt es jedes Opfer, und jedes andre Ding gilt ihm ohne Wert.

Der Mann fürchte sich vor dem Weibe, wenn es haßt: denn der Mann ist im Grunde der Seele nur böse, das Weib aber ist dort schlecht.

Wen haßt das Weib am meisten? – Also sprach das Eisen zum Magneten: »ich hasse dich am meisten, weil du anziehst, aber nicht stark genug bist, an dich zu ziehen.«

Das Glück des Mannes heißt: ich will. Das Glück des Weibes heißt: er will.

»Siehe, jetzt eben ward die Welt vollkommen!« – also denkt ein jedes Weib, wenn es aus ganzer Liebe gehorcht.

Und gehorchen muß das Weib und eine Tiefe finden zu seiner Oberfläche. Oberfläche ist des Weibes Gemüt, eine bewegliche stürmische Haut auf einem seichten Gewässer.

Des Mannes Gemüt aber ist tief, sein Strom rauscht in unterirdischen Höhlen: das Weib ahnt seine Kraft, aber begreift sie nicht. –

Da entgegnete mir das alte Weiblein: »Vieles Artige sagte Zarathustra und sonderlich für Die, welche jung genug dazu sind.

Seltsam ist's, Zarathustra kennt wenig die Weiber, und doch hat er über sie recht! Geschieht dies deshalb, weil beim Weibe kein Ding unmöglich ist?

Und nun nimm zum Danke eine kleine Wahrheit! Bin ich doch alt genug für sie!

Wickle sie ein und halte ihr den Mund: sonst schreit sie überlaut, diese kleine Wahrheit.«

»Gib mir, Weib, deine kleine Wahrheit!« sagte ich. Und also sprach das alte Weiblein:

»Du gehst zu Frauen? Vergiß die Peitsche nicht!« –

Also sprach Zarathustra.

"'Let woman be a plaything, pure and delicate, like a jewel, illuminated by the virtues of a world that does not yet exist.

"'Let a ray from a star shine in your love! Let your hope be: "May I give birth to the more-than-man!"

"'Let there be bravery in your love! With your love you should light into anyone who inspires fear in you.

"'Let your honor be in your love! Otherwise woman has very little conception of honor. But let this be your honor: always to love more than you are loved, and never to be the less loving.

"'Let man fear woman when she loves: she then makes every sacrifice, and all else seems worthless to her.

"'Let man fear woman when she hates: for at the bottom of his heart man is merely wicked, whereas woman is really bad.

"'Whom does woman hate most? The iron once said to the magnet: "I hate you most because you attract me but aren't strong enough to draw me to you."

"'Man's happiness is: "I want." Woman's happiness is: "He wants."

"'"Behold, only now has the world become perfect!" That's what each and every woman thinks when she obeys because she's completely in love.

"'And woman must obey and find depths to go with her superficiality. Woman's temperament is a surface, an agitated, stormy film over a shallow body of water.

"'But man's temperament is deep; its current roars in underground caves; woman has an inkling of his strength but doesn't grasp it.'

"Then the little old lady countered: 'Zarathustra has said many bright things, especially for those young enough for them.

"'Strange, Zarathustra has little acquaintance with women, and yet what he says about them is correct! Is that because in woman nothing is impossible?

"'And now, to show my gratitude, let me give you a small truth! I'm certainly old enough for *it!*

"'Wrap it up and keep its mouth closed, or it will yell too loud, this small truth.'

"'Woman, give me your small truth!' I said. And the little old lady spoke as follows:

"'You're going among women? Don't forget your whip!'"

Thus spoke Zarathustra.

VOM BIß DER NATTER (Of the Adder's Bite): Bitten by an adder while asleep, Zarathustra speaks so loftily that the snake licks his wound. The moral: don't requite an enemy with a good action (which would shame him), but prove that he's done you a service. Don't be too just; don't be afraid to get angry, to curse, and to take at least some slight revenge. / VON KIND UND EHE (Of Children and Marriage): Only those men who are self-conquerors building for the future should wish for children; only in that case should they marry—and the woman should be worthy

Von der schenkenden Tugend

1.

Als Zarathustra von der Stadt Abschied genommen hatte, welcher sein Herz zugetan war und deren Name lautet: »die bunte Kuh« – folgten ihm Viele, die sich seine Jünger nannten, und gaben ihm das Geleit. Also kamen sie an einen Kreuzweg: da sagte ihnen Zarathustra, daß er nunmehr allein gehen wolle; denn er war ein Freund des Alleingehens. Seine Jünger aber reichten ihm zum Abschiede einen Stab, an dessen goldnem Griffe sich eine Schlange um die Sonne ringelte. Zarathustra freute sich des Stabes und stützte sich darauf; dann sprach er also zu seinen Jüngern:

Sagt mir doch: wie kam Gold zum höchsten Werte? Darum, daß es ungemein ist und unnützlich und leuchtend und mild im Glanze; es schenkt sich immer.

Nur als Abbild der höchsten Tugend kam Gold zum höchsten Werte. Goldgleich leuchtet der Blick dem Schenkenden. Goldes-Glanz schließt Friede zwischen Mond und Sonne.

Ungemein ist die höchste Tugend und unnützlich, leuchtend ist sie und mild im Glanze: eine schenkende Tugend ist die höchste Tugend.

Wahrlich, ich errate euch wohl, meine Jünger: ihr trachtet, gleich mir, nach der schenkenden Tugend. Was hättet ihr mit Katzen und Wölfen gemeinsam?

Das ist euer Durst, selber zu Opfern und Geschenken zu werden: und darum habt ihr den Durst, alle Reichtümer in eure Seele zu häufen.

Unersättlich trachtet eure Seele nach Schätzen und Kleinodien, weil eure Tugend unersättlich ist im Verschenken-Wollen.

Ihr zwingt alle Dinge zu euch und in euch, daß sie aus eurem Borne zurückströmen sollen als die Gaben eurer Liebe.

Wahrlich, zum Räuber an allen Werten muß solche schenkende Liebe werden; aber heil und heilig heiße ich diese Selbstsucht.

of him (a rarity!). VOM FREIEN TODE (Of Voluntary Death): Die at the proper time (as soon as you are victorious, fulfilled, and a model for others)! Second best is to die nobly in battle. It was a misfortune for many that Jesus died too soon, before he could see the shortcomings of "the good and the just"; if he had remained in the wilderness, he would have learned to love life on earth; if he had lived longer, he would have recanted.

Of the Virtue That Gives of Itself

1.

After Zarathustra took leave of the city to which his heart was attached, the one named Spotted Cow, he was followed by many who called themselves his disciples and were seeing him off. And so they came to a crossroads; there Zarathustra told them that he now wanted to continue by himself, for he was fond of walking alone. But his disciples, on departing, handed him a staff, on the golden handle of which a serpent was coiled around the sun. Zarathustra was pleased with the staff and leaned on it; then he spoke thus to his disciples:

"Tell me, then, how did gold attain the highest value? Because it is of rare occurrence, and of no intrinsic use, and it gleams with a gentle glow; it always gives of itself.

"Only as the image of the highest virtue did gold attain the highest value. The eyes of the man who gives gleam like gold. The shine of gold makes peace between moon and sun.

"The highest virtue is rare, not utilitarian, and it gleams with a gentle glow: the highest virtue is a virtue that gives of itself.

"Truly, I guess your thoughts, my disciples: like me, you strive for the virtue that gives of itself. What would you have in common with cats and wolves?

"Your thirst is to become offerings and gifts yourselves, and therefore you feel the thirst to amass all riches in your soul.

"Your soul strives insatiably for treasures and jewels, because your virtue is insatiable in its desire to give.

"You compel all things to come to you and into you, so that they can flow back out of your fountain as the gifts of your love.

"Truly, such generous love must become a robber to all old values; but I proclaim that such egotism is healthy and holy.

Eine andre Selbstsucht gibt es, eine allzuarme, eine hungernde, die immer stehlen will, jene Selbstsucht der Kranken, die kranke Selbstsucht.

Mit dem Auge des Diebes blickt sie auf alles Glänzende; mit der Gier des Hungers mißt sie Den, der reich zu essen hat; und immer schleicht sie um den Tisch der Schenkenden.

Krankheit redet aus solcher Begierde und unsichtbare Entartung; von siechem Leibe redet die diebische Gier dieser Selbstsucht.

Sagt mir, meine Brüder: was gilt uns als Schlechtes und Schlechtestes? Ist es nicht *Entartung*? – Und auf Entartung raten wir immer, wo die schenkende Seele fehlt.

Aufwärts geht unser Weg, von der Art hinüber zur Über-Art. Aber ein Grauen ist uns der entartende Sinn, welcher spricht: »Alles für mich.«

Aufwärts fliegt unser Sinn: so ist er ein Gleichnis unsres Leibes, einer Erhöhung Gleichnis. Solcher Erhöhungen Gleichnisse sind die Namen der Tugenden.

Also geht der Leib durch die Geschichte, ein Werdender und ein Kämpfender. Und der Geist – was ist er ihm? Seiner Kämpfe und Siege Herold, Genoß und Widerhall.

Gleichnisse sind alle Namen von Gut und Böse: sie sprechen nicht aus, sie winken nur. Ein Tor, welcher von ihnen Wissen will!

Achtet mir, meine Brüder, auf jede Stunde, wo euer Geist in Gleichnissen reden will: da ist der Ursprung eurer Tugend.

Erhöht ist da euer Leib und auferstanden; mit seiner Wonne entzückt er den Geist, daß er Schöpfer wird und Schätzer und Liebender und aller Dinge Wohltäter.

Wenn euer Herz breit und voll wallt, dem Strome gleich, ein Segen und eine Gefahr den Anwohnenden: da ist der Ursprung eurer Tugend.

Wenn ihr erhaben seid über Lob und Tadel, und euer Wille allen Dingen befehlen will, als eines Liebenden Wille: da ist der Ursprung eurer Tugend.

Wenn ihr das Angenehme verachtet und das weiche Bett, von den Weichlichen euch nicht weit genug betten könnt: da ist der Ursprung eurer Tugend.

Wenn ihr Eines Willens Wollende seid, und diese Wende aller Not euch Notwendigkeit heißt: da ist der Ursprung eurer Tugend.

"There is another egotism, one that is far too poor, a starving one, which always wants to steal: the egotism of the sick; sick egotism.

"It looks upon all that glitters with the eyes of a thief; with the ravening of hunger it measures the man who has abundant food; and it always slinks around the table of those who give.

"Such craving and invisible degeneracy bespeak sickness; the thievish ravening of this egotism bespeaks a sick body.

"Tell me, my brothers: what do we consider bad and extremely bad? It is not *degeneracy*? And we always detect degeneracy when the generous soul is absent.

"Our path leads upward, from the species to the super-species. But we're horrified by the degenerate mind that says: 'Everything for me!'

"Our mind flies upward, and so it is a metaphor for our body, a metaphor for an elevation. The names of the virtues are metaphors for such elevations.

"Thus our body proceeds through history, evolving and struggling. And the intellect—what is it for the body? The herald, comrade, and echo of its battles and victories.

"All designations of good and evil are metaphors: they do not express, they merely indicate. Only a fool would demand knowledge from them!

"My brothers, watch for that hour when your intellect is ready to speak in metaphors: that will be the origin of your virtue.

"Then your body will be exalted and resurrected; with its bliss it will enrapture the intellect, so that it may become a creator, evaluator, the loving benefactor of all things.

"When your heart surges in broad, full spate like a river, a blessing and peril to those who live along its banks, that will be the origin of your virtue.

"When you are uplifted above praise and blame, and your will is ready to give orders to all things, as the will of a loving man, that will be the origin of your virtue.

"When you despise what is pleasant, such as soft beds, and can't make your bed far enough away from flabby people, that will be the origin of your virtue.

"When all of you are men who will with a single will, and when this point at which all need is left behind becomes necessity[10] for you, that will be the origin of your virtue.

---

10. *Wende der Not* is literally "turning [point] of need (or: distress)." It's impossible to convey in English the German wordplay on *Wende, Not,* and *Notwendigkeit* ("necessity").

Wahrlich, ein neues Gutes und Böses ist sie! Wahrlich, ein neues tiefes Tauschen und eines neuen Quelles Stimme!

Macht ist sie, diese neue Tugend; ein herrschender Gedanke ist sie, und um ihn eine kluge Seele: eine goldene Sonne, und um sie die Schlange der Erkenntnis.

2.

Hier schwieg Zarathustra eine Weile und sah mit Liebe auf seine Jünger. Dann fuhr er also fort zu reden: – und seine Stimme hatte sich verwandelt.

Bleibt mir der Erde treu, meine Brüder, mit der Macht eurer Tugend! Eure schenkende Liebe und eure Erkenntnis diene dem Sinn der Erde! Also bitte und beschwöre ich euch.

Laßt sie nicht davonfliegen vom Irdischen und mit den Flügeln gegen ewige Wände schlagen! Ach, es gab immer so viel verflogene Tugend!

Führt, gleich mir, die verflogene Tugend zur Erde zurück – ja, zurück zu Leib und Leben: daß sie der Erde ihren Sinn gebe, einen Menschen-Sinn!

Hundertfältig verflog und vergriff sich bisher so Geist wie Tugend. Ach, in unsrem Leibe wohnt jetzt noch all dieser Wahn und Fehlgriff: Leib und Wille ist er da geworden.

Hundertfältig versuchte und verirrte sich bisher so Geist wie Tugend. Ja, ein Versuch war der Mensch. Ach, viel Unwissen und Irrtum ist an uns Leib geworden!

Nicht nur die Vernunft von Jahrtausenden – auch ihr Wahnsinn bricht an uns aus. Gefährlich ist es, Erbe zu sein.

Noch kämpfen wir Schritt um Schritt mit dem Riesen Zufall, und über der ganzen Menschheit waltete bisher noch der Unsinn, der Ohne-Sinn.

Euer Geist und eure Tugend diene dem Sinn der Erde, meine Brüder: und aller Dinge Wert werde neu von euch gesetzt! Darum sollt ihr Kämpfende sein! Darum sollt ihr Schaffende sein!

Wissend reinigt sich der Leib; mit Wissen versuchend erhöht er sich; dem Erkennenden heiligen sich alle Triebe; dem Erhöhten wird die Seele fröhlich.

Arzt, hilf dir selber: so hilfst du auch deinem Kranken noch. Das sei seine beste Hilfe, daß er Den mit Augen sehe, der sich selber heil macht.

Tausend Pfade gibt es, die nie noch gegangen sind, tausend

"Truly, it is a new good and evil! Truly, a new, deep roaring of waters and the voice of a new fountain!

"This new virtue is power; it is a dominating idea and, around that idea, a wise soul: a golden sun and, around that sun, the serpent of knowledge."

2.

Here Zarathustra was silent for a time, gazing lovingly at his disciples. Then he continued speaking as follows (and his voice was different):

"Remain faithful to the earth, my brothers, with the power of your virtue! Let your generous love and your knowledge serve the meaning of the earth! That is what I ask and beseech of you.

"Don't let them fly away from earthly things and beat their wings against walls of eternity! Alas, there has always been so much virtue that has flown astray!

"Like me, lead your straying virtue back to earth—yes, back to the body and life, so that it can give the earth its meaning, a human meaning!

"Until now, both intellect and virtue have flown astray and erred in a hundred ways. Alas, all this delusion and error still dwells in our body, where it has become body and will.

"Until now, both intellect and virtue have experimented and gone astray. Yes, mankind was an experiment. Alas, much ignorance and error has become part of our body!

"Not only the rationality of millennia—their madness, too, breaks out in us. It is dangerous to be an heir.

"We are still battling every step of the way with the giant Chance, and until now all mankind has been governed by senselessness, non-sense.

"Let your intellect and your virtue serve the meaning of the earth, my brothers, and let the value of all things be newly established by you! It is for this that you must fight! It is for this that you must create!

"By knowledge the body is cleansed; experimenting with knowledge, it raises itself higher; in the man who knows, all urges become sanctified; the soul of the uplifted man becomes happy.

"Physician, help yourself; in that way you help your patient, as well. Let the best help for him be to behold the man who cures himself.

"There are a thousand paths never yet trodden, a thousand states of

Gesundheiten und verborgene Eilande des Lebens. Unerschöpft und unentdeckt ist immer noch Mensch und Menschen-Erde.

Wachet und horcht, ihr Einsamen! Von der Zukunft her kommen Winde mit heimlichem Flügelschlagen; und an feine Ohren ergeht gute Botschaft.

Ihr Einsamen von heute, ihr Ausscheidenden, ihr sollt einst ein Volk sein: aus euch, die ihr euch selber auswähltet, soll ein auserwähltes Volk erwachsen: – und aus ihm der Übermensch.

Wahrlich, eine Stätte der Genesung soll noch die Erde werden! Und schon liegt ein neuer Geruch um sie, ein heilbringender – und eine neue Hoffnung!

3.

Als Zarathustra diese Worte gesagt hatte, schwieg er, wie Einer, der nicht sein letztes Wort gesagt hat; lange wog er den Stab zweifelnd in seiner Hand. Endlich sprach er also: – und seine Stimme hatte sich verwandelt.

Allein gehe ich nun, meine Jünger! Auch ihr geht nun davon und allein! So will ich es.

Wahrlich, ich rate euch: geht fort von mir und wehrt euch gegen Zarathustra! Und besser noch: schämt euch seiner! Vielleicht betrog er euch.

Der Mensch der Erkenntnis muß nicht nur seine Feinde lieben, sondern auch seine Freunde hassen können.

Man vergilt einem Lehrer schlecht, wenn man immer nur der Schüler bleibt. Und warum wollt ihr nicht an meinem Kranze rupfen?

Ihr verehrt mich; aber wie, wenn eure Verehrung eines Tages umfällt? Hütet euch, daß euch nicht eine Bildsäule erschlage!

Ihr sagt, ihr glaubt an Zarathustra? Aber was liegt an Zarathustra! Ihr seid meine Gläubigen: aber was liegt an allen Gläubigen!

Ihr hattet euch noch nicht gesucht: da fandet ihr mich. So tun alle Gläubigen; darum ist es so wenig mit allem Glauben.

Nun heiße ich euch, mich verlieren und euch finden; und erst, wenn ihr mich Alle verleugnet habt, will ich euch widerkehren.

Wahrlich, mit andern Augen, meine Brüder, werde ich mir dann meine Verlorenen suchen; mit einer andern Liebe werde ich euch dann lieben.

Und einst noch sollt ihr mir Freunde geworden sein und Kinder

health and hidden islands of life. Man and man's earth are still unexhausted and undiscovered.

"Be wakeful and alert, you solitary ones! Winds are blowing this way from the future with secret beating of wings, and good news reaches subtle ears.

"You solitary ones of today, you who separate out, some day you shall be a nation: from you, who have chosen yourselves out of the mass, a chosen people shall grow—and from it, the more-than-man.

"Truly, the earth will yet become a place of recovery from illness! And even now there is a new fragrance to it, one that brings salvation—there is new hope!"

3.

After Zarathustra said this, he fell silent like one who hasn't spoken his last word; for a long time he weighed the staff in his hand dubiously. Finally he spoke as follows (and his voice had changed):

"Now I go off alone, my disciples! You, too, are departing, and alone! That is what I wish.

"Truly, I counsel you: leave me and protect yourselves against Zarathustra! Better yet: be ashamed of your association with him! Perhaps he has deceived you.

"The man of knowledge must not only love his enemies, but also be able to hate his friends.

"A teacher is repaid badly when you always remain merely his pupil. And why don't you want to pluck at my laurel wreath?

"You revere me, but what if your reverence falls over some day? Beware of being crushed by a statue![11]

"You say you believe in Zarathustra? But what is there to Zarathustra? You are believers in me, but what is there to all believers?

"You had not yet sought yourselves; then you found me. That's what all believers do; that's why all faith amounts to so little.

"Now I bid you to lose me and find yourselves; only when all of you have denied me will I return to you.

"Truly, my brothers, I shall then seek my lost ones with other eyes; I shall then love you with another love.

"And some day you will have become my friends and children of

---

11. Aristotle, in the *Poetics*, tells of the statue of a great man which fell and crushed his killer at a public festival.

Einer Hoffnung: dann will ich zum dritten Male bei euch sein, daß ich den großen Mittag mit euch feiere.

Und das ist der große Mittag, da der Mensch auf der Mitte seiner Bahn steht zwischen Tier und Übermensch und seinen Weg zum Abende als seine höchste Hoffnung feiert: denn es ist der Weg zu einem neuen Morgen.

Alsda wird sich der Untergehende selber segnen, daß er ein Hinübergehender sei; und die Sonne seiner Erkenntnis wird ihm im Mittage stehn.

»*Tot sind alle Götter: nun wollen wir, daß der Übermensch lebe.*« – Dies sei einst am großen Mittage unser letzter Wille! –

Also sprach Zarathustra.

one hope; then I will be with you for the third time, so I can celebrate the great noonday with you.

"And the great noonday is when mankind is midway on its journey between animal and more-than-man, and is celebrating its way toward evening as its highest hope; for it is the way to a new morning.

"Then man in his sunset will bless himself because he is a transitional figure; and the sun of his knowledge will be at its noonday zenith.

"'*All gods are dead; let it now be our will that the more-than-man may live.*' Let this, some day, at the great noonday, be our final will!"

Thus spoke Zarathustra.

ZWEITER TEIL

Das Kind mit dem Spiegel

Hierauf ging Zarathustra wieder zurück in das Gebirge und in die Einsamkeit seiner Höhle und entzog sich den Menschen: wartend gleich einem Sämann, der seinen Samen ausgeworfen hat. Seine Seele aber wurde voll von Ungeduld und Begierde nach Denen, welche er liebte: denn er hatte ihnen noch Viel zu geben. Dies nämlich ist das Schwerste: aus Liebe die offne Hand schließen und als Schenkender die Scham bewahren.

Also vergingen dem Einsamen Monde und Jahre; seine Weisheit aber wuchs und machte ihm Schmerzen durch ihre Fülle.

Eines Morgens aber wachte er schon vor der Morgenröte auf, besann sich lange auf seinem Lager und sprach endlich zu seinem Herzen:

»Was erschrak ich doch so in meinem Traume, daß ich aufwachte? Trat nicht ein Kind zu mir, das einen Spiegel trug?

›Oh Zarathustra‹ – sprach das Kind zu mir – ›schaue Dich an im Spiegel!‹

Aber als ich in den Spiegel schaute, da schrie ich auf, und mein Herz war erschüttert: denn nicht mich sahe ich darin, sondern eines Teufels Fratze und Hohnlachen.

Wahrlich, allzugut verstehe ich des Traumes Zeichen und Mahnung: meine *Lehre* ist in Gefahr, Unkraut will Weizen heißen!

Meine Feinde sind mächtig worden und haben meiner Lehre Bildnis entstellt, also, daß meine Liebsten sich der Gaben schämen müssen, die ich ihnen gab.

Verloren gingen mir meine Freunde; die Stunde kam mir, meine Verlornen zu suchen!« –

Mit diesen Worten sprang Zarathustra auf, aber nicht wie ein Geängstigter, der nach Luft sucht, sondern eher wie ein Seher und Sänger, welchen der Geist anfällt. Verwundert sahen sein Adler und seine Schlange auf ihn hin: denn gleich dem Morgenrote lag ein kommendes Glück auf seinem Antlitze.

PART TWO

The Child with the Mirror

Thereupon Zarathustra returned to the mountains and the solitude of his cave, withdrawing from people: waiting like a sower who has scattered his seed. But his soul became full of impatience and craving for those he loved, for he still had much to give them. For this is the hardest thing: to close one's open hand out of love and to preserve one's modesty though generous.

In that way months and years passed by for the solitary man; but his wisdom increased and caused him pain by its abundance.

But one morning he awoke before dawn, meditated a long time in his bed, and finally said to his heart:

"Why, then, was I so frightened in my dream that I awoke? Didn't a child come up to me carrying a mirror?

"'O Zarathustra,' the child said to me, 'look at yourself in the mirror!'

"But when I looked in the mirror, I cried out, and my heart was shaken, for I saw in it, not myself, but a devil's ugly face and mocking laughter.

"Truly, I understand only too well the dream's symbolic warning: my *doctrine* is in peril, weeds are trying to pass themselves off as wheat!

"My enemies have grown powerful and have disfigured the portrait of my doctrine in such a way that those dearest to me must be ashamed of the gifts I gave them.

"My friends have been lost to me; the time has come for me to look for my lost ones!"

Saying this, Zarathustra leapt up, but not like an anxious man gasping for breath, rather like a seer and bard inspired by the spirit. His eagle and serpent looked at him in amazement, for a coming happiness lay on his face like the flush of dawn.

75

Was geschah mir doch, meine Tiere? – sagte Zarathustra. Bin ich nicht verwandelt? Kam mir nicht die Seligkeit wie ein Sturmwind?

Töricht ist mein Glück und Törichtes wird es reden: zu jung noch ist es – so habt Geduld mit ihm!

Verwundet bin ich von meinem Glücke: alle Leidenden sollen mir Ärzte sein!

Zu meinen Freunden darf ich wieder hinab und auch zu meinen Feinden! Zarathustra darf wieder reden und schenken und Lieben das Liebste tun!

Meine ungeduldige Liebe fließt über in Strömen, abwärts, nach Aufgang und Niedergang. Aus schweigsamem Gebirge und Gewittern des Schmerzes rauscht meine Seele in die Täler.

Zu lange sehnte ich mich und schaute in die Ferne. Zu lange gehörte ich der Einsamkeit: so verlernte ich das Schweigen.

Mund bin ich worden ganz und gar, und Brausen eines Bachs aus hohen Felsen: hinab will ich meine Rede stürzen in die Täler.

Und mag mein Strom der Liebe in Unwegsames stürzen! Wie sollte ein Strom nicht endlich den Weg zum Meere finden!

Wohl ist ein See in mir, ein einsiedlerischer, selbstgenugsamer; aber mein Strom der Liebe reißt ihn mit sich hinab – zum Meere!

Neue Wege gehe ich, eine neue Rede kommt mir; müde wurde ich, gleich allen Schaffenden, der alten Zungen. Nicht will mein Geist mehr auf abgelaufnen Sohlen wandeln.

Zu langsam läuft mir alles Reden: – in deinen Wagen springe ich, Sturm! Und auch dich will ich noch peitschen mit meiner Bosheit!

Wie ein Schrei und ein Jauchzen will ich über weite Meere hinfahren, bis ich die glückseligen Inseln finde, wo meine Freunde weilen: –

Und meine Feinde unter ihnen! Wie liebe ich nun Jeden, zu dem ich nur reden darf! Auch meine Feinde gehören zu meiner Seligkeit.

Und wenn ich auf mein wildestes Pferd steigen will, so hilft mir mein Speer immer am besten hinauf: der ist meines Fußes allzeit bereiter Diener: –

Der Speer, den ich gegen meine Feinde schleudere! Wie danke ich es meinen Feinden, daß ich endlich ihn schleudern darf!

Zu groß war die Spannung meiner Wolke: zwischen Gelächtern der Blitze will ich Hagelschauer in die Tiefe werfen.

Gewaltig wird sich da meine Brust heben, gewaltig wird sie ihren Sturm über die Berge hinblasen: so kommt ihr Erleichterung.

Wahrlich, einem Sturme gleich kommt mein Glück und meine Freiheit! Aber meine Feinde sollen glauben, *der Böse* rase über ihren Häuptern.

"What has happened to me, my animals?" said Zarathustra. "Am I not transformed? Hasn't bliss come to me like a storm wind?

"My happiness is foolish and will say foolish things; it's still too young—so be patient with it!

"I am wounded by my happiness: let all sufferers be my physicians!

"I am once again permitted to go down to my friends and to my enemies, also! Zarathustra is once again free to speak and give and do loving service to those he loves!

"My impatient love is overflowing in streams, downward, toward sunrise and sunset. From the silent mountains and the storms of sorrow my soul is roaring into the valleys.

"For too long I have yearned and gazed into the distance. For too long I have belonged to solitude, and so I have forgotten how to be silent.

"I have become entirely lips, and the sound of a brook tumbling from high crags: I want my speech to plunge into the valleys.

"And may my current of love plunge into impassable places! How could a stream fail to find its way to the sea at last?

"There is surely a lake in me, a self-sufficient hermit's lake; but my current of love is tearing it downward along with it—to the sea!

"I tread new paths, a new speech comes to me; like all creators, I have grown tired of the old tongues. No longer does my mind wish to walk on worn-down soles.

"All speech runs too slowly for me: I shall leap into your chariot, storm! And even you I shall lash to higher speed with my malice!

"Like a cry and a shout of joy I shall travel across wide seas until I find the Fortunate Islands where my friends are residing—

"And my foes among them! How I now love anyone I can talk to! Even my foes are part of my bliss.

"And when I wish to mount my wildest horse, my spear will always help me up best: it is my foot's ever-ready servant—

The spear that I shall fling at my foes! How I thank my foes for the chance to fling it at last!

"The tension in my cloud was too great: between the lightning's bursts of laughter I shall hurl showers of hail onto the lowlands.

"My bosom will then heave mightily, mightily it will blow its storm over the mountains: in that way it will gain relief.

"Truly, my happiness and my freedom come like a storm! But I want my enemies to think that the Evil One is raging over their heads.

Ja, auch ihr werdet erschreckt sein, meine Freunde, ob meiner wilden Weisheit; und vielleicht flieht ihr davon samt meinen Feinden.

Ach, daß ich's verstünde, euch mit Hirtenflöten zurückzulocken! Ach, daß meine Löwin Weisheit zärtlich brüllen lernte! Und Vieles lernten wir schon miteinander!

Meine wilde Weisheit wurde trächtig auf einsamen Bergen; auf rauhen Steinen gebar sie ihr Junges, Jüngstes.

Nun läuft sie närrisch durch die harte Wüste und sucht und sucht nach sanftem Rasen – meine alte wilde Weisheit!

Auf eurer Herzen sanften Rasen, meine Freunde! – auf eure Liebe möchte sie ihr Liebstes betten! –

Also sprach Zarathustra.

Auf den glückseligen Inseln

Die Feigen fallen von den Bäumen, sie sind gut und süß; und indem sie fallen, reißt ihnen die rote Haut. Ein Nordwind bin ich reifen Feigen.

Also, gleich Feigen, fallen euch diese Lehren zu, meine Freunde: nun trinkt ihren Saft und ihr süßes Fleisch! Herbst ist es umher und reiner Himmel und Nachmittag.

Seht, welche Fülle ist um uns! Und aus dem Überflusse heraus ist es schön hinauszublicken auf ferne Meere.

Einst sagte man Gott, wenn man auf ferne Meere blickte; nun aber lehrte ich euch sagen: Übermensch.

Gott ist eine Mutmaßung; aber ich will, daß euer Mutmaßen nicht weiter reiche, als euer schaffender Wille.

Könntet ihr einen Gott *schaffen?* – So schweigt mir doch von allen Göttern! Wohl aber könntet ihr den Übermenschen schaffen.

Nicht ihr vielleicht selber, meine Brüder! Aber zu Vätern und Vorfahren könntet ihr euch umschaffen des Übermenschen: und Dies sei euer bestes Schaffen! –

Gott ist eine Mutmaßung: aber ich will, daß euer Mutmaßen begrenzt sei in der Denkbarkeit.

Könntet ihr einen Gott *denken?* – Aber dies bedeute euch Wille zur Wahrheit, daß Alles verwandelt werde in Menschen-Denkbares, Menschen-Sichtbares, Menschen-Fühlbares! Eure eignen Sinne sollt ihr zu Ende denken!

Und was ihr Welt nanntet, das soll erst von euch geschaffen werden: eure Vernunft, euer Bild, euer Wille, eure Liebe soll es selber werden! Und wahrlich, zu eurer Seligkeit, ihr Erkennenden!

"Yes, you, too, will be frightened, my friends, at my wild wisdom; and perhaps you will run away along with my foes.

"Oh, if I only knew how to lure you back with shepherds' flutes! Oh, if my wisdom, that lioness, learned how to roar tenderly! And we've already learnt a lot together!

"My wild wisdom became pregnant on lonely mountains; on rough rocks she gave birth to her young, youngest.

"Now she runs foolishly through the hard desert, looking and looking for soft grass—my old, wild wisdom!

"On the soft grass of your hearts, my friends—on your love—may she prepare a bed for her dearest one!"

Thus spoke Zarathustra.

On the Fortunate Islands

The figs are falling from the trees; they're tasty and sweet; and as they fall their red skin splits open. I am a north wind for ripe figs.

And so, like figs, these teachings are falling for you, my friends: now drink their juice and eat their sweet flesh! It is autumn round about, and clear sky and afternoon.

See what abundance lies around us! And from the midst of this abundance it is pleasant to look out toward distant seas.

In the past people spoke of God when they beheld distant seas; but now I teach you to say: "More-than-man."

God is an assumption, but I don't want your assumptions to go further than your creative will.

Could you *create* a god? If not, don't speak to me about any gods! But you probably could create the more-than-man.

Perhaps not you yourselves, my brothers! But you could transform yourselves into fathers and forebears of the more-than-man; and let this be your best creativity!

God is an assumption; but I want your assumptions to be confined to what is conceivable.

Could you *think* of a god? But let that mean to you the will to truth, wherein everything is transformed into things humanly conceivable, visible to man, perceptible to man! Your own senses should be thoroughly thought through!

And that which you called world must first be created by you: it must become your reason, your image, your will, your love! And truly, for happiness, you men of knowledge!

Und wie wolltet ihr das Leben ertragen ohne diese Hoffnung, ihr Erkennenden? Weder ins Unbegreifliche dürftet ihr eingeboren sein, noch ins Unvernünftige.

Aber daß ich euch ganz mein Herz offenbare, ihr Freunde: *wenn es Götter gäbe, wie hielte ich's aus, kein Gott zu sein! Also* gibt es keine Götter.

Wohl zog ich den Schluß; nun aber zieht er mich. –

Gott ist eine Mutmaßung: aber wer tränke alle Qual dieser Mutmaßung, ohne zu sterben? Soll dem Schaffenden sein Glaube genommen sein und dem Adler sein Schweben in Adler-Fernen?

Gott ist ein Gedanke, der macht alles Gerade krumm und Alles, was steht, drehend. Wie? Die Zeit wäre hinweg, und alles Vergängliche nur Lüge?

Dies zu denken ist Wirbel und Schwindel menschlichen Gebeinen, und noch dem Magen ein Erbrechen: wahrlich, die drehende Krankheit heiße ich's, Solches zu mutmaßen.

Böse heiße ich's und menschenfeindlich: all dies Lehren vom Einen und Vollen und Unbewegten und Satten und Unvergänglichen!

Alles Unvergängliche – das ist nur ein Gleichnis! Und die Dichter lügen zuviel. –

Aber von Zeit und Werden sollen die besten Gleichnisse reden: ein Lob sollen sie sein und eine Rechtfertigung aller Vergänglichkeit!

Schaffen – das ist die große Erlösung vom Leiden, und des Lebens Leichtwerden. Aber daß der Schaffende sei, dazu selber tut Leid not und viel Verwandelung.

Ja, viel bitteres Sterben muß in eurem Leben sein, ihr Schaffenden! Also seid ihr Fürsprecher und Rechtfertiger aller Vergänglichkeit.

Daß der Schaffende selber das Kind sei, das neu geboren werde, dazu muß er auch die Gebärerin sein wollen und der Schmerz der Gebärerin.

Wahrlich, durch hundert Seelen ging ich meinen Weg und durch hundert Wiegen und Geburtswehen. Manchen Abschied nahm ich schon, ich kenne die herzbrechenden letzten Stunden.

Aber so will's mein schaffender Wille, mein Schicksal. Oder, daß ich's euch redlicher sage: solches Schicksal gerade – will mein Wille.

Alles Fühlende leidet an mir und ist in Gefängnissen: aber mein Wollen kommt mir stets als mein Befreier und Freudebringer.

Wollen befreit: das ist die wahre Lehre von Wille und Freiheit – so lehrt sie euch Zarathustra.

And how could you bear this life without that hope, you men of knowledge? You mustn't be born natives of either the incomprehensible or the irrational.

But, to open my whole heart to you, friends: *if* gods existed, how could I bear not being a god! *Therefore* there are no gods.

Yes, I drew the conclusion, but now it's drawing me.—

God is an assumption, but who could drink in all the torment of that assumption without dying? Is the creative man's faith to be taken away, and the eagle's ability to soar in eagle's heights?

God is an idea that makes everything straight crooked and sets everything stationary spinning. What?! Are we to eliminate time and call all transitory things a mere lie?

To think this is a turmoil and dizziness for human constitutions, and makes our stomach vomit, too: truly, I call this kind of assumption "the spinning sickness."

I call it evil and hostile to man, all this doctrine of the One, Full, Immovable, Replete, and Imperishable!

Everything imperishable is merely a metaphor![12] And poets tell too many lies.

But the best metaphors ought to speak of time and becoming: they should be an encomium and a justification of all that is transitory!

Creativity is the great redemption from suffering, the removal of a weight from life. But for the creative man to exist, pain is needed and much transformation.

Yes, there must be much bitter dying in your life, O creative men! In that way you are spokesmen and justifiers of all that is transitory.

For the creative man himself to be the child that is to be newly born, he must also consent to be the woman in labor and her pain.

Truly, I have made my way through a hundred souls and through a hundred cradles and labor pains. I have already taken leave countless times, and I am familiar with the heartbreak of final hours.

But that's what my creative will, my fate, demands. Or, to put it to you more forthrightly: that is precisely the fate which my will demands.

All that has feeling suffers in me and is imprisoned: but my will always comes to set me free and bring me joy.

The will sets you free: that is the true doctrine of will and freedom—that is what Zarathustra teaches you.

---

12. A parody of the very end of Goethe's *Faust* (Part Two).

Nicht-mehr-Wollen und Nicht-mehr-Schätzen und Nicht-mehr-Schaffen! ach, daß diese große Müdigkeit mir stets ferne bleibe!

Auch im Erkennen fühle ich nur meines Willens Zeuge- und Werde-Lust; und wenn Unschuld in meiner Erkenntnis ist, so geschieht dies, weil Wille zu Zeugung in ihr ist.

Hinweg von Gott und Göttern lockte mich dieser Wille; was wäre denn zu schaffen, wenn Götter – da wären!

Aber zum Menschen treibt er mich stets von neuem, mein inbrünstiger Schaffens-Wille; so treibt's den Hammer hin zum Steine.

Ach, ihr Menschen, im Steine schläft mir ein Bild, das Bild meiner Bilder! Ach, daß es im härtesten, häßlichsten Steine schlafen muß!

Nun wütet mein Hammer grausam gegen sein Gefängnis. Vom Steine stäuben Stücke: was schiert mich das?

Vollenden will ich's: denn ein Schatten kam zu mir – aller Dinge Stillstes und Leichtestes kam einst zu mir!

Des Übermenschen Schönheit kam zu mir als Schatten. Ach, meine Brüder! Was gehen mich noch – die Götter an! –

Also sprach Zarathustra.

VON DEN MITLEIDIGEN (Of the Compassionate): Christian charity, which injures the pride of those being aided, is inferior to a general feeling of joy, which will prevent one from harming others. Abolish pangs of conscience and petty thoughts! True love seeks the self-respect and self-reliance of the one loved. God died of his compassion for mankind. / VON DEN PRIESTERN (Of Priests): The humility of priests is vengeful; they are victims of delusion and false values. They can only

---

Vom Gesindel

Das Leben ist ein Born der Lust; aber wo das Gesindel mittrinkt, da sind alle Brunnen vergiftet.

Allem Reinlichen bin ich hold; aber ich mag die grinsenden Mäuler nicht sehn und den Durst der Unreinen.

Sie warfen ihr Auge hinab in den Brunnen: nun glänzt mir ihr widriges Lächeln herauf aus dem Brunnen.

Das heilige Wasser haben sie vergiftet mit ihrer Lüsternheit; und als sie ihre schmutzigen Träume Lust nannten, vergifteten sie auch noch die Worte.

No longer to will, no longer to evaluate, no longer to create! Ah, may that great weariness always be far from me!

In acquiring knowledge, as well, I feel only my will's pleasure in begetting and becoming; and if there is innocence in my knowledge, this is because it contains the will to procreate.

This will lured me away from God and gods; what would be left to create if gods existed?

But it always drives me back to mankind again, this ardently creative will of mine; in the same way, the hammer is driven into the stone.

Ah, people, in the stone I see an image sleeping, the image of my images! Alas, that it is forced to sleep in the hardest, ugliest stone!

Now my hammer rages cruelly against its prison. Bits of the stone scatter into powder: what do I care?[13]

I want to complete the task, because a shadow came to me—the quietest and lightest of all things came to me once!

The beauty of the more-than-man came to me as a shadow. Ah, my brothers! What further use do I have for the gods?

Thus spoke Zarathustra.

---

love God by crucifying man; they smell of death. They are mean-spirited and narrow-minded. / VON DEN TUGENDHAFTEN (Of the Virtuous): The virtuous seek a reward in heaven, but no paymaster exists. Virtue is the essential trait of the truly virtuous, and not anything extrinsic—as opposed to the virtues which are only vices grown old and feeble, or which are used as a weapon or a safety measure.

Of the Rabble

Life is a fountain of pleasure, but when the rabble partakes, all wells are poisoned.

I look kindly on all that is clean, but I don't want to see the grinning mugs and the thirst of the unclean.

They have cast their glances down into the well: now their repellent laughter glitters up to me out of the well.

They have poisoned the holy water with their lustfulness; and when they called their filthy dreams "pleasure," they poisoned language, too.

---

13. Note the obsessive alliteration in the German original.

Unwillig wird die Flamme, wenn sie ihre feuchten Herzen ans Feuer legen; der Geist selber brodelt und raucht, wo das Gesindel ans Feuer tritt.

Süßlich und übermürbe wird in ihrer Hand die Frucht: windfällig und wipfeldürr macht ihr Blick den Fruchtbaum.

Und Mancher, der sich vom Leben abkehrte, kehrte sich nun vom Gesindel ab: er wollte nicht Brunnen und Flamme und Frucht mit dem Gesindel teilen.

Und Mancher, der in die Wüste ging und mit Raubtieren Durst litt, wollte nur nicht mit schmutzigen Kameltreibern um die Zisterne sitzen.

Und Mancher, der wie ein Vernichter daherkam und wie ein Hagelschlag allen Fruchtfeldern, wollte nur seinen Fuß dem Gesindel in den Rachen setzen und also seinen Schlund stopfen.

Und nicht Das ist der Bissen, an dem ich am meisten würgte, zu wissen, daß das Leben selber Feindschaft nötig hat und Sterben und Marterkreuze: –

Sondern ich fragte einst und erstickte fast an meiner Frage: wie? hat das Leben auch das Gesindel *nötig*?

Sind vergiftete Brunnen nötig und stinkende Feuer und beschmutzte Träume und Maden im Lebensbrode?

Nicht mein Haß, sondern mein Ekel fraß mir hungrig am Leben! Ach, des Geistes wurde ich oft müde, als ich auch das Gesindel geistreich fand!

Und den Herrschenden wandt' ich den Rücken, als ich sah, was sie jetzt Herrschen nennen: Schachern und Markten um Macht – mit dem Gesindel!

Unter Völkern wohnte ich fremder Zunge, mit verschlossenen Ohren: daß mir ihres Schacherns Zunge fremd bliebe und ihr Markten um Macht.

Und die Nase mir haltend, ging ich unmutig durch alles Gestern und Heute: wahrlich, übel riecht alles Gestern und Heute nach dem schreibenden Gesindel!

Einem Krüppel gleich, der taub und blind und stumm wurde: also lebte ich lange, daß ich nicht mit Macht- und Schreib- und Lust-Gesindel lebte.

Mühsam stieg mein Geist Treppen und vorsichtig; Almosen der Lust waren sein Labsal; am Stabe schlich dem Blinden das Leben.

Was geschah mir doch? Wie erlöste ich mich vom Ekel? Wer verjüngte mein Auge? Wie erflog ich die Höhe, wo kein Gesindel mehr am Brunnen sitzt?

Schuf mein Ekel selber mir Flügel und quellenahnende Kräfte?

The flame grows hesitant when they place their damp hearts by the fire; the mind itself seethes and smokes whenever the rabble steps up to the fire.

In their hands fruit becomes sickly-sweet and overripe; their glance makes the fruit tree liable to be blown over and dries up its top branches.

And many a man who turned away from life has now turned away from the rabble; he didn't want to share the well and the flame and the fruit with the rabble.

And many a man who went to the desert, and suffered thirst there along with the beasts of prey, was merely unwilling to sit around the cistern with filthy camel drivers.

And many a man who came along as an annihilator, and a hailstorm for all grainfields, merely wished to thrust his foot into the rabble's jaws and thus block up its maw.

The morsel on which I gagged most was not the knowledge that life itself needs enmity, dying, and martyrs' crosses—

But I once asked and nearly choked on my question: "What? Does life *need* the rabble, as well?

"Are poisoned wells necessary, and stinking fire and sullied dreams and maggots in the bread of life?"

Not my hate, but my disgust, gnawed away hungrily at my life! Ah, I was often weary of my wit when I found even the rabble witty!

And I turned my back on rulers when I saw what they now call ruling: trafficking and haggling for power—with the rabble!

I dwelt among peoples who spoke foreign tongues, my ears shut so that the language of their trafficking and their haggling for power would remain foreign to me.

And, holding my nose, I walked in ill humor through all of yesterday and today: truly, all of yesterday and today has the bad odor of the rabble of writers!

Like a lame man who became deaf, blind, and mute, I lived for a long time, so that I wouldn't have to live with the power, writing, and pleasure rabble.

My mind climbed stairs laboriously and cautiously; its balm was handouts of pleasure; the blind man's life stole away as he leaned on his staff.

What happened to me? How did I redeem myself from that disgust? Who rejuvenated my eyes? How did I fly up to the heights where no more rabble is sitting by the well?

Did my very disgust give me wings and the power to discover water

Wahrlich, ins Höchste mußte ich fliegen, daß ich den Born der Lust wiederfände!

Oh, ich fand ihn, meine Brüder! Hier im Höchsten quillt mir der Born der Lust! Und es gibt ein Leben, an dem kein Gesindel mittrinkt!

Fast zu heftig strömst du mir, Quell der Lust! Und oft leerst du den Becher wieder, dadurch daß du ihn füllen willst!

Und noch muß ich lernen, bescheidener dir zu nahen: allzuheftig strömt dir noch mein Herz entgegen: –

Mein Herz, auf dem mein Sommer brennt, der kurze, heiße, schwermütige, überselige: wie verlangt mein Sommer-Herz nach deiner Kühle!

Vorbei die zögernde Trübsal meines Frühlings! Vorüber die Bosheit meiner Schneeflocken im Juni! Sommer wurde ich ganz und Sommer-Mittag!

Ein Sommer im Höchsten mit kalten Quellen und seliger Stille: oh kommt, meine Freunde, daß die Stille noch seliger werde!

Denn dies ist *unsre* Höhe und unsre Heimat: zu hoch und steil wohnen wir hier allen Unreinen und ihrem Durste.

Werft nur eure reinen Augen in den Born meiner Lust, ihr Freunde! Wie sollt er darob trübe werden! Entgegenlachen soll er euch mit *seiner* Reinheit.

Auf dem Baume Zukunft bauen wir unser Nest; Adler sollen uns Einsamen Speise bringen in ihren Schnäbeln!

Wahrlich, keine Speise, an der Unsaubere mitessen dürften! Feuer würden sie zu fressen wähnen und sich die Mäuler verbrennen!

Wahrlich, keine Heimstätten halten wir hier bereit für Unsaubere! Eishöhle würde ihren Leibern unser Glück heißen und ihren Geistern!

Und wie starke Winde wollen wir über ihnen leben, Nachbarn den Adlern, Nachbarn dem Schnee, Nachbarn der Sonne: also leben starke Winde.

Und einem Winde gleich will ich einst noch zwischen sie blasen und mit meinem Geiste ihrem Geiste den Atem nehmen: so will es meine Zukunft.

Wahrlich, ein starker Wind ist Zarathustra allen Niederungen; und solchen Rat rät er seinen Feinden und Allem, was spuckt und speit: »hütet euch, *gegen* den Wind zu speien!« –

Also sprach Zarathustra.

sources? Truly, I had to fly to the highest levels in order to find the fountain of pleasure again!

Oh, I found it, my brother! Here at the highest level the fountain of pleasure is gushing for me! And a life exists at which no rabble shares the water!

You are flowing almost too violently for me, spring of pleasure! And often you empty the cup again in your urge to fill it!

And I must still learn to approach you more modestly: my heart is still flowing toward you too violently—

My heart, in which my summer is burning, brief, hot, melancholy, too blissful: how my summer heart longs for your coolness!

Gone is the hesitant tribulation of my springtime! Past is the malice of my snowflakes in June! I have become entirely summer and summer noon!

A summer at the highest level, with cool fountains and blissful silence: oh, come, my friends, so the silence will become even more blissful!

For these are *our* heights, this is our homeland: here we dwell too high up, on slopes too steep, for all unclean people and their thirst.

Just cast your clean glance into the fountain of my pleasure, friends! How could it be muddied by it? It will smile up to you with its own purity.

Let's build our nest on the tree Future; eagles shall bring food for us solitary ones in their beaks!

Truly, no food that an unclean man is permitted to share! They'd think they were swilling fire, and they'd burn their dirty mouths!

Truly, we have no homesteads ready here for the unclean! Our happiness would be an ice cave for their bodies and their spirits!

And like strong winds we shall live above them, neighbors to the eagles, neighbors to the snow, neighbors to the sun: that's how strong winds live.

And like a wind I will some day blow into their midst, and with my spirit take the breath away from theirs: that is what my future promises.

Truly, Zarathustra is a strong wind for all lowlands; and this advice he gives to his enemies and all who spit and expectorate: "Be careful not to spit *into* the wind!"

Thus spoke Zarathustra.

VON DEN TARANTELN (Of the Tarantulas): Vengeance out of envy is the
tarantulas' poison; they stand for the tyrannical preachers of "equality"
(leveling) and "justice" (punishment). People are not all alike, and the
best among them must prepare the way for the more-than-man by
striving and strife: Zarathustra dances, but not to the tarantella. / VON

Das Nachtlied

Nacht ist es: nun reden lauter alle springenden Brunnen. Und auch
meine Seele ist ein springender Brunnen.

Nacht ist es: nun erst erwachen alle Lieder der Liebenden. Und
auch meine Seele ist das Lied eines Liebenden.

Ein Ungestilltes, Unstillbares ist in mir; das will laut werden. Eine
Begierde nach Liebe ist in mir, die redet selber die Sprache der
Liebe.

Licht bin ich: ach, daß ich Nacht wäre! Aber dies ist meine
Einsamkeit, daß ich von Licht umgürtet bin.

Ach, daß ich dunkel wäre und nächtig! Wie wollte ich an den
Brüsten des Lichts saugen!

Und euch selber wollte ich noch segnen, ihr kleinen Funkelsterne
und Leuchtwürmer droben! – und selig sein ob eurer Licht-Geschenke.

Aber ich lebe in meinem eignen Lichte, ich trinke die Flammen in
mich zurück, die aus mir brechen.

Ich kenne das Glück des Nehmenden nicht; und oft träumte mir
davon, daß Stehlen noch seliger sein müsse als Nehmen.

Das ist meine Armut, daß meine Hand niemals ausruht vom
Schenken; das ist mein Neid, daß ich wartende Augen sehe und die
erhellten Nächte der Sehnsucht.

Oh Unseligkeit aller Schenkenden! Oh Verfinsterung meiner Sonne!
Oh Begierde nach Begehren! Oh Heißhunger in der Sättigung!

Sie nehmen von mir: aber rühre ich noch an ihre Seele? Eine Kluft
ist zwischen Geben und Nehmen; und die kleinste Kluft ist am letzten
zu überbrücken.

Ein Hunger wächst aus meiner Schönheit: wehe tun möchte ich
Denen, welchen ich leuchte, berauben möchte ich meine
Beschenkten: – also hungere ich nach Bosheit.

Die Hand zurückziehend, wenn sich schon ihr die Hand entgegen-
streckt; dem Wasserfalle gleich zögernd, der noch im Sturze zögert: –
also hungere ich nach Bosheit.

Solche Rache sinnt meine Fülle aus: solche Tücke quillt aus meiner
Einsamkeit.

DEN BERÜHMTEN WEISEN (Of Famous Wise Men): The sages of old served popular superstition, not truth—like masters amusing their slaves. The populace hates freethinkers; their own sages are donkeys in lions' skins. The true lion, the free spirit, dwells alone in the wilderness; he cares nothing for popular acclaim, but is proud and adventurous.

The Night Song

It is night: now all spurting fountains speak more loudly. And my soul, too, is a spurting fountain.

It is night: only now do all the songs of lovers awaken. And my soul, too, is the song of a lover.

There is something unquenched, unquenchable, in me; it wants to speak out. There is a craving for love in me which itself speaks the language of love.

I am a bright light: oh, if only I were night! But this is my solitude: I am surrounded by light.

Oh, if only I were dark and nocturnal! How I would suck at the breasts of the light!

And I would also bless you yourselves, you little twinkling stars and fireflies up there, and I'd be happy over your gifts of light.

But I live in my own light, I resorb the flames that issue from me.

I don't know the happiness of the one who takes, and I have often dreamt that stealing must be even more blissful than taking.

It is the way of my poverty that my hand never ceases giving; it is the way of my envy that I see expectant eyes and the illuminated nights of longing.

Oh, the unhappiness of all who give! Oh, the eclipse of my sun! Oh, my craving for desire! Oh, my great hunger though I am replete!

They take from me: but do I still touch their soul? There is a chasm between giving and taking, and the smallest gap is the hardest to bridge over.

A hunger grows from my beauty: I'd like to do harm to those I illuminate, I'd like to rob those to whom I have made gifts: so much do I hunger for malice.

Withdrawing my hand while another hand is already held out to it; hesitating like the waterfall that still hesitates even as it plunges: so much do I hunger for malice.

Such revenge is devised by my abundance; such guile flows from my solitude.

Mein Glück im Schenken erstarb im Schenken, meine Tugend wurde ihrer selber müde an ihrem Überflusse!

Wer immer schenkt, dessen Gefahr ist, daß er die Scham verliere; wer immer austeilt, dessen Hand und Herz hat Schwielen vor lauter Austeilen.

Mein Auge quillt nicht mehr über vor der Scham der Bittenden; meine Hand wurde zu hart für das Zittern gefüllter Hände.

Wohin kam die Träne meinem Auge und der Flaum meinem Herzen? Oh Einsamkeit aller Schenkenden! Oh Schweigsamkeit aller Leuchtenden!

Viel Sonnen kreisen im öden Raume: zu Allem, was dunkel ist, reden sie mit ihrem Lichte, – mir schweigen sie.

Oh dies ist die Feindschaft des Lichts gegen Leuchtendes: erbarmungslos wandelt es seine Bahnen.

Unbillig gegen Leuchtendes im tiefsten Herzen, kalt gegen Sonnen – also wandelt jede Sonne.

Einem Sturme gleich fliegen die Sonnen ihre Bahnen, das ist ihr Wandeln. Ihrem unerbittlichen Willen folgen sie, das ist ihre Kälte.

Oh, ihr erst seid es, ihr Dunklen, ihr Nächtigen, die ihr Wärme schafft aus Leuchtendem! Oh, ihr erst trinkt euch Milch und Labsal aus des Lichtes Eutern!

Ach, Eis ist um mich, meine Hand verbrennt sich an Eisigem! Ach, Durst ist in mir, der schmachtet nach eurem Durste!

Nacht ist es: ach daß ich Licht sein muß! Und Durst nach Nächtigem! Und Einsamkeit!

Nacht ist es: nun bricht wie ein Born aus mir mein Verlangen, – nach Rede verlangt mich.

Nacht ist es: nun reden lauter alle springenden Brunnen. Und auch meine Seele ist ein springender Brunnen.

Nacht ist es: nun erwachen alle Lieder der Liebenden. Und auch meine Seele ist das Lied eines Liebenden. –

Also sang Zarathustra.

DAS TANZLIED (The Dance Song): Finding girls dancing on a meadow, Zarathustra assures them he is not their enemy; he is fond of dancing, and Cupid lies sleeping amid his dark cypresses. The devil, "lord of the world," is the spirit of gravity. Life is not inscrutable; it is a fickle, mischievous woman. Zarathustra loves life and wisdom, which are alike. /

My happiness in giving died of the very giving; my virtue has always grown weary of itself because of its overabundance!

The man who always gives is in danger of losing his modesty; the man who always distributes has a hand and heart callused from constantly handing out.

My eyes no longer shed tears for the shame of those who ask; my hand has become too hard for the trembling of filled hands.

Where did the tears in my eyes go, and the down in my heart? Oh, solitude of all who give of themselves! O taciturnity of all who glow!

Many suns circulate in empty space: to all that is dark they speak with their light—to me they are silent.

Oh, this is the hostility of light to that which glows: it pursues its own paths mercilessly.

Unjust to that which glows at the bottom of its heart, cold to suns— thus each sun journeys.

Like a storm the suns fly along their orbits; such is their journeying. They follow their inexorable will; such is their coldness.

Oh, you dark, nocturnal ones, it is you who first create warmth out of that which glows! Oh, you are the first to drink milk and balm from the udders of the light!

Alas, ice is around me, my hand is burned by iciness! Alas, thirst is in me, which languishes for your thirst!

It is night: ah, that I must be a light! And thirst for the nocturnal! And solitude!

It is night: now my longing bursts from me like a fountain—I long for speech.

It is night: now all spurting fountains speak more loudly. And my soul, too, is a spurting fountain.

It is night: now all the songs of lovers awaken. And my soul, too, is the song of a lover.

Thus sang Zarathustra.

DAS GRABLIED (The Funeral Song): The dead whom Zarathustra laments are his cherished youthful visions and hopes, killed by his enemies. Once, when he was ready to perform his most ecstatic dance, his foes persuaded his singer [Wagner?] to perform doleful music [*Parsifal?*]. But his will is intact.

Von der Selbst-Überwindung

»Wille zur Wahrheit« heißt ihr's, ihr Weisesten, was euch treibt und brünstig macht?

Wille zur Denkbarkeit alles Seienden: also heiße *ich* euren Willen!

Alles Seiende wollt ihr erst denkbar *machen*: denn ihr zweifelt mit gutem Mißtrauen, ob es schon denkbar ist.

Aber es soll sich euch fügen und biegen! So will's euer Wille. Glatt soll es werden und dem Geiste untertan, als sein Spiegel und Widerbild.

Das ist euer ganzer Wille, ihr Weisesten, als ein Wille zur Macht; und auch wenn ihr vom Guten und Bösen redet und von den Wertschätzungen.

Schaffen wollt ihr noch die Welt, vor der ihr knien könnt: so ist es eure letzte Hoffnung und Trunkenheit.

Die Unweisen freilich, das Volk – die sind gleich dem Flusse, auf dem ein Nachen weiter schwimmt: und im Nachen sitzen feierlich und vermummt die Wertschätzungen.

Euren Willen und eure Werte setztet ihr auf den Fluß des Werdens; einen alten Willen zur Macht verrät mir, was vom Volke als Gut und Böse geglaubt wird.

Ihr wart es, Ihr Weisesten, die solche Gäste in diesen Nachen setzten und ihnen Prunk und stolze Namen gaben – ihr und euer herrschender Wille!

Weiter trägt nun der Fluß euren Nachen: er *muß* ihn tragen. Wenig tut's, ob die gebrochene Welle schäumt und zornig dem Kiele widerspricht!

Nicht der Fluß ist eure Gefahr und das Ende eures Guten und Bösen, ihr Weisesten: sondern jener Wille selber, der Wille zur Macht – der unerschöpfte zeugende Lebens-Wille.

Aber damit ihr mein Wort versteht vom Guten und Bösen: dazu will ich euch noch mein Wort vom Leben sagen und von der Art alles Lebendigen.

Dem Lebendigen ging ich nach, ich ging die größten und die kleinsten Wege, daß ich seine Art erkenne.

Mit hundertfachem Spiegel fing ich noch seinen Blick auf, wenn ihm der Mund geschlossen war: daß sein Auge mir rede. Und sein Auge redete mir.

Aber, wo ich nur Lebendiges fand, da hörte ich auch die Rede vom Gehorsame. Alles Lebendige ist ein Gehorchendes.

Und dies ist das Zweite: Dem wird befohlen, der sich nicht selber gehorchen kann. So ist es des Lebendigen Art.

Of Self-Overcoming

You call it the "will to truth," you great sages, that which urges you on and makes you ruttish?

The will to conceivability of all being: that's what *I* call your will!

You want to begin *making* being conceivable, because, with a legitimate distrust, you doubt whether it is conceivable already.

But it must submit and yield to you! That is what your will demands. It must become smooth and subservient to the mind, as its mirror and reflection.

That is your entire will, you great sages, as a will to power; and even when you speak of good and evil and of evaluations.

You still want to create a world to which you can kneel: such is your final hope and intoxication.

Of course, those not wise, the populace—they are like a river on which a boat keeps sailing; and in the boat the evaluations sit solemnly, all wrapped up.

You placed your will and your values on the river of becoming; I detect an old will to power in that which the populace believes to be good or evil.

It was you, great sages, who put such passengers in that boat, lending them pomp and proud names—you and your dominant will!

Now the river bears your boat along; it *must* bear it. It matters little whether the choppy waters foam and contend angrily against the keel!

It is not the river that is your peril and the end of your good and evil, sages, but that will itself, the will to power—the unexhausted, procreative will to live.

But, in order for you to understand my teaching about good and evil, I shall now tell you my teaching about life and the nature of all living things.

I have pursued that which lives, I have followed the widest and the narrowest paths in order to learn its nature.

With a hundred-faceted mirror I have caught the reflection of its eyes, when its lips were closed: so that its eyes could talk to me. And its eyes did talk to me.

But wherever I found living things, I also heard talk of obedience. All that lives is obedient.

And this is the second point: he who can't obey himself takes orders from others. Such is the nature of the living.

Dies aber ist das Dritte, was ich hörte: daß Befehlen schwerer ist, als Gehorchen. Und nicht nur, daß der Befehlende die Last aller Gehorchenden trägt, und daß leicht ihn diese Last zerdrückt: –

Ein Versuch und Wagnis erschien mir in allem Befehlen; und stets, wenn es befiehlt, wagt das Lebendige sich selber dran.

Ja noch, wenn es sich selber befiehlt: auch da noch muß es sein Befehlen büßen. Seinem eignen Gesetze muß es Richter und Rächer und Opfer werden.

Wie geschieht dies doch! so fragte ich mich. Was überredet das Lebendige, daß es gehorcht und befiehlt und befehlend noch Gehorsam übt?

Hört mir nun mein Wort, ihr Weisesten! Prüft es ernstlich, ob ich dem Leben selber ins Herz kroch, und bis in die Wurzeln seines Herzens!

Wo ich Lebendiges fand, da fand ich Willen zur Macht; und noch im Willen des Dienenden fand ich den Willen, Herr zu sein.

Daß dem Stärkeren diene das Schwächere, dazu überredet es sein Wille, der über noch Schwächeres Herr sein will: dieser Lust allein mag es nicht entraten.

Und wie das Kleinere sich dem Größeren hingibt, daß es Lust und Macht am Kleinsten habe: also gibt sich auch das Größte noch hin und setzt um der Macht willen – das Leben dran.

Das ist die Hingebung des Größten, daß es Wagnis ist und Gefahr, und um den Tod ein Würfelspielen.

Und wo Opferung und Dienste und Liebesblicke sind: auch da ist Wille, Herr zu sein. Auf Schleichwegen schleicht sich da der Schwächere in die Burg und bis ins Herz dem Mächtigeren – und stiehlt da Macht.

Und dies Geheimnis redete das Leben selber zu mir: »Siehe«, sprach es, »ich bin Das, *was sich immer selber überwinden muß*.

Freilich, ihr heißt es Wille zur Zeugung oder Trieb zum Zwecke, zum Höheren, Ferneren, Vielfacheren: aber all Dies ist Eins und Ein Geheimnis.

Lieber noch gehe ich unter, als daß ich diesem Einen absagte; und wahrlich, wo es Untergang gibt und Blätterfallen, siehe, da opfert sich Leben – um Macht!

Daß ich Kampf sein muß und Werden und Zweck und der Zwecke Widerspruch: ach, wer meinen Willen errät, errät wohl auch, auf welchen *krummen* Wegen er gehen muß!

Was ich auch schaffe und wie ich's auch liebe, – bald muß ich Gegner ihm sein und meiner Liebe: so will es mein Wille.

Und auch du, Erkennender, bist nur ein Pfad und Fußstapfen

Now this is the third thing I heard: that giving orders is harder than obeying. And not merely because the man giving the orders bears the responsibility for all who obey him, and is readily crushed by that responsibility—

I saw a risky experiment in all giving of orders; and whenever they give orders, living things put themselves at risk.

Yes, even when they give orders to themselves: even then they must make amends for those orders. They must become judge and avenger and victim to their own laws.

"How does this come about?" I wondered. What persuades living things to obey and command and still obey while commanding?

Now hear my teaching, you sages! Test it carefully to see whether I have crept into the very heart of life, and to the very root of its heart!

Wherever I found life, I found the will to power; even in the will of the servant I found the will to be master.

The weaker is persuaded to serve the stronger by its own will, which wishes to lord it over those that are weaker yet; this pleasure alone it cannot do without.

And just as the smaller submits to the greater in order to have pleasurable power over the smallest of all, in the same way the greater, too, submits and stakes its life for the sake of power.

This is the submissiveness of the greatest: it is risk and danger and a dice game that can be fatal.

And wherever sacrifice, service, and loving looks occur, there, too, you will find the will to dominate. Then the weaker man steals into the fortress by devious routes, into the very heart of the more powerful man—and robs him of his power.

And life once told me this secret: "See," it said, "I am that *which must constantly overcome itself.*

"Of course, you call it the will to procreate or the urge toward a purpose, toward something higher, more distant, more diversified, but it is all one, all one mystery.

"I'd rather perish than renounce this one thing; and truly, where there is perishing and falling of leaves, behold, there life is sacrificing itself—for power!

"That I must be a battle and becoming and a purpose and the contradiction between purposes: ah, whoever guesses my will probably also guesses how *tortuous* the paths are that it must travel!

"Whatever I create, and no matter how much I love it—soon I must oppose it and my love: thus my will demands.

"And you, too, man of knowledge, are only a path and a footprint of

meines Willens: wahrlich, mein Wille zur Macht wandelt auch auf den Füßen deines Willens zur Wahrheit!

Der traf freilich die Wahrheit nicht, der das Wort nach ihr schoß vom ›Willen zum Dasein‹: diesen Willen – gibt es nicht!

Denn: was nicht ist, das kann nicht wollen; was aber im Dasein ist, wie könnte das noch zum Dasein wollen!

Nur, wo Leben ist, da ist auch Wille: aber nicht Wille zum Leben, sondern – so lehre ich's dich – Wille zur Macht!

Vieles ist dem Lebenden höher geschätzt, als Leben selber; doch aus dem Schätzen selber heraus redet – der Wille zur Macht!« –

Also lehrte mich einst das Leben: und daraus löse ich euch, ihr Weisesten, noch das Rätsel eures Herzens.

Wahrlich, ich sage euch: Gutes und Böses, das unvergänglich wäre – das gibt es nicht! Aus sich selber muß es sich immer wieder überwinden.

Mit euren Werten und Worten von Gut und Böse übt ihr Gewalt, ihr Wertschätzenden: und Dies ist eure verborgene Liebe und eurer Seele Glänzen, Zittern und Überwallen.

Aber eine stärkere Gewalt wächst aus euren Werten und eine neue Überwindung: an der zerbricht Ei und Eierschale.

Und wer ein Schöpfer sein muß im Guten und Bösen: wahrlich, der muß ein Vernichter erst sein und Werte zerbrechen.

Also gehört das höchste Böse zur höchsten Güte: diese aber ist die schöpferische. –

Reden wir nur davon, ihr Weisesten, ob es gleich schlimm ist. Schweigen ist schlimmer; alle verschwiegenen Wahrheiten werden giftig.

Und mag doch Alles zerbrechen, was an unseren Wahrheiten zerbrechen – kann! Manches Haus gibt es noch zu bauen! –

Also sprach Zarathustra.

Von den Erhabenen (Of the Lofty Ones): Zarathustra laughs at the ugliness of a solemn "lofty man," an "intellectual penitent" (ascetic). All of life is a fight over questions of good taste. The "lofty man" looks down on life; he is gloomy, envious, restless; if he's good, it's only because he's weak. / Vom Lande der Bildung (Of the Land of Culture): The cultured people of the day make Zarathustra laugh; they wear colorful face paint and are surrounded by flattering mirrors; their learning is a light mantle. They are equally ugly when naked, though they pride themselves on their realism. They have no future. Zarathustra must remain homeless. / Von der unbefleckten Erkenntnis (Of the Immaculate Perception): Those who despise earthly things are lustful hypocrites. Their "immaculate perception" of the world is a cowardly shirking of life

my will; truly, my will to power even walks on the feet of your will to truth!

"To be sure, that man missed the truth when he shot at her that phrase 'the will to existence': such a will—doesn't exist!

"For: that which is not, cannot will; but how could that which is in existence still wish to exist?

"Only where there is life is there also will; but not will to life, rather—this is my doctrine—will to power!

"The living esteems many things more highly than life itself; but from that very evaluation can be heard—the will to power!"

That is what I was once taught by life; and from this, you sages, I shall now solve for you the riddle of your heart.

Truly, I say to you: imperishable good and evil—do not exist! They must constantly supersede themselves by drawing on themselves.

You exert force, you value-givers, with your values and doctrines of good and evil: and this is your concealed love and the shining, trembling, and boiling over of your soul.

But a stronger force, and a new overcoming, develop from your values; dashing against them, the egg and the eggshell are destroyed.

And whoever must be a creator in good and evil, truly, he must first be an annihilator and shatter values.

Thus the greatest evil is allied to the greatest kindliness: and the latter is of the creative kind.

Let us *speak* of it, sages, even if it's bad. Silence is worse; all truths kept under wraps become poisonous.

And may everything shatter that *can* shatter against our truths! Many a house is still to be built!

Thus spoke Zarathustra.

---

and love, and a fear of death; love and death are linked. Zarathustra's dawn light exposes those people. / VON DEN GELEHRTEN (Of Scholars): Zarathustra has been boycotted by the scholars, whose house he abandoned because they left him hungry. He has to be an experimental thinker, not a mere spectator or a machine that needs constant rewinding. / VON DEN DICHTERN (Of Poets): Poets tell too many lies because they believe in popular wisdom and old wives' tales (the "eternal feminine"), and in inspiration (thus, in gods). [The passage is full of parodies of Goethe.] Poets are too superficial and vain. / VON GROßEN EREIGNISSEN (Of Great Events): After a disappearance lasting several days, Zarathustra reports to his disciples about his alleged visit to hell. Our greatest events, he says, are our quietest hours. New values make

the world go round. New life arises out of iconoclasm and contempt.
Old institutions should let themselves be overturned. / DER
WAHRSAGER (The Soothsayer): Zarathustra becomes dejected when he
hears a soothsayer declare that all is barren emptiness. He dreams of

Von der Erlösung

Als Zarathustra eines Tages über die große Brücke ging, umringten
ihn die Krüppel und Bettler, und ein Bucklichter redete also zu ihm:
»Siehe, Zarathustra! Auch das Volk lernt von dir und gewinnt
Glauben an deine Lehre: aber daß es ganz dir glauben soll, dazu bedarf es noch Eines – du mußt erst noch uns Krüppel überreden! Hier
hast du nun eine schöne Auswahl und wahrlich, eine Gelegenheit mit
mehr als Einem Schopfe! Blinde kannst du heilen und Lahme laufen
machen; und Dem, der zuviel hinter sich hat, könntest du wohl auch
ein Wenig abnehmen: – Das, meine ich, wäre die rechte Art, die
Krüppel an Zarathustra glauben zu machen!«

Zarathustra aber erwiderte Dem, der da redete, also: Wenn man dem
Bucklichten seinen Buckel nimmt, so nimmt man ihm seinen Geist – also
lehrt das Volk. Und wenn man dem Blinden seine Augen gibt, so sieht er
zuviel schlimme Dinge auf Erden: also daß er den verflucht, der ihn heilte.
Der aber, welcher den Lahmen laufen macht, der tut ihm den größten
Schaden an: denn kaum kann er laufen, so gehn seine Laster mit ihm
durch – also lehrt das Volk über Krüppel. Und warum sollte Zarathustra
nicht auch vom Volke lernen, wenn das Volk von Zarathustra lernt?

Das ist mir aber das Geringste, seit ich unter Menschen bin, daß ich
sehe: »Diesem fehlt ein Auge und Jenem ein Ohr und einem Dritten
das Bein, und Andre gibt es, die verloren die Zunge oder die Nase
oder den Kopf.«

Ich sehe und sah Schlimmeres und mancherlei so Abscheuliches,
daß ich nicht von Jeglichem reden und von Einigem nicht einmal
schweigen möchte: nämlich Menschen, denen es an allem fehlt, außer
daß sie Eins zuviel haben – Menschen, welche Nichts weiter sind, als
ein großes Auge oder ein großes Maul oder ein großer Bauch oder ir-
gendetwas Großes, – umgekehrte Krüppel heiße ich Solche.

Und als ich aus meiner Einsamkeit kam und zum ersten Male über
diese Brücke ging: da traute ich meinen Augen nicht und sah hin, und
wieder hin, und sagte endlich: »das ist ein Ohr! Ein Ohr, so groß wie
ein Mensch!« Ich sah noch besser hin: und wirklich, unter dem Ohre
bewegte sich noch Etwas, das zum Erbarmen klein und ärmlich und

frightening laughter issuing from a bursting coffin. His favorite disciple interprets the dream: Zarathustra's own healthy laughter reinvigorates the world, and he will survive periods of spiritual darkness.

Of Redemption

One day, as Zarathustra was crossing the big bridge, he was surrounded by cripples and beggars, and a hunchback addressed him as follows:

"Behold, Zarathustra! The commoners, too, learn from you and are gaining faith in your doctrine; but if they are to have complete faith in you, one thing more is necessary: you must convince us cripples first! Here you now have a fine selection and, truly, an opportunity with more than one forelock! You can cure blind men and make lame men run; and from the man who has too much in back of him you could surely also remove a little. This, in my opinion, would be the proper way of making the cripples believe in Zarathustra!"

But Zarathustra responded to the speaker as follows: "When a hunchback's hump is taken away, so is his intelligence—that's what the populace says. And when the blind man's sight is restored, he sees too many bad things in the world, so that he curses his healer. But whoever makes the lame man run does him the greatest harm, for the minute he can run, his vices run away with him—that's what the populace says about cripples. And why shouldn't Zarathustra, too, learn from the people when the people learn from Zarathustra?

"But ever since I have been among human beings, it's of the slightest importance to me to see that one man is missing an eye; a second man, an ear; and a third, a leg; and that there are others who have lost their tongue, nose, or head.

"I see, and have seen, worse and, at times, such abominable things that I prefer not to speak about each one, and there are some things I don't even want to keep silent about: that is, people who are missing everything, except that they have too much of one thing—people who are nothing but a big eye or a big yap or a big belly or some other big thing; I call such people "reverse cripples."

And when I left my solitude and first crossed this bridge, I couldn't believe my eyes; I took a look, and then another look, and finally said: "It's an ear! An ear as big as a man!" I took a better look, and, truly, under the ear something else was moving, something pathetically small, shabby, and frail. And actually the enormous ear was sitting on

schmächtig war. Und wahrhaftig, das ungeheure Ohr saß auf einem kleinen dünnen Stiele, – der Stiel aber war ein Mensch! Wer ein Glas vor das Auge nahm, konnte sogar noch ein kleines neidisches Gesichtchen erkennen; auch, daß ein gedunsenes Seelchen am Stiele baumelte. Das Volk sagte mir aber, das große Ohr sei nicht nur ein Mensch, sondern ein großer Mensch, ein Genie. Aber ich glaubte dem Volke niemals, wenn es von großen Menschen redete – und behielt meinen Glauben bei, daß es ein umgekehrter Krüppel sei, der an Allem zu wenig und an Einem zu viel habe.

Als Zarathustra so zu dem Bucklichten geredet hatte und zu Denen, welchen er Mundstück und Fürsprecher war, wandte er sich mit tiefem Unmute zu seinen Jüngern und sagte:

Wahrlich, meine Freunde, ich wandle unter den Menschen wie unter den Bruchstücken und Gliedmaßen von Menschen!

Dies ist meinem Auge das Fürchterliche, daß ich den Menschen zertrümmert finde und zerstreuet wie über ein Schlacht- und Schlächterfeld hin.

Und flüchtet mein Auge vom Jetzt zum Ehemals: es findet immer das gleiche: Bruchstücke und Gliedmaßen und grause Zufälle – aber keine Menschen!

Das Jetzt und das Ehemals auf Erden – ach! meine Freunde – das ist *mein* Unerträglichstes; und ich wüßte nicht zu leben, wenn ich nicht noch ein Seher wäre, Dessen, was kommen muß.

Ein Seher, ein Wollender, Ein Schaffender, eine Zukunft selber und eine Brücke zur Zukunft – und ach, auch noch gleichsam ein Krüppel an dieser Brücke: das Alles ist Zarathustra.

Und auch ihr fragtet euch oft: »wer ist uns Zarathustra? Wie soll er uns heißen?« Und gleich mir selber gabt ihr euch Fragen zur Antwort.

Ist er ein Versprechender? Oder ein Erfüller? Ein Erobernder? Oder ein Erbender? Ein Herbst? Oder eine Pflugschar? Ein Arzt? Oder ein Genesener?

Ist er ein Dichter? Oder ein Wahrhaftiger? Ein Befreier? Oder ein Bändiger? Ein Guter? Oder ein Böser?

Ich wandle unter Menschen als den Bruchstücken der Zukunft: jener Zukunft, die ich schaue.

Und das ist all mein Dichten und Trachten, daß ich in Eins dichte und zusammentrage, was Bruchstück ist und Rätsel und grauser Zufall.

Und wie ertrüge ich es, Mensch zu sein, wenn der Mensch nicht auch Dichter und Rätselrater und der Erlöser des Zufalls wäre!

Die Vergangnen zu erlösen und alles »Es war« umzuschaffen in ein »So wollte ich es!« – das hieße mir erst Erlösung!

Wille – so heißt der Befreier und Freudebringer: also lehrte ich

a small, thin stem—and the stem was a person! If you looked through a magnifying glass, you could even make out a small, envious face; you could also see that a bloated little soul was dangling from the stem. But people told me that the big ear was not only a person, but a great person, a genius. But I have never believed the people when they spoke about great men—and I have retained my belief that it was a reverse cripple who had too little of everything and too much of one thing."

After Zarathustra had said this to the hunchback and to those whose mouthpiece and spokesman he was, he turned to his disciples in great ill humor, saying:

"Truly, my friends, I walk among men as if amid the fragments and limbs of men!

"The most frightful thing to my eyes is to find man broken into bits and scattered as if across a battlefield or a butchers' field.

"And when my eyes flit from the present to the past, they always find the same thing: fragments and limbs and dire accidents—but no people!

"The present and the past on earth—alas, my friends!—are what *I* find hardest to bear; and I'd be unable to go on living if I didn't foresee that which must come.

"A seer, one who wills, a creator, myself a future and a bridge to the future—and, alas, still as if I, too, were a cripple on this bridge: Zarathustra is all of this.

"And you, too, have often wondered: 'Who is Zarathustra to us? How should we define him?' And, like me, you answered yourselves with new questions.

"Is he one who promises? Or one who fulfills? A conqueror? Or an inheritor? An autumn? Or a plowshare? A physician? Or one who has recovered?

"Is he a poet? Or a truthful man? A liberator? Or a tamer? A good man? Or an evil man?

"I walk among men as if they were the fragments of the future: that future which I behold.

"And all my thought and endeavor is to compose and collect into a unity that which is a fragment, riddle, and dire accident.

"And how could I bear to be a human being if man weren't also a poet and riddle solver and the redeemer of chance?

"To redeem those of the past and to change all 'There was' into an 'I wanted it that way!'—only that would I call redemption!

"The will is the liberator and joybringer: this I have taught you,

euch, meine Freunde! Aber nun lernt Dies hinzu: der Wille selbst ist noch ein Gefangener.

Wollen befreit: aber wie heißt Das, was auch den Befreier noch in Ketten schlägt?

»Es war«: also heißt des Willens Zähneknirschen und einsamste Trübsal. Ohnmächtig gegen Das, was getan ist – ist er allem Vergangenen ein böser Zuschauer.

Nicht zurück kann der Wille wollen; daß er die Zeit nicht brechen kann und der Zeit Begierde, – das ist des Willens einsamste Trübsal.

Wollen befreit: was ersinnt sich das Wollen selber, daß es los seiner Trübsal werde und seines Kerkers spotte?

Ach, ein Narr wird jeder Gefangene! Närrisch erlöst sich auch der gefangene Wille.

Daß die Zeit nicht zurückläuft, das ist sein Ingrimm; »Das, was war« – so heißt der Stein, den er nicht wälzen kann.

Und so wälzt er Steine aus Ingrimm und Unmut und übt Rache an Dem, was nicht gleich ihm Grimm und Unmut fühlt.

Also wurde der Wille, der Befreier, ein Wehetäter: und an Allem, was leiden kann, nimmt er Rache dafür, daß er nicht zurückkann.

Dies, ja dies allein ist *Rache* selber: des Willens Widerwille gegen die Zeit und ihr »Es war«.

Wahrlich, eine große Narrheit wohnt in unserm Willen; und zum Fluche wurde es allem Menschlichen, daß diese Narrheit Geist lernte!

Der Geist der Rache: meine Freunde, das war bisher der Menschen bestes Nachdenken; und wo Leid war, da sollte immer Strafe sein.

»Strafe«, nämlich, so heißt sich die Rache selber: mit einem Lügenwort heuchelt sie sich ein gutes Gewissen.

Und weil im Wollenden selber Leid ist, darob, daß es nicht zurückwollen kann, – also sollte Wollen selber und alles Leben – Strafe sein!

Und nun wälzte sich Wolke auf Wolke über den Geist: bis endlich der Wahnsinn predigte: »Alles vergeht, darum ist Alles wert zu vergehn!«

»Und dies ist selber Gerechtigkeit, jenes Gesetz der Zeit, daß sie ihre Kinder fressen muß«: also predigte der Wahnsinn.

»Sittlich sind die Dinge geordnet nach Recht und Strafe. Oh wo ist die Erlösung vom Fluß der Dinge und der Strafe ›Dasein‹?« Also predigte der Wahnsinn.

»Kann es Erlösung geben, wenn es ein ewiges Recht gibt? Ach, un-

my friends! But now learn this in addition: the will itself is still a prisoner.

"The will liberates, but what is the thing that still enchains even the liberator?

"'There was': that is the will's gnashing of teeth and loneliest tribulation. Powerless against things already done, it is an angry spectator of everything in the past.

"The will cannot will backwards; its inability to break time and time's craving—that is the will's loneliest tribulation.

"The will liberates; what does the will itself devise to be rid of its tribulation and to mock at its dungeon?

"Alas, every prisoner becomes a fool! The imprisoned will, too, redeems itself in a foolish way.

"It's furious because time doesn't run backward; 'That which was' is the stone it can't roll away.

"And so, in its fury and displeasure, it rolls stones and wreaks vengeance on that which doesn't feel fury and displeasure in the same way.

"Thus the will, the liberator, became a doer of harm; and from everything that can suffer it exacts vengeance for being unable to go back in time.

"This, yes, this alone is *vengeance* itself: the will's grudge against time and its 'There was.'

"Truly, there is great folly in our will, and it has become a curse to all mankind that this folly acquired intelligence!

"*The spirit of revenge:* this, my friends, has hitherto been man's chief subject of meditation; and wherever there was sorrow, punishment always had to follow.

"You see, 'punishment' is the term for revenge itself: with a lying word it acquires an easy conscience hypocritically.

"And because the will itself feels sorrow because it cannot exert itself on the past, the will itself and all of life were to be punishment!

"And now cloud after cloud rolled over the intellect, until madness finally preached: 'All things pass away, therefore all things deserve to pass away!'

"'And this is justice itself, that law of time: that it must devour its children'—thus did madness preach.

"'Things are morally ordered according to right and punishment. Oh, where is the redemption from the flow of things and from the punishment Existence?' Thus did madness preach.

"'Can there be any redemption when there is an eternal right? Alas,

wälzbar ist der Stein ›Es war‹: ewig müssen auch alle Strafen sein!«
Also predigte der Wahnsinn.

»Keine Tat kann vernichtet werden: wie könnte sie durch die Strafe
ungetan werden! Dies, dies ist das Ewige an der Strafe ›Dasein‹, daß
das Dasein auch ewig wieder Tat und Schuld sein muß!

»Es sei denn, daß der Wille endlich sich selber erlöste und Wollen
zu Nicht-Wollen würde –«: doch ihr kennt, meine Brüder, dies
Fabellied des Wahnsinns!

Weg führte ich euch von diesen Fabelliedern, als ich euch lehrte:
»der Wille ist ein Schaffender.«

Alles »Es war« ist ein Bruchstück, ein Rätsel, ein grauser Zufall –
bis der schaffende Wille dazu sagt: »aber so wollte ich es!«

– Bis der schaffende Wille dazu sagt: »Aber so will ich es! So werde
ich's wollen!«

Aber sprach er schon so? Und wann geschieht dies? Ist der Wille
schon abgeschirrt von seiner eignen Torheit?

Wurde der Wille sich selber schon Erlöser und Freudebringer?
Verlernte er den Geist der Rache und alles Zähneknirschen?

Und wer lehrte ihn Versöhnung mit der Zeit, und Höheres, als alle
Versöhnung ist?

Höheres als alle Versöhnung muß der Wille wollen, welcher der
Wille zur Macht ist –: doch wie geschieht ihm das? Wer lehrte ihn
auch noch das Zurückwollen?

– Aber an dieser Stelle seiner Rede geschah es, daß Zarathustra plötzlich innehielt und ganz einem Solchen gleichsah, der auf das Äußer-
ste erschrickt. Mit erschrecktem Auge blickte er auf seine Jünger; sein
Auge durchbohrte wie mit Pfeilen ihre Gedanken und Hintergedanken. Aber nach einer kleinen Weile lachte er schon wieder und
sagte begütigt:

»Es ist schwer, mit Menschen zu leben, weil Schweigen so schwer
ist. Sonderlich für einen Geschwätzigen.« –

Also sprach Zarathustra. Der Bucklichte aber hatte dem Gespräche
zugehört und sein Gesicht dabei bedeckt; als er aber Zarathustra
lachen hörte, blickte er neugierig auf und sagte langsam:

»Aber warum redet Zarathustra anders zu uns, als zu seinen
Jüngern?«

Zarathustra antwortete: »Was ist da zum Verwundern! Mit
Bucklichten darf man schon bucklicht reden!«

»Gut«, sagte der Bucklichte; »und mit Schülern darf man schon aus
der Schule schwätzen.

the stone "There was" can't be rolled away; all punishments must be eternal, as well!' Thus did madness preach.

"'No deed can be annihilated: how could it be made undone by punishment? This, this is what is eternal about the punishment Existence: Existence, too, must be eternally new deed and guilt!

"'Unless the will finally redeems itself and willing becomes non-willing'—but, my brothers, you know this fable told by madness!

"I led you away from such fables when I taught you: 'The will is creative.'

"All 'there was' is a fragment, a riddle, a dire accident—until the creative will adds: 'But that's the way I wanted it!'

"Until the creative will adds: 'But that's the way I want it! That's the way I will want it!'

"But has it already said it? And when does that occur? Is the will already unyoked from its own folly?

"Has the will already become its own redeemer and joybringer? Has it forgotten the spirit of revenge and all gnashing of teeth?

"And who taught it reconciliation with time, and something higher than all reconciliation?

"Something higher than all reconciliation must be willed by that will which is the will to power; but how does it achieve this? Who can teach it the power to exert itself backwards, as well?"

But at this point in his address it came about that Zarathustra suddenly stopped short and resembled in every way a man who is extremely frightened. With terrified eyes he gazed at his disciples; as if with arrows, his eyes penetrated their thoughts and ulterior motives. But after a little while he was already laughing again, and, appeased, he said:

"It's hard to live with people because it's so hard to keep quiet. Especially for a talkative man."

Thus spoke Zarathustra. But the hunchback had listened to the conversation, covering his face as he did so; but when he heard Zarathustra laugh, he looked up in curiosity and said slowly:

"But why does Zarathustra speak one way to us and another to his disciples?"

Zarathustra replied: "Why should you be surprised? To hunchbacks it's all right to speak in hunchback fashion!"

"Fine," said the hunchback, "and to pupils it's all right to tell tales out of school.

Aber warum redet Zarathustra anders zu seinen Schülern – als zu sich selber?« –

Die stillste Stunde

Was geschah mir, meine Freunde? Ihr seht mich verstört, fortgetrieben, unwillig-folgsam, bereit zu gehen – ach, *von euch* fortzugehen!

Ja, noch Ein Mal muß Zarathustra in seine Einsamkeit: aber unlustig geht diesmal der Bär zurück in seine Höhle!

Was geschah mir? Wer gebeut dies? – Ach, meine zornige Herrin will es so, sie sprach zu mir; nannte ich je euch schon ihren Namen?

Gestern gen Abend sprach zu mir *meine stillste Stunde*: das ist der Name meiner furchtbaren Herrin.

Und so geschah's, – denn Alles muß ich euch sagen, daß euer Herz sich nicht verhärte gegen den plötzlich Scheidenden!

Kennt ihr den Schrecken des Einschlafenden? –

Bis in die Zehen hinein erschrickt er, darob, daß ihm der Boden weicht und der Traum beginnt.

Dieses sage ich euch zum Gleichnis. Gestern, zur stillsten Stunde, wich mir der Boden: der Traum begann.

Der Zeiger rückte, die Uhr meines Lebens holte Atem –, nie hörte ich solche Stille um mich: also daß mein Herz erschrak.

Dann sprach es ohne Stimme zu mir: »*Du weißt es, Zarathustra?*« –

Und ich schrie vor Schrecken bei diesem Flüstern, und das Blut wich aus meinem Gesichte: aber ich schwieg.

Da sprach es abermals ohne Stimme zu mir: »Du weißt es, Zarathustra, aber du redest es nicht!« –

Und ich antwortete endlich gleich einem Trotzigen: »Ja, ich weiß es, aber ich will es nicht reden!«

"But why does Zarathustra speak one way to his pupils—and another way to himself?"

Von der Menschen-Klugheit (Of Human Wisdom): Zarathustra is suspended between man and more-than-man. To remain accessible, he lets himself be deceived. Vain people are good actors in the drama of life, and Zarathustra esteems the entertainment they afford; they're modest because they rely on praise from others. Also, Zarathustra likes to observe the wicked, who are less wicked than they're reputed to be. When the more-than-man appears, the "good and just" will call him a devil.

The Quietest Hour

What has happened to me, my friends? You see me perturbed, driven away, reluctantly obedient, ready to go—alas, to depart *from you!*

Yes, once again Zarathustra must return to his solitude; but this time the bear is reentering his cave unwillingly!

What has happened to me? Who is giving these orders?—Alas, my wrathful mistress wishes it to be; she spoke to me; have I ever told you her name?

Yesterday, toward evening, *my quietest hour* spoke to me; that's the name of my terrifying mistress.

And so it came about—for I must tell you everything, lest your hearts grow hard against the one who suddenly departs!

Are you familiar with the terror of the man falling asleep?

He is frightened down to his toes because the ground is giving way beneath him and the dream is beginning.

I say this to you metaphorically. Yesterday, at the quietest hour, the ground gave way beneath me: the dream began.

The minute hand moved, the clock of my life drew a breath—never have I heard such stillness around me; so that my heart was frightened.

Then a voiceless something[14] said to me: "Do you know, Zarathustra?"

"And I cried out in fright at that whispering, and the blood drained from my face; but I kept silent.

Then the voiceless something spoke to me again: "You do know, Zarathustra, but you don't say it!"

And I finally replied, as if in defiance: "Yes, I know, but I won't say it!"

---

14. Or (just barely possible): "it [my heart] voicelessly . . ."

Da sprach es wieder ohne Stimme zu mir: »Du *willst* nicht, Zarathustra? Ist dies auch wahr? Verstecke dich nicht in deinen Trotz!« –

Und ich weinte und zitterte wie ein Kind und sprach: »Ach, ich wollte schon, aber wie kann ich es! Erlaß mir Dies nur! Es ist über meine Kraft!«

Da sprach es wieder ohne Stimme zu mir: »Was liegt an dir, Zarathustra! Sprich dein Wort und zerbrich!« –

Und ich antwortete: »Ach, es ist *mein* Wort? Wer bin *ich*? Ich warte des Würdigeren; ich bin nicht wert, an ihm auch nur zu zerbrechen.«

Da sprach es wieder ohne Stimme zu mir: »Was liegt an dir? Du bist mir noch nicht demütig genug. Die Demut hat das härteste Fell.« –

Und ich antwortete: »Was trug nicht schon das Fell meiner Demut! Am Fuße wohne ich meiner Höhe: wie hoch meine Gipfel sind? Niemand sagte es mir noch. Aber gut kenne ich meine Täler.«

Da sprach es wieder ohne Stimme zu mir: »Oh Zarathustra, wer Berge zu versetzen hat, der versetzt auch Täler und Niederungen.« –

Und ich antwortete: »Noch versetzte mein Wort keine Berge, und was ich redete, erreichte die Menschen nicht. Ich ging wohl zu den Menschen, aber noch langte ich nicht bei ihnen an.«

Da sprach es wieder ohne Stimme zu mir: »Was weißt du *davon*! Der Tau fällt auf das Gras, wenn die Nacht am verschwiegensten ist.« –

Und ich antwortete: »Sie verspotteten mich, als ich meinen eigenen Weg fand und ging; und in Wahrheit zitterten damals meine Füße.

Und so sprachen sie zu mir: du verlerntest den Weg, nun verlernst du auch das Gehen!«

Da sprach es wieder ohne Stimme zu mir: »Was liegt an ihrem Spotte! Du bist Einer, der das Gehorchen verlernt hat: nun sollst du befehlen!

Weißt du nicht, wer Allen am nötigsten tut? Der Großes befiehlt.

Großes vollführen ist schwer: aber das Schwerere ist, Großes befehlen.

Das ist dein Unverzeihlichstes: du hast die Macht, und du willst nicht herrschen.« –

Und ich antwortete: »Mir fehlt des Löwen Stimme zu allem Befehlen.«

Da sprach es wieder wie ein Flüstern zu mir: »Die stillsten Worte sind es, welche den Sturm bringen. Gedanken, die mit Taubenfüßen kommen, lenken die Welt.

Oh Zarathustra, du sollst gehen als ein Schatten Dessen, was kommen muß: so wirst du befehlen und befehlend vorangehen.« –

Then the voiceless something spoke to me again: "You don't *want* to, Zarathustra? Is that true, too? Don't hide in your defiance!"

And I wept and trembled like a child, and said: "Ah, I'm willing by now, but how can I? Spare me this only! It's beyond my strength!"

Then the voiceless something spoke to me again: "You're too unimportant, Zarathustra! Speak your piece and burst!"

And I replied: "Ah, it's for *me* to say? Who am *I*? I am awaiting the worthier man; I'm not even worthy to be shattered against him."

Then the voiceless something spoke to me again: "You don't count. You aren't humble enough to suit me. Humility has the toughest hide."

And I replied: "What hasn't the hide of my humility already endured? I dwell at the foot of my heights: how high are my summits? No one has told me yet. But I'm well acquainted with my valleys."

Then the voiceless something spoke to me again: "O Zarathustra, the man who is to move mountains can also move valleys and hollows."

And I replied: "My words have never yet moved mountains; and my speech hasn't reached mankind. Oh, yes, I set out for the people, but I have not yet arrived among them."

Then the voiceless something spoke to me again: "What do you know *of that*? The dew falls on the grass when night is at its most discreetly silent."

And I replied: "They laughed at me when I found and followed my own path; and, in truth, my feet were trembling then.

"And so they said to me: 'You have forgotten the path, now you're even forgetting how to walk!' "

Then the voiceless something said to me: "What does their mockery matter? You're a man who has forgotten how to obey; now you must give orders!

"Don't you know who is most needed by everyone? The man who orders great things to be done.

"To carry out great things is difficult, but it's more difficult to order great things to be done.

"This is what is most unforgivable about you: you have the power, but you don't wish to govern."

And I replied: "I lack the lion's voice for all commanding."

Then it spoke to me again as if in whisper: "It's the quietest words that conjure up the storm. Ideas that come on the feet of doves direct the world.

"O Zarathustra, you must proceed as a shadow of that which is sure to come; in that way you will command and lead the way as a commander."

Und ich antwortete: »Ich schäme mich.«

Da sprach es wieder ohne Stimme zu mir: »Du mußt noch Kind werden und ohne Scham.

Der Stolz der Jugend ist noch auf dir, spät bist du jung geworden: aber wer zum Kinde werden will, muß auch noch seine Jugend überwinden.« –

Und ich besann mich lange und zitterte. Endlich aber sagte ich, was ich zuerst sagte: »Ich will nicht.«

Da geschah ein Lachen um mich. Wehe, wie dies Lachen mir die Eingeweide zerriß und das Herz aufschlitzte!

Und es sprach zum letzten Male zu mir: »Oh Zarathustra, deine Früchte sind reif, aber du bist nicht reif für deine Früchte!

So mußt du wieder in die Einsamkeit: denn du sollst noch mürbe werden.« –

Und wieder lachte es und floh: dann wurde es stille um mich wie mit einer zwiefachen Stille. Ich aber lag am Boden, und der Schweiß floß mir von den Gliedern.

– Nun hörtet ihr Alles, und warum ich in meine Einsamkeit zurück muß. Nichts verschwieg ich euch, meine Freunde.

Aber und Dies hörtet ihr von mir, *wer* immer noch aller Menschen Verschwiegenster ist – und es sein will!

Ach, meine Freunde! Ich hätte euch noch Etwas zu sagen, ich hätte euch noch Etwas zu geben! Warum gebe ich es nicht? Bin ich denn geizig?« –

Als Zarathustra aber diese Worte gesprochen hatte, überfiel ihn die Gewalt des Schmerzes und die Nähe des Abschieds von seinen Freunden, also daß er laut weinte; und Niemand wußte ihn zu trösten. Des Nachts aber ging er allein fort und verließ seine Freunde.

And I replied: "I'm ashamed."

Then it said to me again voicelessly: "You have yet to become a child that knows no shame.

"The pride of young manhood is still on you; you grew young belatedly. But whoever wants to become a child must also overcome his youth."

And I thought this over for a long time, trembling. But finally I said what I had first said: "I don't want to."

Then there was a laughter around me. Woe, how that laughter tore up my insides and slit open my heart!

And I was addressed for the last time: "O Zarathustra, your fruits are ripe, but you aren't ripe for your fruits!

"And so you must return to your solitude, for you still have to become tender."

And it laughed again, and fled; then there was stillness around me, a twofold stillness, as it were. But I lay on the ground, and sweat poured from my limbs.

Now you have heard it all, why I must return to my solitude. I have kept nothing back from you, my friends.

But this, too, you have heard from me, who is still the most discreetly silent of all men—and wants to be!

Ah, my friends! I could still tell you something, I could still give you something! Why don't I give it? Am I miserly?

But after Zarathustra spoke these words, he was assailed by violent sorrow and the proximity of departure from his friends, so that he wept out loud; and no one was able to console him. But at night he went away alone, leaving his friends behind.

DRITTER TEIL

Der Wanderer

Um Mitternacht war es, da nahm Zarathustra seinen Weg über den Rücken der Insel, daß er mit dem frühen Morgen an das andre Gestade käme: denn dort wollte er zu Schiff steigen. Es gab nämlich allda eine gute Reede, an der auch fremde Schiffe gern vor Anker gingen; die nahmen Manchen mit sich, der von den glückseligen Inseln über das Meer wollte. Als nun Zarathustra so den Berg hinanstieg, gedachte er unterwegs des vielen einsamen Wanderns von Jugend an, und wie viele Berge und Rücken und Gipfel er schon gestiegen sei.

Ich bin ein Wanderer und ein Bergsteiger, sagte er zu seinem Herzen, ich liebe die Ebenen nicht, und es scheint, ich kann nicht lange still sitzen.

Und was mir nun auch noch als Schicksal und Erlebnis komme, – ein Wandern wird darin sein und ein Bergsteigen: man erlebt endlich nur noch sich selber.

Die Zeit ist abgeflossen, wo mir noch Zufälle begegnen durften; und was *könnte* jetzt noch zu mir fallen, was nicht schon mein Eigen wäre!

Es kehrt nun zurück, es kommt mir endlich heim – mein eigen Selbst, und was von ihm lange in der Fremde war und zerstreut unter alle Dinge und Zufälle.

Und noch Eins weiß ich: ich stehe jetzt vor meinem letzten Gipfel und vor Dem, was mir am längsten aufgespart war. Ach, meine härtesten Wege muß ich hinan! Ach, ich begann meine einsamste Wanderung!

Wer aber meiner Art ist, der entgeht einer solchen Stunde nicht: der Stunde, die zu ihm redet: »Jetzo erst gehst du deinen Weg der Größe! Gipfel und Abgrund – das ist jetzt in Eins beschlossen!

Du gehst deinen Weg der Größe: nun ist deine letzte Zuflucht worden, was bisher deine letzte Gefahr hieß!

Du gehst deinen Weg der Größe: Das muß nun dein bester Mut sein, daß es hinter dir keinen Weg mehr gibt!

PART THREE

The Wayfarer

It was around midnight when Zarathustra made his away across the ridge of the island in order to reach the opposite coast early in the morning, for he wished to board a ship there. You see, there was a good roadstead there, in which even foreign ships were glad to ride at anchor; they took on many passengers who wanted to leave the Fortunate Islands and cross the sea. As Zarathustra now climbed the mountain, on the way he thought of all the lonely journeying he had done since his youth, and of how many mountains, ridges, and peaks he had already ascended.

"I am a wayfarer and a mountain climber," he said to his heart; "I don't like the plains, and apparently I can't sit still for very long.

"And whatever destiny and experience may now come to me, there will be wayfaring and mountain climbing in it: after all, one experiences only oneself.

"The time is past when random events could still befall me, and what *could* come my way that wasn't already mine?

"My own self is now returning, finally coming home—and so is that part of it which was long on foreign soil, dispersed among all things and accidents.

"And one more thing I know: I'm now facing my last peak and that which has been held in reserve for me for the longest time. Alas, I must climb my most difficult paths! Alas, I have begun my lonesomest journey!

"But a man of my nature doesn't elude an hour like this, the hour that tells him: 'Now for the first time you're following your path to greatness! Summit and abyss—they are now combined in one!

"You're following your path to greatness; now that has become your last refuge which was until now your greatest danger!

"You're following your path to greatness; you must derive your utmost courage from the fact that there is no longer any path behind you!

Du gehst deinen Weg der Größe: hier soll dir Keiner nachschlei-
chen! Dein Fuß selber löschte hinter dir den Weg aus, und über ihm
steht geschrieben: Unmöglichkeit.

Und wenn dir nunmehr alle Leitern fehlen, so mußt du verstehen,
noch auf deinen eigenen Kopf zu steigen: wie wolltest du anders
aufwärts steigen?

Auf deinen eigenen Kopf und hinweg über dein eigenes Herz! Jetzt
muß das Mildeste an dir noch zum Härtesten werden.

Wer sich stets viel geschont hat, der kränkelt zuletzt an seiner vielen Schonung. Gelobt sei, was hart macht! Ich lobe das Land nicht,
wo Butter und Honig – fließt!

Von sich *absehn* lernen ist nötig, um Viel zu sehn: – diese Härte tut
jedem Berge-Steigenden not.

Wer aber mit den Augen zudringlich ist als Erkennender, wie sollte
Der von allen Dingen mehr als ihre vorderen Gründe sehn!

Du aber, oh Zarathustra, wolltest aller Dinge Grund schaun und
Hintergrund: so mußt du schon über dich selber steigen, – hinan, hinauf, bis du auch deine Sterne noch *unter* dir hast!

Ja! Hinab auf mich selber sehn und noch auf meine Sterne: Das
erst hieße mir mein *Gipfel*. Das blieb mir noch zurück als mein *letzter*
Gipfel!« –

Also sprach Zarathustra im Steigen zu sich, mit harten Sprüchlein sein
Herz tröstend: denn er war wund am Herzen wie noch niemals zuvor.
Und als er auf die Höhe des Bergrückens kam, siehe, da lag das andre
Meer vor ihm ausgebreitet: und er stand still und schwieg lange. Die
Nacht aber war kalt in dieser Höhe und klar und hellgestirnt.

Ich erkenne Mein Los, sagte er endlich mit Trauer: Wohlan! Ich
bin bereit. Eben begann meine letzte Einsamkeit.

Ach, diese schwarze traurige See unter mir! Ach, diese schwangere
nächtliche Verdrossenheit! Ach, Schicksal und See! Zu euch muß ich
nun *hinab*steigen!

Vor meinem höchsten Berge stehe ich und vor meiner längsten
Wanderung: darum muß ich erst tiefer hinab, als ich jemals stieg:

– tiefer hinab in den Schmerz, als ich jemals stieg, bis hinein in seine
schwärzeste Flut! So will es mein Schicksal: Wohlan! Ich bin bereit.

Woher kommen die höchsten Berge? so fragte ich einst. Da lernte
ich, daß sie aus dem Meere kommen.

Dies Zeugnis ist in ihr Gestein geschrieben und in die Wände ihrer
Gipfel. Aus dem Tiefsten muß das Höchste zu seiner Höhe kommen. –

"You're following your path to greatness: no one shall slink after you here! Your foot itself has obliterated the path behind you, and over it is written: 'Impossibility.'

"And if henceforth you lack all ladders, you must know how to ascend onto your own head: how else did you want to climb upward?

"Onto your own head, and stepping over your own heart! Now your gentlest component must become the toughest.

"The man who has always spared himself a lot finally becomes sickly with all that indulgence. Praised be that which hardens a person! I don't praise the land that flows with butter and honey!

"To learn to *look away* from oneself is necessary if one is to see a lot; every mountain climber needs this toughness.

"But how is the man whose eyes are importunate in the quest for knowledge to see any more of each thing than its foreground?

"But you, O Zarathustra, wanted to behold the foundations of all things, and their background; and so you must ascend beyond yourself, higher, upward, until even your stars are *below* you!

"Yes! To look down at myself and even at my stars: then I could say I was at my *summit*. This is what is still left for me as my *ultimate summit*!"

Thus spoke Zarathustra to himself as he ascended, comforting his heart with tough, short maxims, for he was sore at heart as never before. And when he came to the top of the ridge, behold, there lay the other sea stretched out before him; and he stood still and maintained a long silence. But the night was cold at that altitude, and clear, and bright with stars.

"I recognize my lot," he finally said sadly. "All right! I'm ready. My final solitude has just begun.

"Ah, this black, sad sea below me! Ah, this pregnant nocturnal irritation! Ah, destiny and sea! I must now *descend* to you!

"I am facing my highest mountain and my longest journey; and so I must first descend a greater distance than I have ever ascended:

"Deeper down into sorrow than I have ever gone, all the way to its blackest waters! That's what my fate demands. Very well! I'm ready.

"'Where do the highest mountains come from?' I once asked. Then I learned that they come from the sea.

"The proof of this is engraved in their rock and the walls of their summits. The highest must attain its height from the deepest."

Also sprach Zarathustra auf der Spitze des Berges, wo es kalt war; als
er aber in die Nähe des Meeres kam und zuletzt allein unter den
Klippen stand, da war er unterwegs müde geworden und sehn-
süchtiger als noch zuvor.

Es schläft jetzt Alles noch, sprach er; auch das Meer schläft. Schlaf-
trunken und fremd blickt sein Auge nach mir.

Aber es atmet warm, das fühle ich. Und ich fühle auch, daß es
träumt. Es windet sich träumend auf harten Kissen.

Horch! Horch! Wie es stöhnt von bösen Erinnerungen! Oder bösen
Erwartungen?

Ach, ich bin traurig mit dir, du dunkles Ungeheuer, und mir selber
noch gram um deinetwillen.

Ach, daß meine Hand nicht Stärke genug hat! Gerne, wahrlich,
möchte ich dich von bösen Träumen erlösen! –

Und indem Zarathustra so sprach, lachte er mit Schwermut und
Bitterkeit über sich selber. Wie! Zarathustra! sagte er, willst du noch
dem Meere Trost singen?

Ach, du liebreicher Narr Zarathustra, du Vertrauens-Überseliger!
Aber so warst du immer: immer kamst du vertraulich zu allem
Furchtbaren.

Jedes Ungetüm wolltest du noch streicheln. Ein Hauch warmen
Atems, ein Wenig weiches Gezottel an der Tatze –: und gleich warst
du bereit, es zu lieben und zu locken.

Die *Liebe* ist die Gefahr des Einsamsten, die Liebe zu Allem, *wenn
es nur lebt*! Zum Lachen ist wahrlich meine Narrheit und meine
Bescheidenheit in der Liebe! –

Also sprach Zarathustra und lachte dabei zum andern Male: da aber
gedachte er seiner verlassenen Freunde –, und wie als ob er sich mit
seinen Gedanken an ihnen vergangen habe, zürnte er sich ob seiner
Gedanken. Und alsbald geschah es, daß der Lachende weinte: – vor
Zorn und Sehnsucht weinte Zarathustra bitterlich.

Vom Gesicht und Rätsel

1.

Als es unter den Schiffsleuten ruchbar wurde, daß Zarathustra auf dem
Schiffe sei – denn es war ein Mann zugleich mit ihm an Bord gegangen,

Thus spoke Zarathustra on the pinnacle of the mountain, where it was cold; but when he came near the sea and was finally standing alone under the cliffs, he had grown weary from his march and yearned even more than before.

"All things are still asleep now," he said; "the sea, too, is asleep. Its eyes are looking at me with the intoxication and alienation of sleep.

"But it is exhaling warmth, I feel it. And I also feel that it's dreaming. In a dream it's tossing and turning on hard pillows.

"Listen! Listen! How it moans with bad memories! Or bad expectations?

"Ah, I share your sadness, you dark monster, and I'm still cross with myself for your sake.

"Alas, that my hand isn't strong enough! Truly, I'd like to free you from bad dreams!"

And as Zarathustra said this, he laughed at himself in melancholy and bitterness. "What! Zarathustra!" he said. "Do you want to sing the sea a song of consolation?

"Ah, you amiable fool Zarathustra, excessively blissful in your confidingness! But you've always been that way: you have always approached all fearful things confidingly.

"You have always wanted to pat every monster. A puff of warm breath, a little tuft of soft fur on its paw—and you were ready at once to love it and beckon to it.

"*Love* is the peril of the loneliest man, love for everything *just as long as it's alive!* Truly, my folly is laughable, as are my modest expectations when it comes to love!"

Thus spoke Zarathustra, and, as he did, he laughed again; but then he remembered the friends he had forsaken—and, as if he had offended against them in his thoughts, he was angry at himself for his thoughts. And at once it came about that the laughing man wept—Zarathustra wept bitterly in anger and longing.

Of the Vision and the Riddle

1.

When the sailors found out that Zarathustra was on board—for a man from the Fortunate Islands had embarked at the same time—great

der von den glückseligen Inseln kam –, da entstand eine große
Neugierde und Erwartung. Aber Zarathustra schwieg zwei Tage und
war kalt und taub vor Traurigkeit, also, daß er weder auf Blicke noch auf
Fragen antwortete. Am Abend aber des zweiten Tages tat er seine
Ohren wieder auf, ob er gleich noch schwieg; denn es gab viel Seltsames
und Gefährliches auf diesem Schiffe anzuhören, welches weither kam
und noch weiterhin wollte. Zarathustra aber war ein Freund aller
Solchen, die weite Reisen tun und nicht ohne Gefahr leben mögen. Und
siehe! zuletzt wurde ihm im Zuhören die eigne Zunge gelöst, und das
Eis seines Herzens brach: – da begann er also zu reden:

Euch, den kühnen Suchern, Versuchern, und wer je sich mit listigen
Segeln auf furchtbare Meere einschiffte, –
    euch, den Rätsel-Trunkenen, den Zwielicht-Frohen, deren Seele
mit Flöten zu jedem Irr-Schlunde gelockt wird:
    – denn nicht wollt ihr mit feiger Hand einem Faden nachtasten;
und, wo ihr *erraten* könnt, da haßt ihr es, zu *erschließen* –
    euch allein erzähle ich das Rätsel, das ich *sah*, – das Gesicht des
Einsamsten. –
    Düster ging ich jüngst durch leichenfarbene Dämmerung, – düster
und hart, mit gepreßten Lippen. Nicht nur Eine Sonne war mir un-
tergegangen.
    Ein Pfad, der trotzig durch Geröll stieg, ein boshafter, einsamer,
dem nicht Kraut, nicht Strauch mehr zusprach: ein Berg-Pfad
knirschte unter dem Trotz meines Fußes.
    Stumm über höhnischem Geklirr von Kieseln schreitend, den Stein
zertretend, der ihn gleiten ließ: also zwang mein Fuß sich aufwärts.
    Aufwärts: – dem Geiste zum Trotz, der ihn abwärts zog, abgrund-
wärts zog, dem Geiste der Schwere, meinem Teufel und Erzfeinde.
    Aufwärts: – obwohl er auf mir saß, halb Zwerg, halb Maulwurf;
lahm; lähmend; Blei durch mein Ohr, Bleitropfen-Gedanken in mein
Hirn träufelnd.
    »Oh Zarathustra«, raunte er höhnisch Silb' um Silbe, »du Stein der
Weisheit! Du warfst dich hoch, aber jeder geworfene Stein muß –
fallen!
    Oh Zarathustra, du Stein der Weisheit, du Schleuderstein, du
Stern-Zertrümmerer! Dich selber warfst du so hoch, – aber jeder
geworfene Stein – muß fallen!

curiosity and expectation ensued. But Zarathustra kept silence for two days; he was cold and deaf from sadness, and so responded neither to glances nor to questions. But on the evening of the second day he opened his ears again, though still remaining silent; for there were many unusual and perilous tales to be heard on this ship, which had come from afar and was traveling even farther. But Zarathustra was a friend of all those who make long journeys and don't like to live without danger. And behold! Finally, as he listened, his own tongue was untied, and the ice around his heart broke up—he began to speak as follows:

"To you, the keen seekers and experimenters, and to whoever has embarked on fearful seas with cunning sails—
"To you, men drunk on riddles, rejoicing in twilight, whose souls are lured with flutes into every devious whirlpool—
"(For you refuse to grope along a thread with cowardly hands;[15] and when you can *guess*, you hate to *deduce*)—
"To you alone I tell the riddle that I *saw*—the vision of the loneliest one.
"Recently I was walking somberly through corpse-colored dusk—somber, hard, tight-lipped. Not merely one sun had set for me.
"A path that climbed defiantly through scree, a malicious, lonely path which had no more use for grasses or bushes: a mountain path crunched beneath my foot's defiance.
"Striding mutely over mocking clatter of gravel, crushing the stone that made them slip, my feet forced themselves upward.
"Upward—in spite of the spirit that drew them downward, drew them toward the abyss: the spirit of gravity, my devil and archenemy.
"Upward—even though he was sitting on me, half dwarf, half mole, lame, laming me, dripping lead into my ears, thoughts like drops of lead into my brain.
"'O Zarathustra,' he murmured mockingly, separating the syllables, 'you stone of wisdom! You threw yourself up high, but every thrown stone—must fall!
"'O Zarathustra, you stone of wisdom, you slingstone, you star-smasher! You yourself you threw so high up, but every thrown stone—must fall!

---

15. Presumably, like Theseus escaping from the Labyrinth.

Verurteilt zu dir selber und zur eignen Steinigung: oh Zarathustra, weit warfst du ja den Stein, – aber auf *dich* wird er zurückfallen!«

Darauf schwieg der Zwerg; und das währte lange. Sein Schweigen aber drückte mich; und solchermaßen zu Zwein ist man wahrlich einsamer als zu Einem!

Ich stieg, ich stieg, ich träumte, ich dachte, – aber alles drückte mich. Einem Kranken glich ich, den seine schlimme Marter müde macht und den wieder ein schlimmerer Traum aus dem Einschlafen weckt. –

Aber es gibt Etwas in mir, das ich Mut heiße: das schlug bisher mir jeden Unmut tot. Dieser Mut hieß mich endlich stille stehn und sprechen: »Zwerg! Du! Oder ich!« –

Mut nämlich ist der beste Totschläger – Mut, welcher *angreift:* denn in jedem Angriffe ist klingendes Spiel.

Der Mensch aber ist das mutigste Tier: damit überwand er jedes Tier. Mit klingendem Spiele überwand er noch jeden Schmerz; Menschen-Schmerz aber ist der tiefste Schmerz.

Der Mut schlägt auch den Schwindel tot an Abgründen: und wo stünde der Mensch nicht an Abgründen! Ist Sehen nicht selber – Abgründe sehen?

Mut ist der beste Totschläger: der Mut schlägt auch das Mitleiden tot. Mitleiden aber ist der tiefste Abgrund: so tief der Mensch in das Leben sieht, so tief sieht er auch in das Leiden.

Mut aber ist der beste Totschläger, Mut, der angreift: der schlägt noch den Tod tot, denn er spricht: »*War das* das Leben? Wohlan! Noch Ein Mal!«

In solchem Spruche aber ist viel klingendes Spiel. Wer Ohren hat, der höre. –

2.

»Halt! Zwerg!« sprach ich. »Ich! Oder du! Ich aber bin der Stärkere von uns Beiden –: du kennst meinen abgründlichen Gedanken nicht! *Den* – könntest du nicht tragen!« –

Da geschah, was mich leichter machte: denn der Zwerg sprang mir von der Schulter, der Neugierige! Und er hockte sich auf einen Stein vor mich hin. Es war aber gerade da ein Torweg, wo wir hielten.

»Siehe diesen Torweg! Zwerg!« sprach ich weiter: »der hat zwei Gesichter. Zwei Wege kommen hier zusammen: die ging noch Niemand zu Ende.

Diese lange Gasse zurück: die währt eine Ewigkeit. Und jene lange Gasse hinaus – das ist eine andre Ewigkeit.

"'Condemned to yourself and your own stoning: O Zarathustra, you did throw the stone far—but it will fall back on *you!*'

"Thereupon the dwarf fell silent; and that lasted for some time. But his silence was oppressive to me, and in such company a man is truly lonesomer than when alone!

"I climbed and climbed, I dreamed and pondered—but everything weighed me down. I was like a sick man made weary by his hard torments and awakened from his doze again by a worse dream.

"But there is something in me that I call courage; so far it has killed all ill humor in me. This courage finally bade me to halt and say: 'Dwarf! One of us must go!'

"You see, courage is the best killer—courage that *attacks:* for in every attack music comes into play.

"But man is the most courageous animal: that's how he surpassed all the others. With musical deftness he has even overcome all pain; and human pain is the deepest pain.

"Courage even kills vertigo over abysses, and where does man not stand on the edge of an abyss? Isn't sight itself—the sight of abysses?

"Courage is the best killer: courage kills even compassion. And compassion is the deepest abyss: the deeper man looks into life, the deeper he looks into suffering, as well.

"But courage is the best killer, the courage that attacks: it kills even death, because it says: '*Was that* life? All right! Let's do it again!'

"And in that saying there is much musical play. Whoever has ears, let him listen."

2.

"'Halt, dwarf!' I said. 'One of us must go. And I'm the stronger of us two: you don't know my unfathomable idea. You couldn't support it!'

"Then something occurred to relieve the weight on me: for the inquisitive dwarf jumped off my shoulders! And he squatted on a stone in front of me. Where we halted, there happened to be a gateway.

"'Look at this gateway, dwarf!' I continued. 'It has two faces. Two roads come together here: no one has ever walked to the ends of them.

"'This long lane backward lasts an eternity. And that long lane forward is another eternity.

Sie widersprechen sich, diese Wege; sie stoßen sich gerade vor den Kopf: – und hier, an diesem Torwege, ist es, wo sie zusammenkommen. Der Name des Torwegs steht oben geschrieben: ›Augenblick‹.

Aber wer Einen von ihnen weiter ginge – und immer weiter und immer ferner: glaubst du, Zwerg, daß diese Wege sich ewig widersprechen?« –

»Alles Gerade lügt«, murmelte verächtlich der Zwerg. »Alle Wahrheit ist krumm, die Zeit selber ist ein Kreis.«

»Du Geist der Schwere!« sprach ich zürnend, »mache dir es nicht zu leicht! Oder ich lasse dich hocken, wo du hockst, Lahmfuß, – und ich trug dich *hoch!*

Siehe«, sprach ich weiter, »diesen Augenblick! Von diesem Torwege Augenblick läuft eine lange ewige Gasse *rückwärts:* hinter uns liegt eine Ewigkeit.

Muß nicht, was laufen *kann* von allen Dingen, schon einmal diese Gasse gelaufen sein? Muß nicht, was geschehn *kann* von allen Dingen, schon einmal geschehn, getan, vorübergelaufen sein?

Und wenn Alles schon dagewesen ist: was hältst du Zwerg von diesem Augenblick? Muß auch dieser Torweg nicht schon – dagewesen sein?

Und sind nicht solchermaßen fest alle Dinge verknotet, daß dieser Augenblick *alle* kommenden Dinge nach sich zieht? *Also* – – sich selber noch?

Denn, was laufen *kann* von allen Dingen: auch in dieser langen Gasse *hinaus* – *muß* es einmal noch laufen! –

Und diese langsame Spinne, die im Mondscheine kriecht, und dieser Mondschein selber, und ich und du im Torwege, zusammen flüsternd, von ewigen Dingen flüsternd – müssen wir nicht alle schon dagewesen sein?

– und wiederkommen und in jener anderen Gasse laufen, hinaus, vor uns, in dieser langen schaurigen Gasse – müssen wir nicht ewig wiederkommen? –«

Also redete ich, und immer leiser: denn ich fürchtete mich vor meinen eignen Gedanken und Hintergedanken. Da, plötzlich, hörte ich einen Hund nahe *heulen.*

Hörte ich jemals einen Hund so heulen? Mein Gedanke lief zurück. Ja! Als ich Kind war, in fernster Kindheit:

– da hörte ich einen Hund so heulen. Und sah ihn auch, gesträubt, den Kopf nach Oben, zitternd, in stillster Mitternacht, wo auch Hunde an Gespenster glauben:

– also daß es mich erbarmte. Eben nämlich ging der volle Mond, totschweigsam, über das Haus, eben stand er still, eine runde Glut, – still auf flachem Dache, gleich als auf fremdem Eigentume: –

"'These roads contradict each other; they actually butt their heads together. And it's here, at this gateway, that they come together. The name of the gateway is written at the top: "The Present Moment."

"'But if one were to pursue either of the roads, farther and farther into the distance, do you think, dwarf, that they will eternally contradict each other?'

"'All straight lines are false,' the dwarf mumbled contemptuously. "All truth is curved, time itself is a circle.'

"'You spirit of gravity,' I said angrily, 'don't make things too easy for yourself! Or else I'll leave you squatting where you are, slowpoke— and I carried you *high!*

"'See this moment!' I continued. From this gateway Present Moment a long eternal lane runs *backwards:* an eternity lies behind us.

"'If there is anything that *can* run, must it not have already run down this lane? If there is anything that *can* occur, must it not already have occurred, been done, have run past?

"'And if everything has already been present, what do you think about this moment, dwarf? Must not this gateway, too, already have been present?

"'And aren't all things so firmly interconnected that this moment draws *all* coming things after it? *Thus,* itself, as well?

"'For anything that *can* run *must* also some day run down this long *forward*-pointing lane!

"'And this slow spider crawling in the moonlight, and this moonlight itself, and you and I in the gateway, whispering together, whispering about things eternal, must not all of us have already been present?—

"'And return and run down that other lane, forward, in front of us, down that long, scary lane—must we not return eternally?'

"Thus I spoke, more quietly all the time: for I was afraid of my own thoughts and ulterior motives. Then I suddenly heard a dog *howling* nearby.

"Did I ever hear a dog howl that way? My thought ran back. Yes! When I was a child, in earliest childhood:

"I heard a dog howl that way then. And I saw him, too, his fur bristling, his head looking up, as he trembled, in the dead silence of midnight, when dogs, too, believe in ghosts:

"So that I took pity. For just then the full moon, as silent as the dead, was over the house; it had just stood still, a round blaze—stood still on the flat roof, as if on someone else's property:

darob entsetzte sich damals der Hund: denn Hunde glauben an Diebe und Gespenster. Und als ich wieder so heulen hörte, da erbarmte es mich abermals.

Wohin war jetzt Zwerg? Und Torweg? Und Spinne? Und alles Flüstern? Träumte ich denn? Wachte ich auf? Zwischen wilden Klippen stand ich mit Einem Male, allein, öde, im ödesten Mondscheine.

Aber da lag ein Mensch! Und da! Der Hund, springend, gesträubt, winselnd, – jetzt sah er mich kommen – da heulte er wieder, da *schrie* er: – hörte ich je einen Hund so Hilfe schrein?

Und, wahrlich, was ich sah, desgleichen sah ich nie. Einen jungen Hirten sah ich, sich windend, würgend, zuckend, verzerrten Antlitzes, dem eine schwarze schwere Schlange aus dem Mund hing.

Sah ich je so viel Ekel und bleiches Grauen auf Einem Antlitze? Er hatte wohl geschlafen? Da kroch ihm die Schlange in den Schlund – da biß sie sich fest.

Meine Hand riß die Schlange und riß: – umsonst! sie riß die Schlange nicht aus dem Schlunde. Da schrie es aus mir: »Beiß zu! Beiß zu!

Den Kopf ab! Beiß zu!« – so schrie es aus mir, mein Grauen, mein Haß, mein Ekel, mein Erbarmen, all mein Gutes und Schlimmes schrie mit einem Schrei aus mir. –

Ihr Kühnen um mich! Ihr Sucher, Versucher, und wer von euch mit listigen Segeln sich in unerforschte Meere einschiffte! Ihr Rätsel-Frohen!

So ratet mir doch das Rätsel, das ich damals schaute, so deutet mir doch das Gesicht des Einsamsten!

Denn ein Gesicht war's und ein Vorhersehn: – *was* sah ich damals im Gleichnisse? Und *wer* ist, der einst noch kommen muß?

Wer ist der Hirt, dem also die Schlange in den Schlund kroch? *Wer* ist der Mensch, dem also alles Schwerste, Schwärzeste in den Schlund kriechen wird?

– Der Hirt aber biß, wie mein Schrei ihm riet; er biß mit gutem Bisse! Weit weg spie er den Kopf der Schlange –: und sprang empor. –

Nicht mehr Hirt, nicht mehr Mensch – ein Verwandelter, ein Umleuchteter, welcher *lachte*! Niemals noch auf Erden lachte je ein Mensch, wie *er* lachte!

Oh meine Brüder, ich hörte ein Lachen, das keines Menschen Lachen war, – – und nun frißt ein Durst an mir, eine Sehnsucht, die nimmer stille wird.

"That's what had terrified the dog at that time: because dogs believe in burglars and ghosts. And when I once more heard howling like that, I took pity again.

"What had now become of the dwarf? And the gateway? And the spider? And all the whispering? Had I been dreaming? Was I now awake? All at once I was standing between wild cliffs, alone, desolate, in the most desolate moonlight.

"*But a person was lying there!* And there! The dog, leaping, his fur on end, whining—now he saw me coming—he howled again, he *shouted*—had I ever heard a dog shouting for help that way?

"And, truly, I had never seen anything like what I then saw. I saw a young shepherd writhing, choking, twitching, his features distorted, with a heavy black snake hanging out of his mouth.

"Had I ever seen so much disgust and pale horror on one face? Had he been sleeping? Then the snake had crept into his gullet and taken firm hold with its fangs.

"My hands tugged and tugged at the snake—to no avail! They couldn't pull the snake out of his gullet. Then the words came tumbling out of me in a cry. 'Bite down! Bite down!

"'Off with its head! Bite down!' That cry issued from me; my horror, my hatred, my disgust, my pity, everything good and bad in me, cried out from me in that cry.

"You bold men around me! You seekers, experimenters, and all of you who have embarked on unexplored seas with cunning sails! You lovers of riddles!

"Solve me the riddle that I then beheld, interpret to me the vision of the loneliest one!

"For a vision it was, and a prophecy. *What* did I then see as a parable? And *who* is it that will surely still come some day?

"*Who* is the shepherd into whose gullet the snake crept in that fashion? *Who* is the person into whose gullet all that is heaviest and blackest will thus creep?

"But the shepherd bit down, as my cry had advised; he bit with a strong bite! He spat out the snake's head to a great distance—and he leaped up.

"No longer a shepherd, no longer a human being—one transformed, a radiant one who *was laughing!* Never yet on earth has anyone laughed as *he* laughed!

"Oh, my brothers, I heard a laughter that was not the laughter of any human being—and now a thirst gnaws at me, a longing that is never quenched.

Meine Sehnsucht nach diesem Lachen frißt an mir: oh wie ertrage ich noch zu leben! Und wie ertrüge ich's, jetzt zu sterben! –

Also sprach Zarathustra.

VON DER SELIGKEIT WIDER WILLEN (Of Reluctant Blissfulness): Conquering his grief, Zarathustra addresses his conscience; in the afternoon of his life, he must live and perfect himself for his doctrine and his disciples, each of whom he must test individually. To perform his task he must remain detached. Some day he will summon "the children of his hope" with "a lion's voice." A moment of bliss has come to him against his will; he expects some misfortune. / VOR SONNEN-AUFGANG (Before Sunrise): A clear, cloudless sky corresponds best to Zarathustra's ideal wisdom, but he prefers an outright storm to "partially overcast." He has become a bestower of blessings and an affirmer of life, after years of mental wrestling. All things are "beyond good and evil"; good and evil are intermediate tones and passing clouds. The world is no longer a slave to teleology and the need to "make sense." /

Vom Vorübergehen

Also, durch viel Volk und vielerlei Städte langsam hindurchschreitend, zing Zarathustra auf Umwegen zurück zu seinem Gebirge und seiner Höhle. Und siehe, dabei kam er unversehens auch an das Stadttor der *großen Stadt:* hier aber sprang ein schäumender Narr mit ausgebreiteten Händen auf ihn zu und trat ihm in den Weg. Dies aber war derselbige Narr, welchen das Volk »den Affen Zarathustra« hieß: denn er hatte ihm Etwas vom Satz und Fall der Rede abgemerkt und borgte wohl auch gerne vom Schatze seiner Weisheit. Der Narr aber redete also zu Zarathustra:

»Oh Zarathustra, hier ist die große Stadt: hier hast du Nichts zu suchen und Alles zu verlieren.

Warum wolltest du durch diesen Schlamm waten? Habe doch Mitleiden mit deinem Fuße! Speie lieber auf das Stadttor und – kehre um!

Hier ist die Hölle für Einsiedler-Gedanken: hier werden große Gedanken lebendig gesotten und klein gekocht.

Hier verwesen alle großen Gefühle: hier dürfen nur klapperdürre Gefühlchen klappern!

Riechst du nicht schon die Schlachthäuser und Garküchen des Geistes? Dampft nicht diese Stadt vom Dunst geschlachteten Geistes?

Siehst du nicht die Seelen hängen wie schlaffe schmutzige Lumpen? – Und sie machen noch Zeitungen aus diesen Lumpen!

"My longing for that laughter gnaws at me: oh, how can I bear to go on living? And how could I bear to die now?!"

Thus spoke Zarathustra.

VON DER VERKLEINERNDEN TUGEND (Of the Virtue That Diminishes Things): Back on dry land, Zarathustra wanders about to see whether people have become "bigger" or "smaller"; he finds that the newest houses are too small for him. The small people are hostile to him or indifferent. They are getting smaller all the time because of their doctrine of happiness and virtue; they seek only comfort, and only a few have a will of their own, whereas even the leaders claim to be servants of the public. But "the great noonday" is nigh! / AUF DEM ÖLBERGE (On the Mount of Olives): Winter is a grim but not totally unwelcome guest in the home of Zarathustra, who seeks out a sunny, windless corner of his Mount of Olives. Both he and the winter sky are taciturn; they both present an icy exterior to the mediocre world that can't detect their hidden glow.

Of Passing By

Thus, striding slowly through many human groups and cities of many kinds, Zarathustra was returning by circuitous routes to his mountains and his cave. And behold, as he did so, he unexpectedly also arrived at the gate to the *big city*. But here a fool, foaming at the mouth, hands outspread, leaped toward him and blocked his way. And this was the same fool whom the populace called "Zarathustra's ape" because he had learned to imitate something of the pattern and flow of his speech, and was surely also fond of borrowing from his treasures of wisdom. And the fool addressed Zarathustra as follows:

"O Zarathustra, this is the big city: here you have nothing to seek and everything to lose.

"Why did you want to wade through this mire? At least have pity on your feet! Instead, spit on the city gate and—turn back!

"This is a hell for hermit-thoughts: here great ideas are boiled alive and reduced to a pulp.

"Here all great emotions rot away; here only emaciated little emotions are allowed to rattle!

"Can't you already smell the slaughterhouses and cookshops of the intellect? Doesn't this city steam with the vapor of slaughtered intellect?

"Don't you see the souls hanging like dirty, limp rags?—And they make newspapers out of these rags, too!

Hörst du nicht, wie der Geist hier zum Wortspiel wurde? Widriges Wort-Spülicht bricht er heraus! – Und sie machen noch Zeitungen aus diesem Wort-Spülicht.

Sie hetzen einander und wissen nicht, wohin? Sie erhitzen einander und wissen nicht, warum? Sie klimpern mit ihrem Bleche, sie klingeln mit ihrem Golde.

Sie sind kalt und suchen sich Wärme bei gebrannten Wassern; sie sind erhitzt und suchen Kühle bei gefrorenen Geistern; sie sind Alle siech und süchtig an öffentlichen Meinungen.

Alle Lüste und Laster sind hier zu Hause; aber es gibt hier auch Tugendhafte, es gibt viel anstellige angestellte Tugend: –

Viel anstellige Tugend mit Schreibfingern und hartem Sitz- und Warte-Fleische, gesegnet mit kleinen Bruststernen und ausgestopften steißlosen Töchtern.

Es gibt hier auch viel Frömmigkeit und viel gläubige Speichel-Leckerei, Schmeichel-Bäckerei vor dem Gott der Heerscharen.

›Von Oben‹ her träufelt ja der Stern und der gnädige Speichel; nach Oben hin sehnt sich jeder sternenlose Busen.

Der Mond hat seinen Hof, und der Hof hat seine Mondkälber: zu allem aber, was vom Hofe kommt, betet das Bettel-Volk und alle anstellige Bettel-Tugend.

›Ich diene, du dienst, wir dienen‹ – so betet alle anstellige Tugend hinauf zum Fürsten: daß der verdiente Stern sich endlich an den schmalen Busen hefte!

Aber der Mond dreht sich noch um alles Irdische: so dreht sich auch der Fürst noch um das Aller-Irdischste –: das aber ist das Gold der Krämer.

Der Gott der Heerscharen ist kein Gott der Goldbarren; der Fürst denkt, aber der Krämer – lenkt!

Bei Allem, was licht und stark und gut in dir ist, oh Zarathustra! Speie auf diese Stadt der Krämer und kehre um!

Hier fließt alles Blut faulicht und lauicht und schaumicht durch alle Adern: speie auf die große Stadt, welche der große Abraum ist, wo aller Abschaum zusammenschäumt!

Speie auf die Stadt der eingedrückten Seelen und schmalen Brüste, der spitzen Augen, der klebrigen Finger –

– auf die Stadt der Aufdringlinge, der Unverschämten, der Schreib- und Schreihälse, der überheizten Ehrgeizigen: –

– wo alles Anbrüchige, Anrüchige, Lüsterne, Düstere, Übermürbe, Geschwürige, Verschwörerische zusammenschwärt: –

–speie auf die große Stadt und kehre um!« – –

"Can't you hear how the intellect has become a word game here? It vomits loathsome verbal slops!—and they make newspapers out of these verbal slops, too!

"They hound one another without knowing where to. They excite one another without knowing why. They rattle their tin sheets, they jingle their gold.

"They're cold and seek warmth from brandy; they're overheated and seek coolness from frozen spirits; they're all sick, all addicted to public opinion.

"All pleasures and vices are at home here; but there are also virtuous people here, there's a lot of employable and employed virtue—

"A lot of employable virtue with fingers that write and hard behinds accustomed to sitting and waiting, blessed with little medals on their chest and stuffed, assless daughters.

"There's also a lot of piety here and a lot of religious spittle-licking and flattery-baking before the Lord of Hosts.

"The medals and the noble spittle trickle down 'from higher up'; every chest without a medal longs to move 'up.'

"The moon has its noble court, and the court has its moon-calves; and to everything that proceeds from the court the beggar folk and all the compliant beggar-virtue prays.

"'I serve, you serve, we serve': that's the prayer of all the compliant virtue as it gazes up to the prince: so that the well-earned medal will finally be pinned to the narrow chest!

"But the moon still revolves around everything terrestrial; in the same way, the prince, too, revolves around the most earthly thing of all: the shopkeepers' gold.

"The Lord of Hosts is no god of gold ingots; the prince proposes, but the shopkeeper disposes!

"By all that's bright and strong and good in you, O Zarathustra, spit on this city of shopkeepers and turn back!

"Here all blood flows through all veins lazily, lukewarm, and frothing. Spit on the big city, which is the big sink where all the scum comes together in a froth!

"Spit on the city of crushed souls and narrow chests, pointy eyes, sticky fingers—

"On the city of pushy, shameless people, loudmouths and loud writers, overheated ambitions—

"Where everything that's decayed, disreputable, lustful, somber, overripe, purulent, and conspiratorial festers en masse—

"Spit on the big city and turn back!"

Hier aber unterbrach Zarathustra den schäumenden Narren und hielt ihm den Mund zu.

»Höre endlich auf!« rief Zarathustra, »mich ekelt lange schon deiner Rede und deiner Art!

Warum wohntest du so lange am Sumpfe, daß du selber zum Frosch und zur Kröte werden mußtest?

Fließt dir nicht selber nun ein faulichtes schaumichtes Sumpf-Blut durch die Adern, daß du also quaken und lästern lerntest?

Warum gingst du nicht in den Wald? Oder pflügtest die Erde? Ist das Meer nicht voll von grünen Eilanden?

Ich verachte dein Verachten; und wenn du mich warntest, – warum warntest du dich nicht selber?

Aus der Liebe allein soll mir mein Verachten und mein warnender Vogel auffliegen: aber nicht aus dem Sumpfe! –

Man heißt dich meinen Affen, du schäumender Narr: aber ich heiße dich mein Grunze-Schwein, – durch Grunzen verdirbst du mir noch mein Lob der Narrheit.

Was war es denn, was dich zuerst grunzen machte? Daß Niemand dir genug *geschmeichelt* hat: – darum setztest du dich hin zu diesem Unrate, daß du Grund hättest viel zu grunzen, –

– daß du Grund hättest zu vieler *Rache*! Rache nämlich, du eitler Narr, ist all dein Schäumen, ich erriet dich wohl!

Aber dein Narren-Wort tut *mir* Schaden, selbst wo du recht hast! Und wenn Zarathustras Wort sogar hundertmal recht *hätte*: du würdest mit meinem Wort immer – unrecht *tun*!«

Also sprach Zarathustra; und er blickte die große Stadt an, seufzte und schwieg lange. Endlich redete er also:

Mich ekelt auch dieser großen Stadt und nicht nur dieses Narren. Hier und dort ist Nichts zu bessern, Nichts zu bösern.

Wehe dieser großen Stadt! – Und ich wollte, ich sähe schon die Feuersäule, in der sie verbrannt wird!

Denn solche Feuersäulen müssen dem großen Mittage vorangehn. Doch dies hat seine Zeit und sein eigenes Schicksal. –

Diese Lehre aber gebe ich dir, du Narr, zum Abschiede: wo man nicht mehr lieben kann, da soll man – *vorübergehn!* –

Also sprach Zarathustra und ging an dem Narren und der großen Stadt vorüber.

But here Zarathustra interrupted the foaming fool and held his mouth shut.

"Stop now!" Zarathustra called. "I've long been disgusted with your speech and your nature!

"Why have you dwelt by the swamp so long that you yourself had to become a frog and a toad?

"Doesn't a sluggish, frothy swamp blood now flow through your own veins, teaching you to croak and blaspheme this way?

"Why haven't you gone to the forest? Or plowed the earth? Isn't the sea full of green islands?

"I contemn your contempt; and if you warned me, why didn't you warn yourself?

"My contempt and my warning bird shall fly up out of love alone, but not from the swamp!

"You're called my ape, you foaming fool, but I call you my oink-pig; your oinking will yet spoil my praise of folly.

"What, then, was it that first made you oink? Because nobody *flattered* you enough—that's why you sat down amid this refuse, so you'd have a reason to oink a lot—

"So you'd have a reason for a lot of *revenge!* You see, you vain fool, all your foaming is revenge, I've found you out!

"But your foolish words do *me* harm even when you're right! And even if Zarathustra's words *were* correct a hundred times, you, speaking my words, would always *do* wrong!"

Thus spoke Zarathustra; and he looked at the big city, sighed, and remained silent for some time. Finally he spoke as follows:

"I am disgusted with this big town, too, and not just with this fool. In both cases, there's no room for improvement or for worsening.

"Woe to this big city!—I wish I could already see the pillar of fire in which it's burnt up!

"For such pillars of fire must precede the great noonday. But there's time for that, and a special destiny.

"But I give you this instruction as I depart, fool: where it's no longer possible to love, one should *pass by!*"

Thus spoke Zarathustra, and he bypassed the fool and the big city.

VON DEN ABTRÜNNIGEN (Of Apostates): Even those who were adventurous when young have grown weary, commonplace, "pious." One mustn't become attached to disciples, who may not remain so for long. For a true sage it's disgraceful and cowardly to pray. The old gods didn't die in a "twilight" [Wagner!]; they laughed themselves to death when they heard one of them say he was the only God. / DIE HEIMKEHR (The Homecoming): Back in his mountain cave, Zarathustra realizes he

Vom Geist der Schwere

1.

Mein Mundwerk – ist des Volks: zu grob und herzlich rede ich für die Seidenhasen. Und noch fremder klingt mein Wort allen Tinten-Fischen und Feder-Füchsen.

Meine Hand – ist eine Narrenhand: wehe allen Tischen und Wänden, und was noch Platz hat für Narren-Zierat, Narren-Schmierat!

Mein Fuß – ist ein Pferdefuß; damit trapple und trabe ich über Stock und Stein, kreuz- und quer-feld-ein, und bin des Teufels vor Lust bei allem schnellen Laufen.

Mein Magen – ist wohl eines Adlers-Magen? Denn er liebt am liebsten Lammfleisch. Gewißlich aber ist er eines Vogels Magen.

Von unschuldigen Dingen genährt und von Wenigem, bereit und ungeduldig zu fliegen, davonzufliegen – das ist nun meine Art: wie sollte nicht Etwas daran von Vogel-Art sein!

Und zumal, daß ich dem Geist der Schwere feind bin, das ist Vogel-Art: und wahrlich, todfeind, erzfeind, urfeind! Oh wohin flog und verflog sich nicht schon meine Feindschaft!

Davon könnte ich schon ein Lied singen – – und will es singen: ob ich gleich allein in leerem Hause bin und es meinen eignen Ohren singen muß.

Andre Sänger gibt es freilich, denen macht das volle Haus erst ihre Kehle weich, ihre Hand gesprächig, ihr Auge ausdrücklich, ihr Herz wach: – Denen gleiche ich nicht. –

2.

Wer die Menschen einst fliegen lehrt, der hat alle Grenzsteine verrückt; alle Grenzsteine selber werden ihm in die Luft fliegen, die Erde wird er neu taufen – als »die Leichte«.

was even lonelier when among other people. His preaching couldn't be heard above their babble, and their uncleanliness disgusted him. / VON DEN DREI BÖSEN (Of the Three "Evils"): After dreaming that he was weighing the world, Zarathustra "weighs" the three "evils" that are most denigrated: lust, greed for power, and selfishness. To truly free spirits, lust is an innocent drive. Greed for power is a sign of health. Selfishness arrises from a strong soul, which despises cowardice and humility.

Of the Spirit of Gravity

1.

My way of talking is that of the common people. I speak too coarsely and warmly for the ultra-refined. And my words are even more foreign to the ink-splashers and pen-pushers.

My hands are fool's hands: woe to all tables and walls and anything else that has room for foolish ornaments and bric-a-brac!

My feet are horse's feet: with them I clop and trot over all kinds of terrain, zigzagging across country; and I'm crazy with joy whenever I can run fast.

My stomach is probably an eagle's stomach, because it loves lamb best of all. At any rate, it's surely a bird's stomach.

Feeding on innocent things, and in small amounts, ready and impatient to fly, to fly away—that's my nature. How could there fail to be something birdlike in it?

And especially my hostility to the spirit of gravity, that's birdlike: and, truly, I'm its mortal enemy, archenemy, primordial enemy! Oh, where hasn't my enmity already flown and flown astray?

I could sing a song about that by now—and I will sing it, even though I'm alone in an empty house and I must sing it for my own ears.

Of course, there are other singers who need a packed house before their throat becomes supple, their gestures become communicative, their eyes become expressive, and their heart becomes alert. I'm not like them.

2.

The man who will some day teach people to fly has moved every boundary stone; for him all boundary stones will fly into the air of their own accord; he will give the earth a new name: "the weightless."

Der Vogel Strauß läuft schneller als das schnellste Pferd, aber auch er steckt noch den Kopf schwer in schwere Erde: also der Mensch, der noch nicht fliegen kann.

Schwer heißt ihm Erde und Leben; und so *will* es der Geist der Schwere! Wer aber leicht werden will und ein Vogel, der muß sich selber lieben: – also lehre *ich*.

Nicht freilich mit der Liebe der Siechen und Süchtigen: denn bei denen stinkt auch die Eigenliebe!

Man muß sich selber lieben lernen – also lehre ich – mit einer heilen und gesunden Liebe: daß man es bei sich selber aushalte und nicht umherschweife.

Solches Umherschweifen tauft sich »Nächstenliebe«: mit diesem Worte ist bisher am besten gelogen und geheuchelt worden, und sonderlich von Solchen, die aller Welt schwerfielen.

Und wahrlich, das ist kein Gebot für heute und morgen, sich lieben *lernen*. Vielmehr ist von allen Künsten diese die feinste, listigste, letzte und geduldsamste.

Für seinen Eigener ist nämlich alles Eigene gut versteckt; und von allen Schatzgruben wird die eigne am spätesten ausgegraben, – also schafft es der Geist der Schwere.

Fast in der Wiege gibt man uns schon schwere Worte und Werte mit: »Gut« und »Böse« – so heißt sich diese Mitgift. Um derentwillen vergibt man uns, daß wir leben.

Und dazu läßt man die Kindlein zu sich kommen, daß man ihnen beizeiten wehre, sich selber zu lieben: also schafft es der Geist der Schwere.

Und wir – wir schleppen treulich, was man uns mitgibt, auf harten Schultern und über rauhe Berge! Und schwitzen wir, so sagt man uns: »Ja, das Leben ist schwer zu tragen!«

Aber der Mensch nur ist sich schwer zu tragen! Das macht, er schleppt zu vieles Fremde auf seinen Schultern. Dem Kamele gleich kniet er nieder und läßt sich gut aufladen.

Sonderlich der starke, tragsame Mensch, dem Ehrfurcht innewohnt: zu viele *fremde* schwere Worte und Werte lädt er sich auf, – nun dünkt das Leben ihm eine Wüste!

Und wahrlich! Auch manches *Eigene* ist schwer zu tragen! Und viel Inwendiges am Menschen ist der Auster gleich, nämlich ekel und schlüpfrig und schwer erfaßlich –,

– also daß eine edle Schale mit edler Zierat fürbitten muß. Aber auch diese Kunst muß man lernen: Schale *haben* und schönen Schein und kluge Blindheit!

The ostrich runs faster than the swiftest horse, but it still buries its head heavily in the heavy earth; so does the person who cannot yet fly.

Earth and life are heavy for him; and that's what the spirit of gravity *wants!* But the man who wants to become weightless, like a bird, must love himself: that is *my* doctrine.

Of course, not with the love of the sick and the addicted, because in them even self-love stinks!

One must learn to love oneself—I teach—with a whole, healthy love, so that one can bear one's own company and not go straying.

Such straying is dubbed "Christian charity"; until now, this term has been responsible for the most lies and hypocrisy, especially among those who were hard for the whole world to bear.

And, truly, to *learn* to love oneself is no commandment to be obeyed overnight. Rather, of all arts it's the subtlest, shrewdest, hardest, and most demanding of patience.

You see, all that is one's own is well hidden from its owner; and of all treasure troves one's own is the last to be excavated. This is brought about by the spirit of gravity.

While we're still almost in the cradle we're dowered with heavy words and values: "good" and "evil" this endowment is called. For their sake we're forgiven for living.

And in addition, the children are "suffered to come to them," so they can be forbidden early on to love themselves. This is brought about by the spirit of gravity.

And we—we faithfully drag along our endowment on weary shoulders across rugged mountains! And if we sweat, we're told: "Yes, life is hard to bear!"

But only man is hard for himself to bear. This is because he's dragging around on his back too much that isn't his. Like a camel he kneels and allows himself to be loaded down.

Especially the strong, burden-bearing man who is full of respect: he loads himself down with too many heavy words and values *that aren't his*—and now life is like a desert to him!

And, truly! Even much *that is one's own* is hard to bear! And much that is inside man is like an oyster; that is, disgusting, slippery, and hard to take hold of—

So that an elegant shell with elegant ornament must intercede. But even that art must be learned: *to have* a shell and a fine appearance and wise blindness!

Abermals trügt über Manches am Menschen, daß manche Schale gering und traurig und zu sehr Schale ist. Viel verborgene Güte und Kraft wird nie erraten; die köstlichen Leckerbissen finden keine Schmecker!

Die Frauen wissen das, die köstlichsten: ein Wenig fetter, ein Wenig magerer – oh wie viel Schicksal liegt in so Wenigem!

Der Mensch ist schwer zu entdecken, und sich selber noch am schwersten; oft lügt der Geist über die Seele. Also schafft es der Geist der Schwere.

Der aber hat sich selber entdeckt, welcher spricht: Das ist *mein* Gutes und Böses: damit hat er den Maulwurf und Zwerg stumm gemacht, welcher spricht: »Allen gut, Allen bös.«

Wahrlich, ich mag auch Solche nicht, denen jegliches Ding gut und diese Welt gar die beste heißt. Solche nenne ich die Allgenügsamen.

Allgenügsamkeit, die alles zu schmecken weiß: das ist nicht der beste Geschmack! Ich ehre die widerspänstigen wählerischen Zungen und Mägen, welche »Ich« und »Ja« und »Nein« sagen lernten.

Alles aber kauen und verdauen – das ist eine rechte Schweine-Art! Immer I-A sagen – das lernte allein der Esel, und wer seines Geistes ist! –

Das tiefe Gelb und das heiße Rot: so will es *mein* Geschmack, – der mischt Blut zu allen Farben.

Wer aber sein Haus weiß tüncht, der verrät mir eine weißgetünchte Seele.

In Mumien verliebt die Einen, die Andern in Gespenster; und Beide gleich feind allem Fleisch und Blute – oh wie gehen beide mir wider den Geschmack! Denn ich liebe Blut.

Und dort will ich nicht wohnen und weilen, wo Jedermann spuckt und speit: das ist nun *mein* Geschmack, – lieber noch lebte ich unter Dieben und Meineidigen. Niemand trägt Gold im Munde.

Widriger aber sind mir noch alle Speichellecker; und das widrigste Tier von Mensch, das ich fand, das taufte ich Schmarotzer: das wollte nicht lieben und doch von Liebe leben.

Unselig heiße ich Alle, die nur Eine Wahl haben: böse Tiere zu werden oder böse Tierbändiger: bei Solchen würde ich mir keine Hütten bauen.

Unselig heiße ich auch Die, welche immer *warten* müssen, – die gehen mir wider den Geschmack: alle die Zöllner und Krämer und Könige und andren Länder- und Ladenhüter.

Wahrlich, ich lernte das Warten auch und von Grund aus, – aber

Another very deceptive thing in man is that many a shell is slight or sad or too much of a shell. Much hidden kindness and strength are never guessed at; the tastiest morsels find no connoisseur!

The tastiest women know this: a little plumper, a little thinner—oh, how much fate lies in so little!

Man is hard to discover, most of all to himself; often his intellect tells lies about his soul. This is brought about by the spirit of gravity.

But that man has discovered himself who says: "This is *my* good and evil." Thereby he shuts the mouth of the mole and dwarf who says: "Good and evil are the same for everybody."

Truly, I also dislike those who find each and every thing good, and this world the very best. I call them the too easily contented.

Easy satisfaction, which likes the taste of everything, isn't the best taste! I esteem the reluctant, choosy tongues and stomachs that have learned to say "I" and "yes" and "no."

But to chew and digest everything is really the nature of pigs! Always to say hee-haw—only the donkey has learned that, and those like him!

Deep yellow and hot red: that's *my* taste, which mixes blood in with all paints.

But the man who whitewashes his house reveals to me a white-washed soul.

Some enamored of mummies, others of ghosts, and both groups equally hostile to all flesh and blood—oh, how distasteful they both are to me! For I love blood.

And I don't want to dwell or tarry where everyone spits and expectorates. That's *my* taste—I'd rather live among thieves and perjurers. No one has "gold in his mouth."[16]

But I find all lickspittles even more repulsive; and the most repulsive human beast I've ever found I called the parasite: he refused to love, yet wanted to live on love.

I call all those disastrous who have only one choice: to become either vicious animals or vicious tamers of animals: I wouldn't want to live among them.

I also call disastrous those who must always *wait*—they're not to my taste: all the publicans and shopkeepers and kings and other guardians of nations and shop shelves: unsalable goods.

Truly, I, too, learned how to wait, and learned it thoroughly—but

---

16. Alluding to the proverb *Morgenstunde hat Gold im Munde* (equivalent to "The early bird catches the worm").

nur das Warten auf *mich*. Und über Allem lernte ich stehn und gehn und laufen und springen und klettern und tanzen.

Das ist aber meine Lehre: wer einst fliegen lernen will, der muß erst stehn und gehn und laufen und klettern und tanzen lernen: – man erfliegt das Fliegen nicht!

Mit Strickleitern lernte ich manches Fenster erklettern, mit hurtigen Beinen klomm ich auf hohe Masten: auf hohen Masten der Erkenntnis sitzen dünkte mich keine geringe Seligkeit, –

– gleich kleinen Flammen flackern auf hohen Masten: ein kleines Licht zwar, aber doch ein großer Trost für verschlagene Schiffer und Schiffbrüchige! –

Auf vielerlei Weg und Weise kam ich zu meiner Wahrheit: nicht auf Einer Leiter stieg ich zur Höhe, wo mein Auge in meine Ferne schweift.

Und ungern nur fragte ich stets nach Wegen, – das ging mir immer wider den Geschmack! Lieber fragte und versuchte ich die Wege selber.

Ein Versuchen und Fragen war all mein Gehen: – und wahrlich, auch antworten muß man *lernen* auf solches Fragen! Das aber – ist mein Geschmack:

– kein guter, kein schlechter, aber *mein* Geschmack, dessen ich weder Scham noch Hehl mehr habe.

»Das – ist nun *mein* Weg, – wo ist der eure?« so antwortete ich Denen, welche mich »nach dem Wege« fragten. *Den Weg* nämlich – den gibt es nicht!

Also sprach Zarathustra.

Von alten und neuen Tafeln

1.

Hier sitze ich und warte, alte zerbrochene Tafeln und mich und auch neue halb beschriebene Tafeln. Wann kommt meine Stunde?

– die Stunde meines Niederganges, Unterganges: denn *noch* Ein Mal will ich zu den Menschen gehn.

Des warte ich nun: denn erst müssen mir die Zeichen kommen, daß es *meine* Stunde sei, – nämlich der lachende Löwe mit dem Taubenschwarme.

Inzwischen rede ich als Einer, der Zeit hat, zu mir selber. Niemand erzählt mir Neues: so erzähle ich mir mich selber. –

only waiting for *myself*. And above all I learned how to stand and walk and run and jump and climb and dance.

But this is my doctrine: whoever wants to learn to fly some day must first learn to stand and walk and run and climb and dance: you can't learn to fly in one swoop!

I learned how to reach many high windows with rope ladders; I've climbed tall masts with rapid legs: to sit on tall masts of knowledge seemed no small bliss to me—

To flicker on tall masts like small flames: a small light, to be sure, and yet a great comfort to mariners off course or shipwrecked!

I have contained my truth in many ways and manners: I didn't use one ladder to reach the heights where my eyes roam into my distance.

And I have always been unwilling to ask the way—it was never to my taste! Instead I sought and tried out the ways myself.

My entire journey has been an experimental questioning: and, truly, one must also *learn* how to answer such questions! But that *is* to my taste—

Not good taste, not bad taste, but *my* taste, which I no longer conceal or feel shame for.

"This is *my* way; where's yours?" Thus I have answered those who asked me "for the way." You see, *the* way doesn't exist!

Thus spoke Zarathustra.

Of Old and New Tablets of the Law

1.

Here I sit and wait, old, shattered tablets around me, as well as new, half-inscribed tablets. When will my hour come?—

The hour of my descent, my sunset: for I wish to go to the people *one more* time.

That, I now await, for the signs must first come to me that it is *my* hour; namely: the laughing lion with the flock of doves.

Meanwhile, I speak to myself, as one who has time. No one gives me any news, so I tell myself to myself.

2.

Als ich zu den Menschen kam, da fand ich sie sitzen auf einem alten Dünkel: Alle dünkten sich lange schon zu wissen, was dem Menschen gut und böse sei.

Eine alte müde Sache dünkte ihnen alles Reden von Tugend; und wer gut schlafen wollte, der sprach vor Schlafengehen noch von »Gut« und »Böse«.

Diese Schläferei störte ich auf, als ich lehrte: was gut und böse ist, *das weiß noch Niemand*: – es sei denn der Schaffende!

– Das aber ist Der, welcher des Menschen Ziel schafft und der Erde ihren Sinn gibt und ihre Zukunft: Dieser erst *schafft* es, *daß* Etwas gut und böse ist.

Und ich hieß sie ihre alten Lehr-Stühle umwerfen, und wo nur jener alte Dünkel gesessen hatte; ich hieß sie lachen über ihre großen Tugend-Meister und Heiligen und Dichter und Welt-Erlöser.

Über ihre düsteren Wesen hieß ich sie lachen, und wer je als schwarze Vogelscheuche warnend auf dem Baume des Lebens gesessen hatte.

An ihre große Gräberstraße setzte ich mich und selber zu Aas und Geiern – und ich lachte über all ihr Einst und seine mürbe verfallende Herrlichkeit.

Wahrlich, gleich Bußpredigern und Narren schrie ich Zorn und Zeter über all ihr Großes und Kleines, – daß ihr Bestes so gar klein ist! Daß ihr Bösestes so gar klein ist! – also lachte ich.

Meine weise Sehnsucht schrie und lachte also aus mir, die auf Bergen geboren ist, eine wilde Weisheit wahrlich! – meine große flügelbrausende Sehnsucht.

Und oft riß sie mich fort und hinauf und hinweg und mitten im Lachen: da flog ich wohl schaudernd, ein Pfeil, durch sonnentrunkenes Entzücken:

– hinaus in ferne Zükünfte, die kein Traum noch sah, in heißere Süden, als je sich Bildner träumten: dorthin, wo Götter tanzend sich aller Kleider schämen: –

– daß ich nämlich in Gleichnissen rede, und gleich Dichtern hinke und stammle: und wahrlich, ich schäme mich, daß ich noch Dichter sein muß! –

Wo alles Werden mich Götter-Tanz und Götter-Mutwillen dünkte, und die Welt los- und ausgelassen und zu sich selber zurückfliehend: –

– als ein ewiges Sich-Fliehn und -Wiedersuchen vieler Götter, als das selige Sich-Widersprechen, Sich-Wieder-Hören, Sich-Wieder-Zugehören vieler Götter: –

2.

When I came to the people, I found them sitting on an old delusion: they all imagined that they had long known what is good or bad for mankind.

All talk of virtue seemed to them like an old, worn-out matter; whoever wanted to sleep soundly said something about "good" and "evil" before bedtime.

I disturbed this somnolence by teaching: *no one yet knows* what is good or evil—except the creative man!

And that is the man who creates a goal for mankind and gives the earth its meaning and its future: only this man *causes* anything to be good or evil.

And I bade them overturn their old professorial chairs and anyplace else where that old delusion had sat; I bade them laugh at their great masters of virtue and saints and poets and world-redeemers.

I bade them laugh at their somber nature and anyone else who had ever sat warningly on the tree of life as a black scarecrow.

Beside their great road of graves I sat down, and even with carrion and vultures—and I laughed at all their "once" and its rotting, ramshackle splendor.

Truly, like preachers of repentance and like fools, I raised a hue and cry against everything they considered great or small—to think that their "best" is so small! That their "worst" is so small! Thus I laughed.

And so my wise longing issued from me in cries and laughter, that longing born on mountains, a wild wisdom, truly!—my great wing-beating longing.

And after it carried me away, upward, far off, in the midst of my laughter: then I flew, surely shuddering, an arrow, through sun-drunken rapture—

Out into distant futures never yet seen in any dream, into warmer southlands than artists have ever dreamed of: there where gods in their dance are ashamed to wear any clothing—

So that I speak in metaphors, you see, limping and stammering like poets: and, truly, I'm ashamed that I must still be a poet!—

Where all becoming seemed to me a dance of gods and the sportiveness of gods, and the world seemed freed and exuberant, fleeing back to itself—

Like the eternal self-fleeing and self-reapproaching of many gods, like the blessed self-contradicting, self-rehearing, renewed self-belonging of many gods—

Wo alle Zeit mich ein seliger Hohn auf Augenblicke dünkte, wo die Notwendigkeit die Freiheit selber war, die selig mit dem Stachel der Freiheit spielte: –

Wo ich auch meinen alten Teufel und Erzfeind wiederfand, den Geist der Schwere, und Alles, was er schuf: Zwang, Satzung, Not und Folge und Zweck und Wille und Gut und Böse: –

Denn muß nicht dasein, *über* das getanzt, hinweggetanzt werde? Müssen nicht um der Leichten, Leichtesten willen – Maulwürfe und schwere Zwerge dasein? –

3.

Dort war's auch, wo ich das Wort »Übermensch« vom Wege auflas, und daß der Mensch Etwas sei, das überwunden werden müsse,

– daß der Mensch eine Brücke sei und kein Zweck: sich selig preisend ob seines Mittags und Abends, als Weg zu neuen Morgenröten:

– das Zarathustra-Wort vom großen Mittage, und was sonst ich über den Menschen aufhängte, gleich purpurnen zweiten Abendröten.

Wahrlich, auch neue Sterne ließ ich sie sehen samt neuen Nächten; und über Wolken und Tag und Nacht spannte ich noch das Lachen aus wie ein buntes Gezelt.

Ich lehrte sie all *mein* Dichten und Trachten: in Eins zu dichten und zusammenzutragen, was Bruchstück ist am Menschen und Rätsel und grauser Zufall, –

– als Dichter, Rätselrater und Erlöser des Zufalls lehrte ich sie an der Zukunft schaffen, und Alles, das *war* –, schaffend zu erlösen.

Das Vergangne am Menschen zu erlösen und alles »Es war« umzuschaffen, bis der Wille spricht: »Aber so wollte ich es! So werde ich's wollen –«

– Dies hieß ich ihnen Erlösung, Dies allein lehrte ich sie Erlösung heißen. – –

Nun warte ich *meiner* Erlösung –, daß ich zum letzten Male zu ihnen gehe.

Denn noch Ein Mal will ich zu den Menschen: *unter* ihnen will ich untergehen, sterbend will ich ihnen meine reichste Gabe geben!

Der Sonne lernte ich das ab, wenn sie hinabgeht, die Überreiche: Gold schüttet sie da ins Meer aus unerschöpflichem Reichtume, –

– also, daß der ärmste Fischer noch mit *goldenem* Ruder rudert! Dies nämlich sah ich einst und wurde der Tränen nicht satt im Zuschauen. – –

Der Sonne gleich will auch Zarathustra untergehn: nun sitzt er hier

Where all time seemed to me like a blessed mockery of moments, where necessity was freedom itself, playing happily with the goad of freedom—

Where I found again my old devil and archenemy, too, the spirit of gravity, and all he created: compulsion, regulations, need and following and purpose and will and good and evil—

For must not something exist *beyond* which one must dance, dancing past it? For the sake of the weightless, the most weightless, must not moles and heavy dwarfs exist?

3.

It was there, too, that I picked up the word "more-than-man" from the road, and realized that man is something that must be superseded,—

That man is a bridge, not a final purpose: counting himself blessed for his noonday and evening, as a road to new dawns—

The Zarathustra phrase of the great noonday, and all the other things I set up to guide man, like second purple twilights.

Truly, I also showed them new stars and new nights; and over clouds and day and night I also spread out laughter like a motley-colored tent.

I taught them all *my* thoughts and endeavors: to compose and assemble into a whole that in man which is a fragment and a puzzle and dire accident—

As poet, puzzle solver, and redeemer from chance, I taught them to work for the future, and to redeem creatively all that *has been*.

To redeem man's past and to transform all "There was," until the will says: "But that's the way I wanted it! That's the way I will want it—"

That is what I told them was redemption, this alone I taught them to call redemption.

Now I await *my* redemption—that I go to them for the last time.

For one more time I want to go to the people: I want to perish *among* them; dying, I want to give them my richest gift!

I have learned it by watching the sun set, the overabundant sun: it then pours gold into the sea from its inexhaustible treasury—

So that even the poorest fisherman rows with a *golden* oar! For I saw this once and never became sated with tears as I beheld it.

Like the sun Zarathustra, too, wishes to set; now he sits here and

und wartet, alte zerbrochne Tafeln um sich und auch neue Tafeln, –
halbbeschriebene.

4.

Siehe, hier ist eine neue Tafel: aber wo sind meine Brüder, die sie mit
mir zu Tale und in fleischerne Herzen tragen? –

Also heischt es meine große Liebe zu den Fernsten: *schone deinen
Nächsten nicht!* Der Mensch ist Etwas, das überwunden werden muß.

Es gibt vielerlei Weg und Weise der Überwindung: da siehe *du* zu!
Aber nur ein Possenreißer denkt: »Der Mensch kann auch *über-
sprungen* werden.«

Überwinde dich selber noch in deinem Nächsten: und ein Recht,
das du dir rauben kannst, sollst du dir nicht geben lassen!

Was du tust, das kann dir Keiner wieder tun. Siehe, es gibt keine
Vergeltung.

Wer sich nicht befehlen kann, der soll gehorchen. Und Mancher
kann sich befehlen, aber da fehlt noch Viel, daß er sich auch
gehorche!

5.

Also will es die Art edler Seelen: sie wollen Nichts *umsonst* haben, am
wenigsten das Leben.

Wer vom Pöbel ist, der will umsonst leben; wir Anderen aber,
denen das Leben sich gab, – wir sinnen immer darüber, *was* wir am
besten *dagegen* geben!

Und wahrlich, dies ist eine vornehme Rede, welche spricht: »was
uns das Leben verspricht, das wollen *wir* – dem Leben halten!«

Man soll nicht genießen wollen, wo man nicht zu genießen gibt.
Und – man soll nicht genießen *wollen!*

Genuß und Unschuld nämlich sind die schamhaftesten Dinge:
Beide wollen nicht gesucht sein. Man soll sie *haben* –, aber man soll
eher noch nach Schuld und Schmerzen *suchen!* –

6.

Oh meine Brüder, wer ein Erstling ist, der wird immer geopfert. Nun
aber sind wir Erstlinge.

waits, old, shattered tablets around him and also new tablets—half-inscribed.

4.

Behold, here is a new tablet; but where are my brothers, to help me carry it downhill to hearts of flesh?

This is what my great love for the most distant demands: *don't spare those nearest to you!* Man is something that must be superseded.

There are all sorts of ways and manners of superseding: *you* look to it! But only a clown thinks: "Man can also be *leapt over.*"

Supersede yourself now in your fellow man: and don't let yourself be granted any right that you can seize!

What you do can't be repeated by anyone else. Behold, there is no retribution.

Whoever cannot give himself orders should obey. And many a man *can* give himself orders, but has a long way to go before he can also obey himself!

5.

Such is the nature of noble souls: they want nothing *gratis,* life least of all.

Whoever is of the rabble wants to live gratis; but we others, to whom life has given itself—we're constantly thinking about *what* we can best give in *return!*

And, truly, it's a noble saying that goes: "The promises that life makes to *us, we* shall keep as if we had made them to life!"

One should not wish to enjoy when one doesn't give something to be enjoyed. And—one shouldn't *wish* to enjoy!

For enjoyment and innocence are the shamefulest things: neither one is to be sought. They should be *had*—but it's better to *seek* for guilt and pain instead!

6.

O my brothers, the one who is a firstborn is always sacrificed. Now, we are firstborn.

Wir bluten Alle an geheimen Opfertischen, wir brennen und braten Alle zu Ehren alter Götzenbilder.

Unser Bestes ist noch jung: das reizt alte Gaumen. Unser Fleisch ist zart, unser Fell ist nur ein Lamm-Fell: – wie sollten wir nicht alte Götzenpriester reizen!

In *uns selber* wohnt er noch, der alte Götzenpriester, der unser Bestes sich zum Schmause brät. Ach, meine Brüder, wie sollten Erstlinge nicht Opfer sein!

Aber so will es unsre Art; und ich liebe Die, welche sich nicht bewahren wollen. Die Untergehenden liebe ich mit meiner ganzen Liebe: denn sie gehn hinüber. –

7.

Wahr sein – das *können* Wenige! Und wer es kann, der will es noch nicht! Am wenigsten aber können es die Guten.

Oh diese Guten! – *Gute Menschen reden nie die Wahrheit;* für den Geist ist solchermaßen gut sein eine Krankheit.

Sie geben nach, diese Guten, sie ergeben sich, ihr Herz spricht nach, ihr Grund gehorcht: wer aber gehorcht, *der hört sich selber nicht!*

Alles, was den Guten böse heißt, muß zusammenkommen, daß Eine Wahrheit geboren werde: oh meine Brüder, seid ihr auch böse genug zu *dieser* Wahrheit?

Das verwegene Wagen, das lange Mißtrauen, das grausame Nein, der Überdruß, das Schneiden ins Lebendige – wie selten kommt *das* zusammen! Aus solchem Samen aber wird – Wahrheit gezeugt!

Neben dem bösen Gewissen wuchs bisher alles *Wissen!* Zerbrecht, zerbrecht mir, ihr Erkennenden, die alten Tafeln!

8.

Wenn das Wasser Balken hat, wenn Stege und Geländer über den Fluß springen: wahrlich, da findet Keiner Glauben, der da spricht: »Alles ist im Fluß.«

Sondern selber die Tölpel widersprechen ihm. »Wie?« sagen die Tölpel, »Alles wäre im Flusse? Balken und Geländer sind doch *über* dem Flusse!«

»*Über* dem Flusse ist Alles fest, alle die Werte der Dinge, die Brücken, Begriffe, alles ›Gut‹ und ›Böse‹: das ist Alles *fest!*« –

We all bleed at secret altars, we are all burnt and roasted to honor old idols.

The best in us is still young; that appeals to old palates. Our flesh is tender, our skin is merely a lambskin—how could we fail to appeal to aged priests of idols?

He still dwells within *ourselves,* the aged idol-priest who roasts the best in us for his feast. Alas, my brothers, how can the firstborn help being a victim?

But that is our nature; and I love those who don't wish to preserve themselves. I love those who perish with all my love: for they pass beyond.

7.

To be true—only few *are able!* And whoever can, doesn't want to be! The good are the least able.

Oh, these good people!—*Good people never speak the truth;* for the mind, being all that good is a sickness.

They make concessions, these good men, they devote themselves, their heart repeats the words, they are basically obedient: but the obedient man *doesn't hear himself!*

Everything that the good call evil must come together so that one truth may be born: O my brothers, are you, too, evil enough for *this* truth?

Rash risk-taking, long-held distrust, cruel refusals, world-weariness, cutting to the quick—how rarely are *they* combined! But from such seed—truth germinates!

Up till now, all *knowledge* has grown *alongside* a bad conscience! You men of knowledge, I tell you to shatter, shatter the old tablets!

8.

When there are beams over the water, when footbridges and railings cross the river: truly, no one is believed who says: "Everything is in flux."

Instead, even the fools contradict him. "What?!" the fools say. "Everything is in flux? But there are beams and railings *over* the river!

"*Over* the river everything is stable, all the values of things, the bridges, concepts, everything 'good' and 'evil': all that is *stable!*"

Kommt gar der harte Winter, der Fluß-Tierbändiger: dann lernen auch die Witzigsten Mißtrauen; und, wahrlich, nicht nur die Tölpel sprechen dann: »Sollte nicht Alles – *stille stehn*?«

»Im Grunde steht Alles stille« –, das ist eine rechte Winter-Lehre, ein gut Ding für unfruchtbare Zeit, ein guter Trost für Winterschläfer und Ofenhocker.

»Im Grund steht Alles still« –: *dagegen* aber predigt der Tauwind!

Der Tauwind, ein Stier, der kein pflügender Stier ist, – ein wütender Stier, ein Zerstörer, der mit zornigen Hörnern Eis bricht! Eis aber – – *bricht Stege!*

Oh meine Brüder, ist *jetzt nicht Alles im Flusse?* Sind nicht alle Geländer und Stege ins Wasser gefallen? Wer *hielte* sich noch an »Gut« und »Böse«?

»Wehe uns! Heil uns! Der Tauwind weht!« – Also predigt mir, oh meine Brüder, durch alle Gassen!

9.

Es gibt einen alten Wahn, der heißt Gut und Böse. Um Wahrsager und Sterndeuter drehte sich bisher das Rad dieses Wahns.

Einst *glaubte* man an Wahrsager und Sterndeuter: und *darum* glaubte man »Alles ist Schicksal: du sollst, denn du mußt!«

Dann wieder mißtraute man allen Wahrsagern und Sterndeutern: und *darum* glaubte man »Alles ist Freiheit: du kannst, denn du willst!«

Oh meine Brüder, über Sterne und Zukunft ist bisher nur gewähnt, nicht gewußt worden: und *darum* ist über Gut und Böse bisher nur gewähnt, nicht gewußt worden!

10.

»Du sollst nicht rauben! Du sollst nicht totschlagen!« – solche Worte hieß man einst heilig; vor ihnen beugte man Knie und Köpfe und zog die Schuhe aus.

Aber ich frage euch: wo gab es je bessere Räuber und Totschläger in der Welt, als es solche heilige Worte waren?

Ist in allem Leben selber nicht – Rauben und Totschlagen? Und daß solche Worte heilig hießen, wurde damit die *Wahrheit* selber nicht – totgeschlagen?

Oder war es eine Predigt des Todes, daß heilig hieß, was allem

Then, when hard winter comes, the tamer of wild rivers, even the cleverest learn distrust; and, truly, then not only the fools say: "Isn't everything *stationary?*"

"Basically, all is stationary": that's a real wintertime doctrine, something good for an infertile time, a good consolation for hibernators and those who stay at home by the stove.

"Basically, all is stationary": but the wind that brings the thaw preaches the *opposite!*

The thaw wind: a bull that is no plow-pulling ox, a raging bull, a destroyer that breaks up ice with angry horns! But ice *breaks footbridges!*

O my brothers, *isn't everything now in flux?* Haven't all the railings and footbridges fallen into the water? Who could now still *hold onto* "good" and "evil"?

"Woe is us! Save us! The thaw wind is blowing!" Preach this for me, oh, my brothers, in every street!

9.

There is an old delusion called good and evil. Until now the wheel of this delusion has revolved around soothsayers and astrologers.

Once people *believed* in soothsayers and astrologers, and *therefore* they believed: "All is fate; you shall because you must!"

Then, later, they distrusted all soothsayers and astrologers: and *therefore* they believed: "All is freedom; you can because you want to!"

O my brothers, until now people have been imagining, not knowing, about stars and the future: and *therefore* up till now there have been only imaginings, not knowledge, about good and evil!

10.

"Thou shalt not steal! Thou shalt not kill!" Such phrases were once considered sacred; in their presence, people bent their knees, bowed their heads, and pulled off their shoes.

But I ask you: where in the world have there ever been greater robbers and killers than those sacred phrases were?

Don't robbing and killing occur everywhere in life itself? And for those phrases to be considered sacred, wasn't the *truth* itself thereby killed?

Or was it a sermon of death that sanctified something which con-

Leben widersprach und widerriet? – Oh meine Brüder, zerbrecht,
zerbrecht mir die alten Tafeln!

11.

Dies ist mein Mitleid mit allem Vergangenen, daß ich sehe: es ist
preisgegeben, –

– der Gnade, dem Geiste, dem Wahnsinne jedes Geschlechtes preisgegeben, das kommt und Alles, was war, zu seiner Brücke umdeutet!

Ein großer Gewalt-Herr könnte kommen, ein gewitzter Unhold, der
mit seiner Gnade und Ungnade alles Vergangene zwänge und zwängte:
bis es ihm Brücke würde und Vorzeichen und Herold und Hahnenschrei.

Dies aber ist die andre Gefahr und mein andres Mitleiden: – wer
vom Pöbel ist, dessen Gedenken geht zurück bis zum Großvater, – mit
dem Großvater aber hört die Zeit auf.

Also ist alles Vergangene preisgegeben: denn es könnte einmal
kommen, daß der Pöbel Herr würde, und in seichten Gewässern alle
Zeit ertränke.

Darum, oh meine Brüder, bedarf es eines *neuen Adels,* der allem
Pöbel und allem Gewalt-Herrischen Widersacher ist und auf neue
Tafeln neu das Wort schreibt »edel«.

Vieler Edlen nämlich bedarf es und vielerlei Edlen, *daß es Adel
gebe!* Oder, wie ich einst im Gleichnis sprach: »Das eben ist Gött-
lichkeit, daß es Götter, aber keinen Gott gibt!«

12.

Oh meine Brüder, ich weihe und weise euch zu einem neuen Adel:
ihr sollt mir Zeuger und Züchter werden und Sämänner der
Zukunft, –

– wahrlich, nicht zu einem Adel, den ihr kaufen könntet gleich den
Krämern und mit Krämer-Golde: denn wenig Wert hat Alles, was
seinen Preis hat.

Nicht, woher ihr kommt, mache euch fürderhin eure Ehre, sondern wohin ihr geht! Euer Wille und euer Fuß, der über euch selber
hinaus will, – das mache eure neue Ehre!

Wahrlich nicht, daß ihr einem Fürsten gedient habt – was liegt
noch an Fürsten! – oder dem, was steht, zum Bollwerk wurdet, daß es
fester stünde!

tradicted, and advised against, all of life?—O, my brothers, I tell you to shatter, shatter the old tablets!

11.

My compassion for all that is past comes from my seeing that it is a prey—

A prey, at the mercy of the favor, the spirit, the madness of every generation that comes along and reinterprets all that once occurred, making it a bridge for itself!

A great lord of violence might come, a clever fiend, who might compel and compress all of the past with his favor and disfavor, until it became a bridge for him, a foretokening, herald, and cockcrow.

But this is the second danger and my second cause for compassion: the memory of the common man extends as far back as his grandfather—and with his grandfather history comes to an end.

And so, the whole past is sacrificed: for the time may come when the rabble rules and all of historical time is drowned in shallow water.

Therefore, O my brothers, a *new nobility* is needed to counteract all rabble and all rulers by violence, and to inscribe the word "noble" newly on new tablets.

You see, many noblemen, and of many different sorts, are needed *for a noble class to exist!* Or, as I once said metaphorically: "True deity is the existence of gods, but of no God!"

12.

O my brothers, I consecrate and point you in the direction of a new nobility: I want you to be the begetters, breeders, and sowers of the future—

Truly, not for a nobility which you could purchase as shopkeepers do, with shopkeepers' gold: because everything that has a price has little value.

In the future, let your honor be based, not on where you come from, but on where you're going! Your will, and your feet that wish to go beyond you—let them constitute a new honor!

Truly, not your having served a prince—what do princes matter any more?—or your having become a bulwark for standing institutions so they stood more firmly!

Nicht, daß euer Geschlecht an Höfen höfisch wurde, und ihr lerntet, bunt, einem Flamingo ähnlich, lange Stunden in flachen Teichen stehn.

– Denn Stehen-*Können* ist ein Verdienst bei Höflingen; und alle Höflinge glauben, zur Seligkeit nach dem Tode gehöre – Sitzen-*Dürfen!* –

Nicht auch, daß ein Geist, den sie heilig nennen, eure Vorfahren in gelobte Länder führte, die *ich* nicht lobe: denn wo der schlimmste aller Bäume wuchs, das Kreuz, – an dem Lande ist Nichts zu loben! –

– und wahrlich, wohin dieser »heilige Geist« auch seine Ritter führte, immer liefen bei solchen Zügen – Ziegen und Gänse und Kreuz- und Querköpfe *voran!* –

Oh meine Brüder, nicht zurück soll euer Adel schauen, sondern *hinaus!* Vertriebene sollt ihr sein aus allen Vater- und Urväterländern!

Eurer *Kinder Land* sollt ihr lieben: diese Liebe sei euer neuer Adel, – das unentdeckte, im fernsten Meere! Nach ihm heiße ich eure Segel suchen und suchen!

An euren Kindern sollt ihr *gutmachen,* daß ihr eurer Väter Kinder seid: alles Vergangene sollt ihr so erlösen! Diese neue Tafel stelle ich über euch!

13.

»Wozu leben? Alles ist eitel! Leben – das ist Stroh dreschen; Leben – das ist sich verbrennen und doch nicht warm werden.« –

Solch altertümliches Geschwätz gilt immer noch als »Weisheit«; daß es aber alt ist und dumpfig riecht, *darum* wird es besser geehrt. Auch der Moder adelt. –

Kinder durften so reden: die *scheuen* das Feuer, weil es sie brannte! Es ist viel Kinderei in den alten Büchern der Weisheit.

Und wer immer »Stroh drischt«, wie sollte der auf das Dreschen lästern dürfen! Solchem Narren müßte man doch das Maul verbinden!

Not your family's having become courtiers at courts, and your having learned to stand long hours in shallow pools in gaudy array, like flamingos.

—Because *being able to* stand is meritorious in courtiers, and all courtiers believe that one of the blissful things after death is *being allowed to* sit down!—

Nor that a spirit, dubbed "holy," led your ancestors into praiseworthy promised lands, which *I* don't praise, because there's nothing to praise about the country where that worst of all trees grew: the cross!

—And, truly, wherever that "holy spirit" led even its knights, in such crusades they were always *preceded* by goats, geese, and the muddle-headed!—[17]

Oh, my brothers, your nobility should look not backward, but *forward!* You should be outcasts from every fatherland and patriarchland!

It is the *land of your children* that you should love: let that love be your new nobility—that undiscovered land in the remotest sea! I bid your sails seek and seek for *it!*

You should atone to your children for your being the children of your fathers: in that way you should redeem all of the past! This new tablet I hold up to you!

13.

"Why live? All is vanity! Living means threshing straw; living means burning up and still not getting warm."

Such old-fashioned prattle still counts as "wisdom"; but *just because* it's old and smells musty, it's more highly honored. Even mildew lends nobility.

It was all right for children to talk that way: they *shy away* from fire because it once burned them! There's a lot of childishness in the old books of wisdom.

And if someone keeps on "threshing straw," why should he be allowed to say bad things about threshing? Such a fool should be gagged!

---

17. An outstanding example of Nietzsche's plays on words, *Kreuz- und Querköpfe* combines *Querkopf* ("wrongheaded person") with *kreuz und quer* ("zigzagging"), with the *Kreuz* also contributing another slap at the Christian cross. Note also the cleverly contrived juxtaposition of the near-homonyms *Zügen* ("crusades") and *Ziegen* ("goats").

Solche setzen sich zu Tisch und bringen Nichts mit, selbst den guten Hunger nicht: – und nun lästern sie »Alles ist eitel!«

Aber gut essen und trinken, oh meine Brüder, ist wahrlich keine eitle Kunst! Zerbrecht, zerbrecht mir die Tafeln der Nimmer-Frohen!

14.

»Dem Reinen ist Alles rein« – so spricht das Volk. Ich aber sage euch: den Schweinen wird Alles Schwein!

Darum predigen die Schwärmer und Kopfhänger, denen auch das Herz niederhängt: »die Welt selber ist ein kotiges Ungeheuer.«

Denn diese Alle sind unsäuberlichen Geistes: sonderlich aber Jene, welche nicht Ruhe noch Rast haben, es sei denn, sie sehen die Welt *von hinten*, – die Hinterweltler!

Denen sage ich ins Gesicht, ob es gleich nicht lieblich klingt: die Welt gleicht darin dem Menschen, daß sie einen Hintern hat, – so *Viel* ist wahr!

Es gibt in der Welt viel Kot: So *Viel* ist wahr! Aber darum ist die Welt selber noch kein kotiges Ungeheuer!

Es ist Weisheit darin, daß Vieles in der Welt übel riecht: der Ekel selber schafft Flügel und quellenahnende Kräfte!

An dem Besten ist noch Etwas zum Ekeln; und der Beste ist noch Etwas, das überwunden werden muß! –

Oh meine Brüder, es ist viel Weisheit darin, daß viel Kot in der Welt ist! –

15.

Solche Sprüche hörte ich fromme Hinterweltler zu ihrem Gewissen reden, und wahrlich, ohne Arg und Falsch, – ob es schon nichts Falscheres in der Welt gibt, noch Ärgeres.

»Laß doch die Welt die Welt sein! Hebe dawider auch nicht Einen Finger auf!«

»Laß, wer da wolle, die Leute würgen und stechen und schinden und schaben: hebe dawider auch nicht Einen Finger auf! Darob lernen sie noch der Welt absagen.«

Some people sit down to a meal and bring nothing along, not even a good appetite—and then they blaspheme: "All is vanity!"

But to eat and drink well, O my brothers, is truly no vain art! I tell you to shatter, shatter the tablets of the permanent malcontents!

14.

"To the pure all is pure," goes the popular saying. But I tell you: "To manure all's manure!"[18]

Therefore the fanatics with bowed heads, whose hearts droop, too, preach: "The world itself is a shitty monster."

For they are all unclean in spirit, and especially those who know not a moment's peace unless they're viewing the world *from behind*—those backworldsmen!

I tell *them* to their face, though it doesn't sound charming: the world is like a human being in having a behind—*that much* is true!

There's a lot of excrement in the world: *that much* is true! But that still doesn't make the world itself a shitty monster!

There's wisdom in the statement that much in the world smells bad: but one's very disgust gives one wings and the power to divine water sources!

Even in the best things there's something to be disgusted with; and even the best man is still something that must be superseded!

O my brothers, there's much wisdom in the statement that there's a lot of excrement in the world!

15.

I have heard pious backworldsmen reciting similar maxims to their conscience and, truly, without guile or falsity—even though there's nothing falser in the world, or more guileful.

"Let the world be the world! Don't even lift a finger to change it!"

"Let anyone who wishes throttle people, and stab and skin and scrape them: don't even lift a finger to change it! In that way, they eventually learn to renounce the world."

---

18. A slight liberty for the sake of the rhyme. The German says literally: "To pigs everything becomes pig!"

«Und deine eigne Vernunft –die sollst du selber görgeln und würgen; denn es ist eine Vernunft von dieser Welt, – darob lernst du selber der Welt absagen.« –

– Zerbrecht, zerbrecht mir, oh meine Brüder, diese alten Tafeln der Frommen! Zersprecht mir die Sprüche der Welt-Verleumder!

16.

»Wer viel lernt, der verlernt alles heftige Begehren« – das flüstert man heute sich zu auf allen dunklen Gassen.

»Weisheit macht müde, es lohnt sich – Nichts; du sollst nicht begehren!« – diese neue Tafel fand ich hängen selbst auf offnen Märkten.

Zerbrecht mir, oh meine Brüder, zerbrecht mir auch diese *neue* Tafel! Die Welt-Müden hängten sie hin und die Prediger des Todes, und auch die Stockmeister: denn seht, es ist auch eine Predigt zu Knechtschaft! –

Daß sie schlecht lernten und das Beste nicht, und Alles zu früh und Alles zu geschwind: daß sie schlecht *aßen,* daher kam ihnen jener verdorbene Magen, –

– ein verdorbener Magen ist nämlich ihr Geist: *der* rät zum Tode! Denn wahrlich, meine Brüder, der *Geist ist* ein Magen!

Das Leben ist ein Born der Lust: aber aus wem der verdorbene Magen redet, der Vater der Trübsal, dem sind alle Quellen vergiftet.

Erkennen: das ist *Lust* dem Löwen-willigen! Aber wer müde wurde, der wird selber nur »gewollt«, mit dem spielen alle Wellen.

Und so ist es immer schwacher Menschen Art: sie verlieren sich auf ihren Wegen. Und zuletzt fragt noch ihre Müdigkeit: »wozu gingen wir jemals Wege! Es ist Alles gleich!«

Denen klingt es lieblich zu Ohren, daß gepredigt wird: »Es verlohnt sich Nichts! Ihr sollt nicht wollen!« Dies aber ist eine Predigt zur Knechtschaft.

Oh meine Brüder, ein frischer Brause-Wind kommt Zarathustra allen Weg-Müden; viele Nasen wird er noch niesen machen!

Auch durch Mauern bläst mein freier Atem, und hinein in Gefängnisse und eingefangne Geister!

Wollen befreit: denn Wollen ist Schaffen: so lehre ich. Und *nur* zum Schaffen sollt ihr lernen!

Und auch das Lernen sollt ihr erst von mir *lernen,* das Gut-Lernen! – Wer Ohren hat, der höre!

"And your own power of reason—you should choke and throttle it yourself, because it's reason that belongs to this world. By doing so, you yourself will learn to renounce the world."

O my brothers, I tell you to shatter, shatter these old tablets of the pious! I tell you to undo the maxims of the world-slanderers!

16.

"He who learns much forgets all violent desires": people whisper that to one another nowadays on every dark street.

"Wisdom tires you out; nothing is worthwhile; thou shalt not desire!" I have found this new tablet set up even in public markets.

Oh, my brothers, I tell you to shatter, shatter this *new* tablet, also! It was set up by the world-weary and the preachers of death, and also the prison guards: for, behold, it's a sermon in the cause of servitude!

Because they learned badly, and not the best things, and everything too soon and everything too fast: because they *ate* badly, they got that disordered stomach—

For their spirit is a disordered stomach: *that's* what advises them to die. For, truly, my brothers, the *spirit is* a stomach!

Life is a fount of pleasure, but for the man who speaks from his upset stomach, that father of misery, all springs are poisoned.

To gain knowledge: that is *pleasure* for the lion-willed! But the man who has grown weary has other people's will imposed on him, all willing billows sport with him.

And this is always the nature of weak people: they get lost on their journey. And finally their weariness asks: "Why did we ever undertake a journey? Things are the same everywhere!"

Their ears are charmed by the sermon: "Nothing is worthwhile. You should have no wishes!" But this is a sermon in the cause of servitude.

O my brothers, Zarathustra comes to all those who are way-weary as a brisk, roaring wind; he will yet make many a nose sneeze!

My free breath blows even through walls, and into prisons and imprisoned spirits!

The will liberates, for to will is to create: that is my doctrine. And you should learn *only* in order to create!

And even learning you should first *learn* from me, proper learning![19]—If you have ears, hearken!

19. Or: "learning of the good." Probably both meanings are intended.

17.

Da steht der Nachen, – dort hinüber geht es vielleicht ins große Nichts. – Aber wer will in dies »Vielleicht« einsteigen?

Niemand von euch will in den Todes-Nachen einsteigen! Wieso wollt ihr dann *Welt-Müde* sein!

Weltmüde! Und noch nicht einmal Erd-Entrückte wurdet ihr! Lüstern fand ich euch immer noch nach Erde, verliebt noch in die eigne Erd-Müdigkeit!

Nicht umsonst hängt euch die Lippe herab: – ein kleiner Erden-Wunsch sitzt noch darauf! Und im Auge – schwimmt da nicht ein Wölkchen unvergeßner Erden-Lust?

Es gibt auf Erden viel gute Erfindungen, die einen nützlich, die andern angenehm: derentwegen ist die Erde zu lieben.

Und mancherlei so gut Erfundenes gibt es da, daß es ist wie des Weibes Busen: nützlich zugleich und angenehm.

Ihr Welt-Müden aber! Ihr Erden-Faulen! Euch soll man mit Ruten streichen! Mit Rutenstreichen soll man euch wieder muntre Beine machen.

Denn: seid ihr nicht Kranke und verlebte Wichte, deren die Erde müde ist, so seid ihr schlaue Faultiere oder naschhafte verkrochene Lust-Katzen. Und wollt ihr nicht wieder lustig *laufen,* so sollt ihr – dahinfahren!

An Unheilbaren soll man nicht Arzt sein wollen: also lehrt es Zarathustra: – so sollt ihr dahinfahren!

Aber es gehört mehr *Mut* dazu, ein Ende zu machen, als einen neuen Vers: das wissen alle Ärzte und Dichter. –

18.

Oh meine Brüder, es gibt Tafeln, welche die Ermüdung, und Tafeln, welche die Faulheit schuf, die faulige: ob sie schon gleich reden, so wollen sie doch ungleich gehört sein. –

Seht hier diesen Verschmachtenden! Nur eine Spanne weit ist er noch von seinem Ziele, aber vor Müdigkeit hat er sich trotzig hier in den Staub gelegt: dieser Tapfere!

Vor Müdigkeit gähnt er Weg und Erde und Ziel und sich selber an: keinen Schritt will er noch weiter tun – dieser Tapfere!

Nun glüht die Sonne auf ihn, und die Hunde lecken nach seinem Schweiße: aber er liegt da in seinem Trotze und will lieber verschmachten: –

17.

There waits the boat. Perhaps it will sail into the great nothingness. But who wants to board that "perhaps"?

None of you wants to board the death boat! And so why do you say you're *world-weary?*

World-weary! And you haven't even become detached from the earth yet! I've always found you lusting for the earth, still enamored of your own earth-weariness!

It's not for nothing that your lip droops—a little earthly wish is still sitting on it! And in your eyes—isn't a little cloud of unforgotten earthly pleasure still floating in them?

There are many good inventions on earth, some useful, others pleasant: for their sake the earth should be loved.

And there are so many sorts of well-invented things there that it's like a woman's bosom: useful and pleasant at the same time.

But you world-weary people! You earth-sluggards! You should be whipped with rods! Rod lashes should put some energy in your legs again.

Because: if you aren't sick people and worn-out creatures that the earth is weary of, then you're sly sloths or greedy, holed-up pleasure cats. And if you don't want to *run* at a lively pace again, then you should pass on!

People shouldn't try to cure the incurable: thus teaches Zarathustra—so you should pass on!

But it takes more *courage* to make an end of oneself than to write a new line of poetry: all doctors and poets know that.

18.

O my brothers, there are tablets created by exhaustion and tablets created by sloth, that lazybones: even though they say the same thing, they don't want to be heard the same way.

Look at this man here languishing away! He's only a handbreadth away from his goal, but in his weariness he has stretched out defiantly in the dust here: that brave fellow!

In his weariness he yawns at the road, the earth, his goal, and himself: he refuses to take another step—that brave fellow!

Now the sun is blazing on him, and the dogs are licking his sweat, but he lies there in his defiance and would rather languish away—

– eine Spanne weit von seinem Ziele verschmachten! Wahrlich, ihr werdet ihn noch an den Haaren in seinen Himmel ziehen müssen, – diesen Helden!

Besser noch, ihr laßt ihn liegen, wohin er sich gelegt hat, daß der Schlaf ihm komme, der Tröster, mit kühlendem Rausche-Regen:

Laßt ihn liegen, bis er von selber wach wird, – bis er von selber alle Müdigkeit widerruft und was Müdigkeit aus ihm lehrte!

Nur, meine Brüder, daß ihr die Hunde von ihm scheucht, die faulen Schleicher, und all das schwärmende Geschmeiß: –

– all was schwärmende Geschmeiß der »Gebildeten«, das sich am Schweiße jedes Helden – gütlich tut! –

19.

Ich schließe Kreise um mich und heilige Grenzen; immer Wenigere steigen mit mir auf immer höhere Berge: ich baue ein Gebirge aus immer heiligeren Bergen. –

Wohin ihr aber auch mit mir steigen mögt, oh meine Brüder: seht zu, daß nicht ein *Schmarotzer* mit euch steige!

Schmarotzer: das ist ein Gewürm, ein kriechendes, geschmiegtes, das fett werden will an euren kranken wunden Winkeln.

Und *das* ist seine Kunst, daß er steigende Seelen errät, wo sie müde sind: in euren Gram und Unmut, in eure zarte Scham baut er sein ekles Nest.

Wo der Starke schwach, der Edle allzumild ist, – dahinein baut er sein ekles Nest: der Schmarotzer wohnt, wo der Große kleine wunde Winkel hat.

Was ist die höchste Art alles Seienden und was die geringste? Der Schmarotzer ist die geringste Art; wer aber höchster Art ist, der ernährt die meisten Schmarotzer.

Die Seele nämlich, welche die längste Leiter hat und am tiefsten hinunter kann: wie sollten nicht an der die meisten Schmarotzer sitzen? –

– die umfänglichste Seele, welche am weitesten in sich laufen und irren und schweifen kann; die notwendigste, welche sich aus Lust in den Zufall stürzt: –

– die seiende Seele, welche ins Werden taucht; die habende, welche ins Wollen und Verlangen *will*: –

– die sich selber fliehende, die sich selber im weitesten Kreise einholt; die weiseste Seele, welcher die Narrheit am süßesten zuredet: –

– die sich selber liebendste, in der alle Dinge ihr Strömen und

Languish to death a handbreadth away from his goal! Truly, you'll have to pull him into his heaven by the hair—that hero!

Better yet: let him lie where he has stretched out, so that sleep, the comforter, may come to him with a cool, pattering rain:

Let him lie until he awakens of his own accord, until he spontaneously revokes all weariness, and all that weariness has taught by his example!

My brothers, merely chase away the dogs from him, those lazy sneaks, and all the swarming vermin:

All the swarming vermin of the "cultured," which loves to batten on the sweat of every hero!

19.

I draw circles and hallowed boundaries around myself; fewer people all the time ascend with me to ever-higher mountains: I'm building a range out of ever-holier mountains.

But wherever you may ascend with me, O my brothers: make sure no *parasite* ascends with you!

Parasite: that's a crawling, curled-up worm that wants to grow fat on your sick and sore spots.

And *this* is his art: to detect when ascending souls are weary: he builds his foul nest in your grief and displeasure, in your tender shame.

Where the strong man is weak and the noble man is too gentle, he builds his foul nest: the parasite lives where the great man has small sore spots.

What is the loftiest nature in all existence, and the lowest? The parasite is the lowest nature; but the man who is of the highest nature provides sustenance for the most parasites.

For the soul that has the longest ladder, and can reach farthest down, naturally has the most parasites attached to it—

The most capacious soul, which can run and stray and roam the farthest into itself; the most necessary soul, which plunges into chance for pleasure—

The existing soul, which dives into becoming; the possessing soul, which *wills* to will and desire—

The soul fleeing itself, which forms the widest circle when catching up with itself; the wisest soul, which folly coaxes most sweetly—

The soul that best loves itself, in which all things have their current

Widerströmen und Ebbe und Flut haben: – oh wie sollte die *höchste Seele* nicht die schlimmsten Schmarotzer haben?

20.

Oh meine Brüder, bin ich denn grausam? Aber ich sage: was fällt, das soll man auch noch stoßen!

Das Alles von heute – das fällt, das verfällt: wer wollte es halten! Aber ich – ich will es noch stoßen!

Kennt ihr die Wollust, die Steine in steile Tiefen rollt? – Diese Menschen von heute: seht sie doch wie sie in meine Tiefen rollen!

Ein Vorspiel bin ich besserer Spieler, oh meine Brüder! Ein Beispiel! *Tut* nach meinem Beispiele!

Und wen ihr nicht fliegen lehrt, den lehrt mir – *schneller fallen!* –

21.

Ich liebe die Tapferen: aber es ist nicht genug, Hau-Degen sein, – man muß auch wissen Hau-schau-Wen!

Und oft ist mehr Tapferkeit darin, daß Einer an sich hält und vorübergeht: *damit* er sich dem würdigeren Feinde aufspare!

Ihr sollt nur Feinde haben, die zu hassen sind, aber nicht Feinde zum Verachten: ihr müßt stolz auf euren Feind sein: also lehrte ich schon Ein Mal.

Dem würdigeren Feinde, oh meine Freunde, sollt ihr euch aufsparen: darum müßt ihr an Vielem vorübergehn, –

– sonderlich an vielem Gesindel, das euch in die Ohren lärmt von Volk und Völkern.

Haltet euer Auge rein von ihrem Für und Wider! Da gibt es viel Recht, viel Unrecht: wer da zusieht, wird zornig.

Dreinschaun, dreinhauen – das ist da Eins: darum geht weg in die Wälder und legt euer Schwert schlafen!

Geht *eure* Wege! Und laßt Volk und Völker die ihren gehn! – dunkle Wege wahrlich, auf denen auch nicht Eine Hoffnung mehr wetterleuchtet!

Mag da der Krämer herrschen, wo Alles, was noch glänzt – Krämer-Gold ist! Es ist die Zeit der Könige nicht mehr: was sich heute Volk heißt, verdient keine Könige.

to and fro and their ebb and flow—oh, how could the *highest soul* not have the worst parasites?

20.

O my brothers, am I, then, cruel? But I say: that which is falling should be given an extra push!

All things today are falling, falling apart: who'd want to hold them up? But I—I want to give them an extra push!

Are you familiar with the deep pleasure of rolling stones into steep chasms? These people of today: just watch them rolling into my chasms!

I am a prelude to better musicians, O my brothers! An example! *Follow* my example!

And if there's someone you can't teach how to fly, I tell you: teach him how to *fall faster!*

21.

I love the brave: but it's not enough to be a swashbuckler—you've also got to know whom to tangle with!

And there's often more bravery in controlling yourself and walking away: *in that way* you save yourself for a worthier enemy!

You should have only enemies whom you can hate, but not enemies who arouse your contempt: you must be proud of your enemy; I have already taught you that once.

O my friends, you should save yourself for a worthier enemy: therefore you must walk away from many situations—

Especially from a lot of rabble who din in your ears about the people and peoples.

Keep your eyes clear of their pro and con! There is much justice, much injustice in it: if you look on, you'll get angry.

To look on and to butt in, is all one; and so, depart for the forest and put your sword to bed!

Go *your* ways! And let the people and peoples go theirs: dark ways, truly, on which not even one more hope flashes fitfully!

Let the shopkeeper rule where all that still glitters is shopkeepers' gold! This is no longer the era of kings: that which calls itself a people today deserves no kings.

Seht doch, wie diese Völker jetzt selber den Krämern gleich tun: sie lesen sich die kleinsten Vorteile noch aus jedem Kehricht!

Sie lauern einander auf, sie lauern einander Etwas ab, – das heißen sie »gute Nachbarschaft«. Oh selige ferne Zeit, wo ein Volk sich sagte: »Ich will über Völker – *Herr* sein!«

Denn, meine Brüder: das Beste soll herrschen, das Beste *will* auch herrschen! Und wo die Lehre anders lautet, da – *fehlt* es am Besten.

22.

Wenn Die – Brot umsonst hätten, wehe! Wonach würden Die schrein! Ihr Unterhalt – das ist ihre rechte Unterhaltung; und sie sollen es schwer haben!

Raubtiere sind es: in ihrem »Arbeiten« – da ist auch noch Rauben, in ihrem »Verdienen« – da ist auch noch Überlisten! Darum sollen sie es schwer haben!

Bessere Raubtiere sollen sie also werden, feinere, klügere, *menschen-ähnlichere:* der Mensch nämlich ist das beste Raubtier.

Allen Tieren hat der Mensch schon ihre Tugenden abgeraubt: das macht, von allen Tieren hat es der Mensch am schwersten gehabt.

Nur noch die Vögel sind über ihm. Und wenn der Mensch noch fliegen lernte, wehe! *wohinauf* – würde seine Raublust fliegen!

23.

So will ich Mann und Weib: kriegstüchtig den Einen, gebärtüchtig das Andere, beide aber tanztüchtig mit Kopf und Beinen.

Und verloren sei uns der Tag, wo nicht Ein Mal getanzt wurde! Und falsch heiße uns jede Wahrheit, bei der es nicht Ein Gelächter gab!

24.

Euer Eheschließen: seht zu, daß es nicht ein schlechtes *Schließen* sei! Ihr schlosset zu schnell: *so folgt* daraus – Ehebrechen!

Und besser noch Ehebrechen als Ehe-biegen, Ehe-lügen! – So

Just see how these peoples now behave just like shopkeepers: they pick the slightest benefits to themselves out of every heap of refuse!

They lie in ambush for one another, they trick one another out of something—they call that "being good neighbors." Oh, that blessed long-ago time when a people used to say to itself: "I want to be *master* of other peoples!"

For, my brothers: the best shall rule, the best also *want* to rule! And wherever some doctrine says differently, the best are *lacking* there.

22.

If they had bread for nothing, woe! What would they yell for? Their sustenance is their real pastime—and they should have a hard time of it!

They're beasts of prey: their "working" is still predatory, too; their "earning" also means outsmarting! And so, they should have a hard time of it!

In that way they shall become better predators, shrewder, wiser, *more like human beings:* for man is the best predator.

Man has already stolen the virtues of all the animals: because, of all animals, man has had the hardest time of it.

Only the birds are still above him. And if man once learned how to fly, woe! How high wouldn't his predatory instincts fly!

23.

This is how I'd like man and woman to be: the man accomplished in warfare, the woman accomplished in childbearing, but both accomplished in dancing with head and legs.

And let that day be accounted lost to us on which there hasn't been even one dance! And let every truth be accounted false to us in which there hasn't been one occasion for laughter!

24.

Make sure your wedlocks aren't carelessly *locked!* You locked up too fast, and the *consequence* is adultery—the "breaking" of the marriage!

But even marriage-breaking is better than marriage-bending,

sprach mir ein Weib: »wohl brach ich die Ehe, aber zuerst brach die Ehe – mich!«

Schlimm-Gepaarte fand ich immer als die schlimmsten Rachsüchtigen: sie lassen es aller Welt entgelten, daß sie nicht mehr einzeln laufen.

Deswillen will ich, daß Redliche zueinander reden: »wir lieben uns: laßt uns *zusehn*, daß wir uns liebbehalten! Oder soll unser Versprechen ein Versehen sein?«

– »Gebt uns eine Frist und kleine Ehe, daß wir zusehen, ob wir zur großen Ehe taugen! Es ist ein großes Ding, immer zu Zwein zu sein!«

Also rate ich allen Redlichen; und was wäre denn meine Liebe zum Übermenschen und zu Allem, was kommen soll, wenn ich anders riete und redete!

Nicht nur fort euch zu pflanzen, sondern *hinauf* – dazu, oh meine Brüder, helfe euch der Garten der Ehe!

25.

Wer über alte Ursprünge weise wurde, siehe, der wird zuletzt nach Quellen der Zukunft suchen und nach neuen Ursprüngen. –

Oh meine Brüder, es ist nicht über lange, da werden *neue Völker* entspringen und neue Quellen hinab in neue Tiefen rauschen.

Das Erdbeben nämlich – das verschüttet viel Brunnen, das schafft viel Verschmachten: das hebt auch innre Kräfte und Heimlichkeiten ans Licht.

Das Erdbeben macht neue Quellen offenbar. Im Erdbeben alter Völker brechen neue Quellen aus.

Und wer da ruft: »Siehe hier ein Brunnen für viele Durstige, Ein Herz für viele Sehnsüchtige, Ein Wille für viele Werkzeuge«: – um Den sammelt sich ein *Volk*, das ist: viel Versuchende.

Wer befehlen kann, wer gehorchen muß – *Das wird da versucht!* Ach, mit welch langem Suchen und Raten und Mißraten und Lernen und Neu-Versuchen!

Die Menschen-Gesellschaft: die ist ein Versuch, so lehre ich's, – ein langes Suchen: sie sucht aber den Befehlenden! –

– ein Versuch, oh meine Brüder! Und *kein* »Vertrag«! Zerbrecht, zerbrecht mir solch Wort der Weich-Herzen und Halb- und Halben!

marriage-lies! A woman said to me: "Yes, I 'broke' my marriage, but first my marriage broke me!"

I have always found incompatible spouses to be the most vengeful people: they make the whole world pay for their inability to be lone wolves.

Therefore I want forthright people to tell each other: "We love each other: let's *make sure* that we stay in love! Or were the promises we made a big mistake?

"Give us a period of trial marriage so we can see whether we're suited to a real marriage! It's no small thing to be together always!"

That's my advice to all forthright people; and how could I love the more-than-man and all that is to come, if I advised and spoke differently?

O my brothers, let the garden of marriage help you not merely to procreate, but to create higher beings!

25.

The man who has gained wisdom with regard to old origins: behold, he will finally seek sources of the future and new origins.

O my brothers, before very long *new peoples* will arise, and new fountains will gush noisily into new depths.

For an earthquake obstructs many wells and causes great thirst, but it also brings inner strength and secrets to light.

An earthquake makes new fountains manifest. In the earthquake of old peoples new fountains gush forth.

And the man who calls: "Behold here a well for many who thirst, one heart for many who yearn, one will for many tools"—around that man, a *people* gathers; that is, those who make many experiments.

Those who can give orders, those who must obey: *that is what they are trying to find!* Ah, how time-consuming the quest, the success, the failure, the learning, and the new experiments!

Human society is an experiment—that is my doctrine—a long search: but it is searching for a man who can give orders!—

An experiment, O my brothers! Not a "contract!" I tell you to shatter, shatter those phrases of the softhearted and the half-and-half!

26.

Oh meine Brüder! Bei Welchen liegt doch die größte Gefahr aller Menschen-Zukunft? Ist es nicht bei den Guten und Gerechten? –

– als bei Denen, die sprechen und im Herzen fühlen: »wir wissen schon, was gut ist und gerecht, wir haben es auch; wehe Denen, die hier noch suchen!«

Und was für Schaden auch die Bösen tun mögen: der Schaden der Guten ist der schädlichste Schaden!

Und was für Schaden auch die Welt-Verleumder tun mögen: der Schaden der Guten ist der schädlichste Schaden.

Oh meine Brüder, den Guten und Gerechten sah einer Einmal ins Herz, der da sprach: »es sind die Pharisäer.« Aber man verstand ihn nicht.

Die Guten und Gerechten selber durften ihn nicht verstehen: ihr Geist ist eingefangen in ihr gutes Gewissen. Die Dummheit der Guten ist unergründlich klug.

Das aber ist die Wahrheit: Die Guten *müssen* Pharisäer sein, – sie haben keine Wahl!

Die Guten *müssen* Den kreuzigen, der sich seine eigne Tugend erfindet! Das *ist* die Wahrheit!

Der Zweite aber, der ihr Land entdeckte, Land, Herz und Erdreich der Guten und Gerechten: das war, der da fragte: »wen hassen sie am meisten?«

Den *Schaffenden* hassen sie am meisten: den, der Tafeln bricht und alte Werte, den Brecher – Den heißen sie Verbrecher.

Die Guten nämlich – die *können* nicht schaffen: die sind immer der Anfang vom Ende: –

– sie kreuzigen Den, der neue Werte auf neue Tafeln schreibt, sie opfern *sich* die Zukunft – sie kreuzigen alle Menschen-Zukunft!

Die Guten – die waren immer der Anfang vom Ende. –

27.

Oh meine Brüder, verstandet ihr auch dies Wort? Und was ich einst sagte vom »letzten Menschen«? – –

Bei Welchen liegt die größte Gefahr aller Menschen-Zukunft? Ist es nicht bei den Guten und Gerechten?

Zerbrecht, zerbrecht mir die Guten und Gerechten! – Oh meine Brüder, verstandet ihr auch dies Wort?

26.

O my brothers! In whom does the greatest peril to the entire future of humanity lie? Isn't it in the good and the just?—

They being the ones who say and feel in their heart: "We already know what is good and just, and we have it, too. Woe to those who are still looking for it around here!"

And, no matter what harm the evil may do, the harm done by the good is the most harmful harm!

And, no matter what harm the world-slanderers may do, the harm done by the good is the most harmful harm.

O my brothers, a man once looked into the heart of the good and the just, and he said: "They're the Pharisees." But he wasn't understood.

The good and the just themselves couldn't have understood him; their mind is imprisoned in their good conscience. The stupidity of the good is unfathomably clever.

But the truth is: the good *must* be Pharisees—they have no choice!

The good *must* crucify the man who invents his own virtue! That *is* the truth.

But the second man who discovered their land, the land, heart, and realm of the good and the just, was the man who asked: "Whom do they hate most?"

The *creative man* is the one they hate most, the man who breaks tablets and old values, the breaker—they call him lawbreaker.

For, you see, the good are *unable* to create: they are always the beginning of the end:

They crucify the man who inscribes new values on new tablets, they sacrifice the future to *themselves,* they crucify the entire future of mankind!

The good have always been the beginning of the end.

27.

O my brothers, have you understood this saying, as well? And what I once said about "the last man"?

In whom does the greatest peril lie to the entire future of humanity? Isn't it in the good and the just?

I tell you to shatter, shatter the good and the just! O my brothers, have you understood this saying, as well?

28.

Ihr flieht von mir? Ihr seid erschreckt? Ihr zittert vor diesem Worte?

Oh meine Brüder, als ich euch die Guten zerbrechen hieß und die Tafeln der Guten: da erst schiffte ich den Menschen ein auf seine hohe See.

Und nun erst kommt ihm der große Schrecken, das große Um-sich-Sehn, die große Krankheit, der große Ekel, die große See-Krankheit.

Falsche Küsten und falsche Sicherheiten lehrten euch die Guten; in Lügen der Guten wart ihr geboren und geborgen. Alles ist in den Grund hinein verlogen und verbogen durch die Guten.

Aber wer das Land »Mensch« entdeckte, entdeckte auch das Land »Menschen-Zukunft«. Nun sollt ihr mir Seefahrer sein, wackere, geduldsame!

Aufrecht geht mir beizeiten, oh meine Brüder, lernt aufrecht gehn! Das Meer stürmt: Viele wollen an euch sich wieder aufrichten.

Das Meer stürmt: Alles ist im Meere. Wohlan! Wohlauf! Ihr alten Seemanns-Herzen!

Was Vaterland! *Dorthin* will unser Steuer, wo unser *Kinder-Land* ist! Dorthinaus, stürmischer als das Meer, stürmt unsre große Sehnsucht! –

29.

»Warum so hart!« – sprach zum Diamanten einst die Küchen-Kohle; »sind wir denn nicht Nah-Verwandte?« –

Warum so weich? Oh meine Brüder, also frage *ich* euch: seid ihr denn nicht – meine Brüder?

Warum so weich, so weichend und nachgebend? Warum ist so viel Leugnung, Verleugnung in eurem Herzen? So wenig Schicksal in eurem Blicke?

Und wollt ihr nicht Schicksale sein und Unerbittliche: wie könntet ihr mit mir – siegen?

Und wenn eure Härte nicht blitzen und scheiden und zerschneiden will: wie könntet ihr einst mit mir – schaffen?

Die Schaffenden nämlich sind hart. Und Seligkeit muß es euch dünken, eure Hand auf Jahrtausende zu drücken wie auf Wachs, –

– Seligkeit, auf dem Willen von Jahrtausenden zu schreiben wie auf Erz, – härter als Erz, edler als Erz. Ganz hart ist allein das Edelste.

Diese neue Tafel, oh meine Brüder, stelle ich über euch: *werdet hart!* –

28.

You flee from me? You're frightened? You tremble at that saying?

O my brothers, when I bade you shatter the good and the tablets of the good, that is when I first set man sailing on his high seas.

And it is only now that the great fright befalls him, the great looking around, the great sickness, the great disgust, the great seasickness.

False coasts and false feelings of security were taught you by the good; you were born and sheltered in the lies of the good. Everything has been thoroughly distorted and twisted by the good.

But the man who discovered the land Humanity also discovered the land Future of Humanity. Now I want you to be seafarers, hearty and patient!

Walk upright early on, O my brothers, learn to walk upright! The sea is stormy: many men want to hoist themselves up again, leaning on you.

The sea is stormy: everything is at sea. All right! Perk up, you old sailor hearts!

What is fatherland? Our rudder longs to reach *that shore* where the *land of our children* lies! Our great longing, stormier than the sea, is directed stormily out there!

29.

"Why are you so hard?" the kitchen coal once asked the diamond. "Aren't we close relatives?"

"Why are you so soft?" O my brothers, that's what *I* ask *you*. Aren't you my brothers?

Why so soft, yielding, and pliant? Why is there so much negation and denial in your heart? So little destiny in your gaze?

And if you don't want to be destinies and inexorable men: how could you conquer along with me?

And if your hardness won't flash and sever and cut to bits: how could you create along with me some day?

For creators are hard. And you must consider it bliss to press your hand onto millennia as if onto wax—

Bliss to write on the will of millennia as if on bronze—harder than bronze, nobler than bronze. Only that which is most noble is thoroughly hard.

O my brothers, I hold up this new tablet to you: *"Become hard!"*

30.

Oh du mein Wille! Du Wende aller Not, du meine Notwendigkeit! Bewahre mich vor allen kleinen Siegen!

Du Schickung meiner Seele, die ich Schicksal heiße! Du In-mir! Über-mir! Bewahre und spare mich auf zu Einem großen Schicksale!

Und deine letzte Größe, mein Wille, spare dir für dein Letztes auf, – daß du unerbittlich bist *in* deinem Siege! Ach, wer unterlag nicht seinem Siege!

Ach, wessen Auge dunkelte nicht in dieser trunkenen Dämmerung! Ach, wessen Fuß taumelte nicht und verlernte im Siege – stehen! –

– Daß ich einst bereit und reif sei im großen Mittage: bereit und reif gleich glühendem Erze, blitzschwangrer Wolke und schwellendem Milch-Euter: –

– bereit zu mir selber und zu meinem verborgensten Willen: ein Bogen brünstig nach seinem Pfeile, ein Pfeil brünstig nach seinem Sterne: –

– ein Stern, bereit und reif in seinem Mittage, glühend, durchbohrt, selig vor vernichtenden Sonnen-Pfeilen: –

– eine Sonne selber und ein unerbittlicher Sonnen-Wille, zum Vernichten bereit im Siegen!

Oh Wille, Wende aller Not, du *meine* Notwendigkeit! Spare mich auf zu einem großen Siege! – –

Also sprach Zarathustra.

DER GENESENDE (The Convalescent): After a vision of his most profound idea, Zarathustra falls ill for a week. He realizes that man is the cruelest of animals, cruel even to himself: he invented hell. But a man's bad instincts are necessary for his improvement, and he is not yet bad enough—not yet ready to surpass himself. It is Zarathustra's hard lot to be the first to teach the eternal return. / VON DER GROßEN SEHNSUCHT (Of the Great Yearning): Zarathustra has made his soul clean, self-reliant, wise, and capacious; now it is yearning for the brighter future. /

30.

O my will! You point at which all need is left behind, you my necessity! Save me from all petty victories!

You mission of my soul which I call fate! You in-me! Over-me! Save me and keep me in readiness for one great fate!

And, my will, keep your ultimate greatness in reserve for your final effort, so that you are inexorable *in* your victory! Ah, who has not succumbed to his victory?

Ah, whose eyes haven't grown dark in that drunken twilight? Ah, whose feet haven't stumbled and, at the moment of victory, forgotten how to stand?

Let me be ready some day, ripe at the great noonday: ready and ripe like red-hot bronze, a cloud pregnant with lightning, and an udder swollen with milk—

Ready for myself and for my most deeply concealed will: a bow in hot desire for its arrow, an arrow in hot desire for its star—

A star, ready and ripe at its noonday, glowing, pierced, enraptured by annihilating arrows of the sun—

Myself a sun and an inexorable solar will, ready for annihilation as I conquer!

O will, point at which all need is left behind, you *my* necessity! Keep me in reserve for a great victory!

Thus spoke Zarathustra.

DAS ANDERE TANZLIED (The Second Dance Song): Zarathustra addresses Life as if it were a capricious girl who must dance to the beat of his whip. [A long section is written in rhyming prose.] Life replies that they should love each other because both of them are beyond good and evil. Zarathustra doesn't love Life enough, and a midnight bell makes him think of abandoning it/her. [There follows a first version of the "Oh Mensch!" song that recurs in the chapter "Das trunkne Lied" in Part Four (fully translated in this volume).]

Die sieben Siegel
(Oder: das Ja-und-Amen-Lied)

1.

Wenn ich ein Wahrsager bin und voll jenes wahrsagerischen Geistes,
der auf hohem Joche zwischen zwei Meeren wandelt, –

zwischen Vergangenem und Zukünftigem als schwere Wolke wandelt, – schwülen Niederungen feind und Allem, was müde ist und
nicht sterben noch leben kann:

zum Blitze bereit im dunklen Busen und zum erlösenden
Lichtstrahle, schwanger von Blitzen, die Ja! sagen, Ja! lachen, zu
wahrsagerischen Blitzstrahlen: –

– selig aber ist der also Schwangere! Und wahrlich, lange muß als
schweres Wetter am Berge hängen, wer einst das Licht der Zukunft
zünden soll! –

Oh wie sollte ich nicht nach der Ewigkeit brünstig sein und nach
dem hochzeitlichen Ring der Ringe – dem Ring der Wiederkunft!

Nie noch fand ich das Weib, von dem ich Kinder mochte, es sei
denn dieses Weib, das ich liebe: denn ich liebe dich, oh Ewigkeit!

Denn ich liebe dich, oh Ewigkeit!

2.

Wenn mein Zorn je Gräber brach, Grenzsteine rückte und alte Tafeln
zerbrochen in steile Tiefen rollte:

Wenn mein Hohn je vermoderte Worte zerblies, und ich wie ein
Besen kam den Kreuzspinnen und als Fegewind alten verdumpften
Grabkammern:

Wenn ich je frohlockend saß, wo alte Götter begraben liegen, welt-
segnend, weltliebend neben den Denkmalen alter Welt-Verleumder: –

– denn selbst Kirchen und Gottes-Gräber liebe ich, wenn der
Himmel erst reinen Auges durch ihre zerbrochnen Decken blickt;
gern sitze ich gleich Gras und rotem Mohne auf zerbrochnen
Kirchen –

Oh wie sollte ich nicht nach der Ewigkeit brünstig sein und nach
dem hochzeitlichen Ring der Ringe – dem Ring der Wiederkunft?

The Seven Seals
(Or: The Yea and Amen Song)

1.

If I am a soothsayer, and filled with that prophetic spirit which roams the high pass between two seas—

Roams between the past and the future like a heavy cloud—hostile to sultry hollows and all that is weary but can neither live nor die:

Ready in my dark bosom to emit lightning and the redeeming ray of light, pregnant with lightnings that say "yea," laugh "yea," prophetic flashes of lightning—

And blissful is the one pregnant in that fashion! And, truly, one must cling to the mountain as a heavy stormcloud a long time, if one is some day to ignite the light of the future!—

Oh, how could I fail to yearn ardently for eternity and the wedding-ring of rings: the ring of eternal return!

Never yet have I found a woman from whom I wanted children, except for this woman that I love: for I love you, O eternity!

For I love you, O eternity!

2.

If my wrath has ever broken open graves, moved boundary stones, and sent old shattered tablets rolling into steep chasms;

If my scorn has ever blown apart mildewed words and I have come to cross-spiders as a broom and as a sweeping wind to old, musty mausolea;

If I have ever sat and rejoiced where old gods lie buried, blessing the world and loving the world beside the monuments of old world-slanderers—

(For I love even churches and gods' graves as soon as the sky peers through their shattered roofs with a pure eyes; I like to sit on shattered churches like grass and red poppies)—

Oh, how could I fail to yearn ardently for eternity and the wedding-ring of rings: the ring of eternal return!

Nie noch fand ich das Weib, von dem ich Kinder mochte, es sei
denn dieses Weib, das ich liebe: denn ich liebe dich, oh Ewigkeit!
Denn ich liebe dich, oh Ewigkeit!

3.

Wenn je ein Hauch zu mir kam vom schöpferischen Hauche und von
jener himmlischen Not, die noch Zufälle zwingt, Sternen-Reigen zu
tanzen:

Wenn ich je mit dem Lachen des schöpferischen Blitzes lachte,
dem der lange Donner der Tat grollend, aber gehorsam nachfolgt:

Wenn ich je am Göttertisch der Erde mit Göttern Würfel spielte,
daß die Erde bebte und brach und Feuerflüsse heraufschnob: –

– denn ein Göttertisch ist die Erde, und zitternd von
schöpferischen neuen Worten und Götter-Würfen: –

Oh wie sollte ich nicht nach der Ewigkeit brünstig sein und
nach dem hochzeitlichen Ring der Ringe – dem Ring der Wiederkunft?

Nie noch fand ich das Weib, von dem ich Kinder mochte, es sei
denn dieses Weib, das ich liebe: denn ich liebe dich, oh Ewigkeit!
Denn ich liebe dich, oh Ewigkeit!

4.

Wenn ich je vollen Zuges trank aus jenem schäumenden Würz- und
Mischkruge, in dem alle Dinge gut gemischt sind:

Wenn meine Hand je Fernstes zum Nächsten goß, und Feuer zu
Geist und Lust zu Leid und Schlimmstes zum Gütigsten:

Wenn ich selber ein Korn bin von jenem erlösenden Salze, welches
macht, daß alle Dinge im Mischkruge gut sich mischen: –

– denn es gibt ein Salz, das Gutes mit Bösem bindet; und auch das
Böseste ist zum Würzen würdig und zum letzten Überschäumen: –

Oh wie sollte ich nicht nach der Ewigkeit brünstig sein und nach
dem Hochzeitlichen Ring der Ringe – dem Ring der Wiederkunft?

Nie noch fand ich das Weib, von dem ich Kinder mochte, es sei
denn dieses Weib, das ich liebe: denn ich liebe dich, oh Ewigkeit!
Denn ich liebe dich, oh Ewigkeit!

Never yet have I found a woman from whom I wanted children, except for this woman that I love: for I love you, O eternity!

For I love you, O eternity!

3.

If ever there has reached me a breath of the creative breath and of that heavenly distress that compels even chance to perform starry round-dances;

If I have ever laughed with the laughter of the creative lightning that is followed growlingly, but obediently, by the long thunder of the deed;

If I have ever played dice with gods at the earth's divine table, so that the earth quaked and broke open and snorted up rivers of fire—

(For the earth is a divine table, trembling with creative new words and divine throws of the dice)—

Oh, how could I fail to yearn ardently for eternity and the wedding-ring of rings: the ring of eternal return!

Never yet have I found a woman from whom I wanted children, except for this woman that I love: for I love you, O eternity!

For I love you, O eternity!

4.

If I have ever drunk a full draft from that foaming, spiced mixing vessel in which all things are well mixed;

If my hand has ever poured the farthest into the nearest, fire into spirit, pleasure into pain, and the worst into the kindliest;

If I myself am a grain of that redeeming salt which makes all things mix well in the vessel—

(For there is a salt that combines good and evil; and even the most evil is worthy to be a spice and cause the last foaming-over)—

Oh, how could I fail to yearn ardently for eternity and the wedding-ring of rings: the ring of eternal return!

Never yet have I found a woman from whom I wanted children, except for this woman that I love: for I love you, O eternity!

For I love you, O eternity!

5.

Wenn ich dem Meere hold bin und Allem, was Meeres-Art ist, und am holdesten noch, wenn es mir zornig widerspricht:

Wenn jene suchende Lust in mir ist, die nach Unentdecktem die Segel treibt, wenn eine Seefahrer-Lust in meiner Lust ist:

Wenn je mein Frohlocken rief: »die Küste schwand – nun fiel mir die letzte Kette ab – .

– das Grenzenlose braust um mich, weit hinaus glänzt mir Raum und Zeit, wohlan! wohlauf! altes Herz!« –

Oh wie sollte ich nicht nach der Ewigkeit brünstig sein und nach dem hochzeitlichen Ring der Ringe – dem Ring der Wiederkunft?

Nie noch fand ich das Weib, von dem ich Kinder mochte, es sei denn dieses Weib, das ich liebe: denn ich liebe dich, oh Ewigkeit!

Denn ich liebe dich, oh Ewigkeit!

6.

Wenn meine Tugend eines Tänzers Tugend ist, und ich oft mit beiden Füßen in gold-smaragdenes Entzücken sprang:

Wenn meine Bosheit eine lachende Bosheit ist, heimisch unter Rosenhängen und Lilien-Hecken:

– im Lachen nämlich ist alles Böse beieinander, aber heilig- und losgesprochen durch seine eigne Seligkeit: –

Und wenn das mein A und O ist, daß alles Schwere leicht, aller Leib Tänzer, aller Geist Vogel werde: und wahrlich, das ist mein A und O! –

Oh wie sollte ich nicht nach der Ewigkeit brünstig sein und nach dem hochzeitlichen Ring der Ringe – dem Ring der Wiederkunft?

Nie noch fand ich das Weib, von dem ich Kinder mochte, es sei denn dieses Weib, das ich liebe: denn ich liebe dich, oh Ewigkeit!

Denn ich liebe dich, oh Ewigkeit!

7.

Wenn ich je stille Himmel über mir ausspannte und mit eignen Flügeln in eigne Himmel flog:

Wenn ich spielend in tiefen Licht-Fernen schwamm und meiner Freiheit Vogel-Weisheit kam: –

5.

If I am fond of the sea and everything sealike, and indeed most fond
when it contradicts me angrily;

If there is that questing pleasure in me which drives its sails on toward the undiscovered; if there is a seafarer's pleasure in my pleasure;

If my jubilation has ever cried: "The coast is out of sight; now my
last chain has fallen from me;

"The boundless roars around me, space and time are gleaming at
me far out there; all right, perk up, old heart!"—

Oh, how could I fail to yearn ardently for eternity and the wedding-
ring of rings: the ring of eternal return!

Never yet have I found a woman from whom I wanted children, except for this woman that I love: for I love you, O eternity!

For I love you, O eternity!

6.

If my virtue is the virtue of a dancer, and I have often leapt with both
feet into gold-emerald rapture;

If my malice is a laughing malice, at home among banks of roses
and hedges of lilies—

(For in laughter all evil is together, but sanctified and absolved by
its own bliss)—

And if my alpha and omega is that everything heavy should become
light, every body should become a dance, and all spirit should become
a bird (and truly, that is my alpha and omega!)—

Oh, how could I fail to yearn ardently for eternity and the wedding-
ring of rings: the ring of eternal return!

Never yet have I found a woman from whom I wanted children, except for this woman that I love: for I love you, O eternity!

For I love you, O eternity!

7.

If I have ever spread out quiet skies above me and flown into my own
heaven on my own wings;

If I have ever floated playfully in deep distances of light, and my
freedom's bird-wisdom came—

– so aber spricht Vogel-Weisheit: »Siehe, es gibt kein Oben, kein Unten! Wirf dich umher, hinaus, zurück, du Leichter! Singe! sprich nicht mehr!

– sind alle Worte nicht für die Schweren gemacht? Lügen dem Leichten nicht alle Worte! Singe! sprich nicht mehr!«

Oh wie sollte ich nicht nach der Ewigkeit brünstig sein und nach dem hochzeitlichen Ring der Ringe – dem Ring der Wiederkunft?

Nie noch fand ich das Weib, von dem ich Kinder mochte, es sei denn dieses Weib, das ich liebe: denn ich liebe dich, oh Ewigkeit!

Denn ich liebe dich, oh Ewigkeit!

And bird-wisdom speaks as follows: "Behold, there's no above or below! Toss yourself around, forward, backward, you weightless one! Sing, no longer speak!

"Aren't all words made for heavy ones? Don't all words lie to the lightweight? Sing, no longer speak!"—

Oh, how could I fail to yearn ardently for eternity and the wedding-ring of rings: the ring of eternal return!

Never yet have I found a woman from whom I wanted children, except for this woman that I love: for I love you, O eternity!

For I love you, O eternity!

VIERTER UND LETZTER TEIL

Das Honig-Opfer

– Und wieder liefen Monde und Jahre über Zarathustras Seele, und er achtete dessen nicht; sein Haar aber wurde weiß. Eines Tages, als er auf einem Steine vor seiner Höhle saß und still hinausschaute – man schaut aber dort auf das Meer hinaus, und hinweg über gewundene Abgründe –, da gingen seine Tiere nachdenklich um ihn herum und stellten sich endlich vor ihn hin.

»Oh Zarathustra«, sagten sie, »schaust du wohl aus nach deinem Glücke?« – »Was liegt am Glücke!« antwortete er, »ich trachte lange nicht mehr nach Glücke, ich trachte nach meinem Werke.« – »Oh Zarathustra«, redeten die Tiere abermals, »Das sagst du als Einer, der des Guten übergenug hat. Liegst du nicht in einem himmelblauen See von Glück?« – »Ihr Schalks-Narren«, antwortete Zarathustra und lächelte, »wie gut wähltet ihr das Gleichnis! Aber ihr wißt auch, daß mein Glück schwer ist, und nicht wie eine flüssige Wasserwelle: es drängt mich und will nicht von mir, und tut gleich geschmolzenem Peche.« –

Da gingen die Tiere wieder nachdenklich um ihn herum und stellten sich dann abermals vor ihn hin. »Oh Zarathustra«, sagten sie, »daher also kommt es, daß du selber immer gelber und dunkler wirst, obschon dein Haar weiß und flächsern aussehen will? Siehe doch, du sitzest in deinem Peche!« – »Was sagt ihr da, meine Tiere«, sagte Zarathustra und lachte dazu, »wahrlich, ich lästerte, als ich von Peche sprach. Wie mir geschieht, so geht es allen Früchten, die reif werden. Es ist der *Honig* in meinen Adern, der mein Blut dicker und auch meine Seele stiller macht.« – »So wird es sein, oh Zarathustra«, antworteten die Tiere und drängten sich an ihn: »willst du aber nicht heute auf einen hohen Berg steigen? Die Luft ist rein, und man sieht heute mehr von der Welt als jemals.« – »Ja, meine Tiere«, antwortete er, »ihr ratet trefflich und mir nach dem Herzen: ich will heute auf

182

FOURTH AND LAST PART

The Honey Offering

—And again months and years passed over Zarathustra's soul, and he paid no heed to this; but his hair turned white. One day, as he sat on a stone outside his cave and silently gazed ahead of him—the view there is out to sea, across tortuous chasms—his animals moved around him meditatively and finally came to a stop in front of him.

"O Zarathustra," they said, "are you looking for your happiness?" "What is there to happiness?" he replied. "For some time now I have no longer thought about happiness; I think about my task." "O Zarathustra," said the animals again, "you speak that way since you're a man with an overabundance of good things. Aren't you afloat on a sky-blue sea of happiness?" "You rogues and fools," Zarathustra replied with a smile, "how well you chose the metaphor! But you also know that my happiness is heavy, and not like a liquid wave of water: it presses in on me, and won't let me go, and acts like melted pitch."

Then the animals moved meditatively around him again and then once more came to a stop in front of him. "O Zarathustra," they said, "so *that's* the reason you're becoming yellower and darker all the time, even though your hair looks white and flaxen? You see, you're sitting in your pitch!"[20] "What are you saying there, my animals?" said Zarathustra, laughing. "Truly, I blasphemed when I mentioned pitch. What's happening to me befalls every fruit that ripens. It's the *honey* in my veins that makes my blood thicker and also my soul quieter." "That's probably it, O Zarathustra," replied the animals as they crowded in on him, "but won't you climb a high mountain today? The air is clear, and more of the world can be seen than ever." "Yes, my animals," he replied, "your advice is excellent and after my own heart: today I shall climb a high mountain! But see to it that I have access to

---

20. Colloquially, *Pech* also means "hard luck."

einen hohen Berg steigen! Aber sorgt, daß dort Honig mir zur Hand
sei, gelber, weißer, guter, eisfrischer Waben-Goldhonig. Denn wisset,
ich will droben das Honig-Opfer bringen.« –

Als Zarathustra aber oben auf der Höhe war, sandte er die Tiere
heim, die ihn geleitet hatten, und fand, daß er nunmehr allein sei: –
da lachte er aus ganzem Herzen, sah sich um und sprach also:

Daß ich von Opfern sprach und Honig-Opfern, eine List war's nur
meiner Rede und wahrlich, eine nützliche Torheit! Hier oben darf ich
schon freier reden als vor Einsiedler-Höhlen und Einsiedler-Haustieren.

Was opfern! Ich verschwende, was mir geschenkt wird, ich
Verschwender mit tausend Händen: wie dürfte ich Das noch –
Opfern heißen!

Und als ich nach Honig begehrte, begehrte ich nur nach Köder und
süßem Seime und Schleime, nach dem auch Brummbären und wunderliche mürrische böse Vögel die Zunge lecken:

– nach dem besten Köder, wie er Jägern und Fischfängern nottut.
Denn wenn die Welt wie ein dunkler Tierwald ist und aller wilden
Jäger Lustgarten, so dünkt sie mich noch mehr und lieber ein ab-
gründliches reiches Meer,

– ein Meer voll bunter Fische und Krebse, nach dem es auch
Götter gelüsten möchte, daß sie an ihm zu Fischern würden und zu
Netz-Auswerfern: so reich ist die Welt an Wunderlichem, großem und
kleinem!

Sonderlich die Menschen-Welt, das Menschen-Meer: – nach *dem*
werfe ich nun meine goldene Angelrute aus und spreche: tue dich auf,
du Menschen-Abgrund!

Tue dich auf und wirf mir deine Fische und Glitzer-Krebse zu! Mit
meinem besten Köder ködere ich mir heute die wunderlichsten
Menschen-Fische!

– mein Glück selber werfe ich hinaus in alle Weiten und Fernen,
zwischen Aufgang, Mittag und Niedergang, ob nicht an meinem
Glücke viele Menschen-Fische zerrn und zappeln lernen.

Bis sie, anbeißend an meine spitzen verborgenen Haken, hinauf
müssen in *meine* Höhe, die buntesten Abgrund-Gründlinge zu dem
boshaftigsten aller Menschen-Fischfänger.

Der nämlich bin ich von Grund und Anbeginn, ziehend, her-
anziehend, hinaufziehend, aufziehend, ein Zieher, Züchter und
Zuchtmeister, der sich nicht umsonst einstmals zusprach: »Werde, der
du bist!«

Also mögen nunmehr die Menschen zu mir *hinauf*kommen: denn

honey there, yellow, white, good, cool and fresh golden honey from the comb. For I'll have you know that I intend to make the honey offering up there."

But when Zarathustra was up on the heights, he sent home the animals, which had escorted him, and found that he was now alone. Then he laughed wholeheartedly, looked around, and spoke as follows:

"My speaking of offerings and honey offerings was merely a ruse in my speech and, truly, a useful piece of folly! Up here I may speak more freely than outside hermits' caves and in front of hermits' pets.

"Why make offerings? I squander all that I am given, I squander with a thousand hands. How could I go and call that 'making offerings'?

"And when I asked for honey, I was merely asking for bait, for sweet, sticky, smeary stuff for which even bruins and odd, sullen, malicious birds hanker:

"For the best bait, such as hunters and fishermen need. For, if the world is a dark, animal-filled forest and the pleasure grounds of every wild hunter, I consider it something more: rather, an unfathomable, rich sea—

"A sea full of multicolored fish and crustacea, which can whet the appetite of even gods, so that, beside it, they become anglers and casters of nets: so rich is the world in strange things great and small!

"Especially the world of man, the sea of man: into *it* I now cast the line from my golden fishing rod and say: 'Open, you abyss of mankind!

"'Open and fling me your fish and glittering crustacea! Today, with my best bait, I shall lure the oddest of human fish!'

"I'm casting my happiness itself into every distant corner, between rising, noonday, and setting, to see whether many human fish won't learn how to tug and wriggle on the line of my happiness.

"Until, biting at my sharp hidden hook, they must ascend to *my* heights: the most motley abyssal gudgeons to the most malicious of all fishers of men.

"For *that's* who I've been from the very outset: pulling, drawing higher, drawing up to me, bringing up, a puller, breeder, and disciplinarian, who once urged himself, not in vain: 'Become the man you are!'

"And so, from now on, let the people come *up here* to me: for I still

noch warte ich der Zeichen, daß es Zeit sei zu meinem Niedergange, noch gehe ich selber nicht unter, wie ich muß, unter Menschen.

Dazu warte ich hier, listig und spöttisch auf hohen Bergen, kein Ungeduldiger, kein Geduldiger, vielmehr Einer, der auch die Geduld verlernt hat, – weil er nicht mehr »duldet«.

Mein Schicksal nämlich läßt mir Zeit: es vergaß mich wohl? Oder sitzt es hinter einem großen Steine im Schatten und fängt Fliegen?

Und wahrlich, ich bin ihm gut darob, meinem ewigen Schicksale, daß es mich nicht hetzt und drängt und mir Zeit zu Possen läßt und Bosheiten: also daß ich heute zu einem Fischfange auf diesen hohen Berg stieg.

Fing wohl je ein Mensch auf hohen Bergen Fische? Und wenn es auch eine Torheit ist, was ich hier oben will und treibe: besser noch Dies, als daß ich da unten feierlich würde vor Warten und grün und gelb –

– ein gespreizter Zornschnauber vor Warten, ein heiliger Heule-Sturm aus Bergen, ein Ungeduldiger, der in die Täler hinabruft: »Hört, oder ich peitsche euch mit der Geißel Gottes!«

Nicht daß ich solchen Zürnern darob gram würde: zum Lachen sind sie mir gut genug! Ungeduldig müssen sie schon sein, diese großen Lärmtrommeln, welche heute oder niemals zu Worte kommen!

Ich aber und mein Schicksal – wir reden nicht zum Heute, wir reden auch nicht zum Niemals: wir haben zum Reden schon Geduld und Zeit und Überzeit. Denn einst muß er doch kommen und darf nicht vorübergehn.

Wer muß einst kommen und darf nicht vorübergehn? Unser großer Hazar, das ist unser großes fernes Menschen-Reich, das Zarathustra-Reich von tausend Jahren –

– Wie ferne mag solche »Ferne« sein? was geht's mich an! Aber darum steht es mir doch nicht minder fest –, mit beiden Füßen stehe ich sicher auf diesem Grunde,

– auf einem ewigen Grunde, auf hartem Urgesteine, auf diesem höchsten härtesten Urgebirge, zu dem alle Winde kommen als zur Wetterscheide, fragend nach Wo? und Woher? und Wohinaus?

Hier lache, lache, meine helle heile Bosheit! Von hohen Bergen wirf hinab dein glitzerndes Spott-Gelächter! Ködere mit deinem Glitzern mir die schönsten Menschen-Fische!

Und was in allen Meeren *mir* zugehört, mein An-und-für-mich in allen Dingen – *Das* fische mir heraus, *Das* führe zu mir herauf: des warte ich, der boshaftigste aller Fischfänger.

Hinaus, hinaus, meine Angel! Hinein, hinab, Köder meines Glücks!

await the signs that it's time for my descent; not yet am I myself 'setting,' as I must, amid mankind.

"For that I wait here, a crafty mocker on high mountains, neither impatient nor patient, rather: one who has forgotten even patience—because he no longer 'undergoes' anything.

"You see, my fate grants me time: has it forgotten I exist? Or is it sitting behind a big rock in the shade, catching flies?

"And, truly, I'm grateful to it, that eternal fate of mine, for not hounding and dunning me, and for granting me time for tomfoolery and mischief, so that today I have climbed this high mountain to go fishing.

"Has anyone ever caught fish on high mountains? And even if it's a piece of folly, what I intend and what I'm doing up here, it's still better than if I were to become solemn down there from waiting, and yellow and green—

"A person pompous and irascible from waiting, a holy howling storm out of mountains, an impatient man calling down to the valleys: 'Listen, or I'll lash you with the scourge of God!'

"Not that I'd be cross with such irate people for acting that way: they're just good enough to hand me a laugh! They must surely be impatient, those big rattling drums, which must speak out today or never!

"But I and my fate don't speak to today, nor do we speak to never: before speaking we have patience and time and more than enough time. For some day 'he' must come and can't pass by.

"'Who' must come some day without passing by? Our great Hazar; that is, our great, distant empire of man, Zarathustra's thousand-year empire—

"How distant may that 'distance' be? What do I care!? For all that, it's no less of a certainty to me: I stand firmly on this basis with both feet—

"On an eternal basis, on hard primordial rock, on this loftiest and hardest ancient mountain range, to which every wind comes, as to the weather divide, asking: 'Where? Where from? Where to?'

"Here laugh, laugh, my bright, hale malice! Cast down your glittering laughter of mockery from high mountains! Lure for me with your glittering the loveliest human fish!

"And that which belongs to *me* in all seas, my most personal belongings among all things—fish *that* out for me! Lead *that* up here to me! That's what I await, I the most malicious of all fishermen.

"Outward, outward, my line! In, down, bait of my happiness! Drip

Träufle deinen süßesten Tau, mein Herzens-Honig! Beiße, meine
Angel, in den Bauch aller schwarzen Trübsal!

Hinaus, hinaus, mein Auge! Oh welche vielen Meere rings um
mich, welch dämmernde Menschen-Zukünfte! Und über mir – welch
rosenrote Stille! Welch entwölktes Schweigen!

DER NOTSCHREI (The Cry of Distress): Back at his cave on the following day, Zarathustra is startled by the sudden appearance of the pessimistic, nihilistic soothsayer he had once met. As his guest predicts a
new adventure for him, Zarathustra hears a cry for help; his compassion
will be his final sin. The cry has come from "the higher human being,"
whom Zarathustra will seek in the forests while the soothsayer waits for
him. / GESPRÄCH MIT DEN KÖNIGEN (Conversation with the Kings): [In
this chapter and the six that follow it, Zarathustra, continuing to seek
the man who cried for help, meets a series of moderately "higher men"
whom he sends to his cave, as guests, to await his return.] He meets two
kings who, with a donkey, are fleeing from all the falsity of their existence and are also seeking a person loftier than themselves. They have
heard of Zarathustra and appreciate his praise of war. / DER BLUTEGEL
(The Leech): Zarathustra literally stumbles upon a recumbent man who
draws his bleeding arm out of swamp water. The man, who compares
Zarathustra to a·"leech of conscience," is the "intellectually conscientious man" [a one-sided scholar or scientist], specializing in leeches'
brains. / DER ZAUBERER (The Sorcerer): An old man, shivering convul-
sively, recites a long poem in which he says he is being tortured by an
unknown god, whom he defies but can't live without. It's the sorcerer,
who then says he has only been playing a part, that of "the intellectual
penitent" (ascetic), to test Zarathustra. But he may have been in
earnest, because he always lies and pretends to be greater than he is. /
AUßER DIENST (Unemployed): Zarathustra meets the last pope, who
had served the old God until God died. Seeking the pious hermit of Part
One (now dead), he has lost his way. The old God was hidden and
unloving; vengeful when young, he became a doddering, softhearted
grandmother who choked to death on compassion. / DER HÄßLICHSTE
MENSCH (The Ugliest Man): In a desolate valley Zarathustra meets a repulsive man—the murderer of God, the man who thus took revenge on
the perpetual witness to his thoughts. He is now fleeing from people's
compassion, and he warns Zarathustra against showing pity. / DER FREI-
WILLIGE BETTLER (The Voluntary Beggar): Zarathustra meets a kindly
preacher addressing a group of cows, from whom he wanted to learn the
secret of earthly happiness: how to ruminate. He is the archetypical formerly rich man who cast away his wealth to lead an Early Christian life;
but the paupers he sought as companions proved to be low rabble (as
the wealthy are, too). / DER SCHATTEN (The Shadow): Zarathustra is
pursued by his "shadow," an aimless wanderer and "free spirit" who

your sweetest dew, honey of my heart! Bite, my line, into the belly of every black tribulation!

"Outward, outward, my eyes! Oh, how many seas all around me, what dawning human futures! And above me—what a rose-red calm! What a cloudless silence!"

---

follows him everywhere, emulating his disregard for conventional morality but conscious of his own weakness. / MITTAGS (Noon): Zarathustra dozes beside a grapevine in the noonday heat, and meditates on life, death, and eternity. / DIE BEGRÜBUNG (The Greeting): On his way home, Zarathustra hears the cry of distress, uttered by several voices, coming from his own cave. The "higher man"—comprised of all his guests—is right there! Zarathustra greets them, bidding them not to despair. They are glad to have found him; better men even than themselves are on their way to him. Zarathustra deems that his guests are not "high" enough for him; they still have plebeian traits, and are merely transitional figures. / DAS ABENDMAHL (The [Last] Supper; or, Communion): The sorcerer asks for food and wine. The kings have brought wine on their donkey, but there is no bread; Zarathustra supplies lamb, fruit, roots, and nuts (this is too rich for the abstemious beggar). VOM HÖHEREN MENSCHEN (Of the Higher Human Being): At supper, the "higher man" is the topic of conversation. The rabble, who believe all men are equal, can't be helped. God's death has left room for the "more-than-man." Those who live for the day must be superseded. We must be brave, tough-minded, able to bear suffering, aware of our limitations, distrustful, independent, egoistic, clean but not unnaturally virtuous, willing to make mistakes, optimistic, exalted, lightfooted dancers. / DAS LIED DER SCHWERMUT (The Song of Melancholy): When Zarathustra steps out of his cave for fresh air, the pessimistic sorcerer sings a long song of melancholy: the wisdom-seeker is merely a deceived poet and fool with primitive instincts. / VON DER WISSENSCHAFT (Of Scholarship and Science): The "intellectually conscientious" man berates the secretly lustful sorcerer; he himself seeks security in knowledge. Science, he says, originated in fear of the uncertain. Zarathustra, returning, refutes him, declaring that all of human progress has come from courage. / UNTER TÖCHTERN DER WÜSTE (Among Daughters of the Desert): At the time of dessert, to cheer up the guests, who are still gloomy from the sorcerer's song, the wanderer (Zarathustra's "shadow") sings a song he once wrote when he was in the warm, bright Near Eastern desert, and which he sang to the local girls. His long song is called "The Desert Grows; Woe to Him Who Conceals Deserts Within Him": the oasis is hospitable to him, as the whale's belly was to Jonah; he is like a date yearning for the girls' bite; the palm tree is like a supple female dancer, but with one leg lost; as a European he can't help roaring words of virtue, dignity, and morality.

Die Erweckung

1.

Nach dem Liede des Wandrers und Schattens wurde die Höhle mit einem Male voll Lärmens und Lachens: und da die versammelten Gäste alle zugleich redeten, und auch der Esel, bei einer solchen Ermutigung, nicht mehr still blieb, überkam Zarathustra ein kleiner Widerwille und Spott gegen seinen Besuch: ob er sich gleich ihrer Fröhlichkeit erfreute. Denn sie dünkte ihm ein Zeichen der Genesung. So schlüpfte er hinaus ins Freie und sprach zu seinen Tieren.

»Wo ist nun ihre Not hin?« sprach er, und schon atmete er selber von seinem kleinen Überdrusse auf, – »bei mir verlernten sie, wie mich dünkt, das Notschrein!

– wenn auch, leider, noch nicht das Schrein.« Und Zarathustra hielt sich die Ohren zu, denn eben mischte sich das I-A des Esels wunderlich mit dem Jubel-Lärm dieser höheren Menschen.

»Sie sind lustig«, begann er wieder, »und wer weiß? vielleicht auf ihres Wirtes Unkosten; und lernten sie von mir lachen, so ist es doch nicht *mein* Lachen, das sie lernten.

Aber was liegt daran! Es sind alte Leute: sie genesen auf ihre Art, sie lachen auf ihre Art; meine Ohren haben schon Schlimmeres erduldet und wurden nicht unwirsch.

Dieser Tag ist ein Sieg: er weicht schon, er flieht, *der Geist der Schwere,* mein alter Erzfeind! Wie gut will dieser Tag enden, der so schlimm und schwer begann!

Und enden *will* er. Schon kommt der Abend: über das Meer her reitet er, der gute Reiter! Wie er sich wiegt, der Selige, Heimkehrende, in seinen purpurnen Sätteln!

Der Himmel blickt klar dazu, die Welt liegt tief: oh all ihr Wunderlichen, die ihr zu mir kamt, es lohnt sich schon, bei mir zu leben!«

Also sprach Zarathustra. Und wieder kam da das Geschrei und Gelächter der höheren Menschen aus der Höhle: da begann er von neuem.

»Sie beißen an, mein Köder wirkt, es weicht auch ihnen ihr Feind, der Geist der Schwere. Schon lernen sie über sich selber lachen: höre ich recht?

Meine Manns-Kost wirkt, mein Saft- und Kraft-Spruch: und

The Awakening

1.

After the song of the wanderer and shadow the cave all at once was filled with noise and laughter; since all the assembled guests were talking at the same time, and even the donkey, thus encouraged, no longer kept silent, Zarathustra was affected by a slight mocking repugnance to his guests, even though he rejoiced in their merriment, which he considered a sign of convalescence. And so he slipped outdoors and spoke to his animals.

"What has become of their distress?" he said, and by now he was feeling relief from his slight vexation. "In my home, I think, they've forgotten how to shout for help!

—"But, unfortunately, not yet how to shout." And Zarathustra covered his ears, because just then the donkey's hee-haw was oddly blended with the jubilant noises of those higher men.

"They're jolly," he resumed, "and who knows? Maybe at their host's expense. And if they learned from me how to laugh, still it wasn't *my* laughter that they learned.

"But what does that matter? They're old people: they're convalescing in their fashion, they're laughing in their fashion; my ears have already put up with worse without becoming surly.

"This day is a victory; he's already yielding, he's fleeing, *that spirit of gravity*, my old archenemy! How well this day will end, which began so badly and heavily!

"And it *will* end. The evening is already coming; it's riding this way across the sea, like a good horseman! How it rocks, the blissful, homecoming evening, on its purple saddles!

"The sky looks on brightly, the world is deep: oh, all you odd people who have come to me, it's worthwhile now to live with me!"

Thus spoke Zarathustra. And again the shouting and laughter of the higher people issued from the cave; then he resumed speaking:

"They're biting; my bait is working, my charm for health and strength; and, truly, their enemy the spirit of gravity is succumbing to them, too. By now they're learning to laugh at themselves: am I hearing correctly?

"My masculine food is working, my charm for health and strength;

wahrlich, ich nährte sie nicht mit Bläh-Gemüsen! Sondern mit Krieger-Kost, mit Eroberer-Kost: neue Begierden weckte ich.

Neue Hoffnungen sind in ihren Armen und Beinen, ihr Herz streckt sich aus. Sie finden neue Worte, bald wird ihr Geist Mutwillen atmen.

Solche Kost mag freilich nicht für Kinder sein, noch auch für sehnsüchtige alte und junge Weibchen. Denen überredet man anders die Eingeweide; deren Arzt und Lehrer bin ich nicht.

Der *Ekel* weicht diesen höheren Menschen: wohlan! das ist mein Sieg. In meinem Reiche werden sie sicher, alle dumme Scham läuft davon, sie schütten sich aus.

Sie schütten ihr Herz aus, gute Stunden kehren ihnen zurück, sie feiern und käuen wieder, – sie werden *dankbar*.

Das nehme ich als das beste Zeichen: sie werden dankbar. Nicht lange noch, und sie denken sich Feste aus und stellen Denksteine ihren alten Freunden auf.

Es sind *Genesende!*« Also sprach Zarathustra fröhlich zu seinem Herzen und schaute hinaus; seine Tiere aber drängten sich an ihn und ehrten sein Glück und sein Stillschweigen.

2.

Plötzlich aber erschrak das Ohr Zarathustras: die Höhle nämlich, welche bisher voller Lärmens und Gelächters war, wurde mit Einem Male totenstill; – seine Nase aber roch einen wohlriechenden Qualm und Weihrauch, wie von brennenden Pinien-Zapfen.

»Was geschieht? Was treiben sie?« fragte er sich und schlich zum Eingange heran, daß er seinen Gästen, unvermerkt, zusehn könne. Aber, Wunder über Wunder! was mußte er da mit seinen eigenen Augen sehen!

»Sie sind alle wieder *fromm* geworden, sie *beten,* sie sind toll!« – sprach er und verwunderte sich über die Maßen. Und, fürwahr! Alle diese höheren Menschen, die zwei Könige, der Papst außer Dienst, der schlimme Zauberer, der freiwillige Bettler, der Wandrer und Schatten, der alte Wahrsager, der Gewissenhafte des Geistes und der häßlichste Mensch: sie lagen Alle gleich Kindern und gläubigen alten Weibchen auf den Knien und beteten den Esel an. Und eben begann der häßlichste Mensch zu gurgeln und zu schnauben, wie als ob etwas Unaussprechliches aus ihm heraus wolle; als er es aber wirklich bis zu Worten gebracht hatte, siehe, da war es eine fromme seltsame Litanei zur Lobpreisung des angebeteten und angeräucherten Esels. Diese Litanei aber klang also:

and, truly, I didn't feed them gassy vegetables, but warriors' food, conquerors' food; I awakened new desires.

"There are new hopes in their arms and legs, their heart is expanding. They're finding new words; soon their spirit will breathe sportiveness.

"Of course, such food may not be for children, or for females old and young sick with longing. *Their* bowels have to be convinced differently; I'm not *their* physician and teacher.

"*Disgust* is fleeing from these higher men. Good! That's my victory. In my realm they're becoming sure of themselves; all false modesty is leaving them; they're pouring themselves out.

"They're pouring their heart out; they're having good times again, they're celebrating and ruminating—they're becoming *grateful*.

"I take *that* as the best sign: they're becoming grateful. Before very long, they'll be devising holidays and setting up memorial stones to their old friends.

"They're *convalescing!*" Thus spoke Zarathustra cheerfully to his heart, looking into the distance, while his animals pressed close to him, honoring his happiness and his silence.

2.

But suddenly Zarathustra's ears were startled: for the cave, which had hitherto been filled with noise and laughter, suddenly became as still as death—but his nose smelled a fragrant vapor and incense, as of burning pinecones.

"What's going on? What are they up to?" he wondered, as he stole up to the entrance so he could watch his guests without being seen. But, wonder of wonders, what did he see with his own eyes?

"They've all become *pious* again, they're *praying*, they're crazy!" he said, in exceeding amazement. And indeed! All those higher men—the two kings, the unemployed pope, the evil sorcerer, the voluntary beggar, the wandering shadow, the old soothsayer, the intellectually conscientious man, and the ugliest man— were all on their knees like children or religious old women, and were worshipping the donkey. And just at that moment the ugliest man began to gurgle and snort as if something unspeakable were trying to make its way out of him; but when he had really formulated it in words, behold: it was a peculiar pious litany in praise of the worshipped and incense-perfumed donkey. And that litany went as follows:

Amen! Und Lob und Ehre und Weisheit und Dank und Preis und
Stärke sei unserm Gott, von Ewigkeit zu Ewigkeit!

– Der Esel aber schrie dazu I-A.

Er trägt unsere Last, er nahm Knechtsgestalt an, er ist geduldsam
von Herzen und redet niemals Nein; und wer seinen Gott liebt, der
züchtigt ihn.

– Der Esel aber schrie dazu I-A.

Er redet nicht: es sei denn, daß er zur Welt, die er schuf, immer Ja
sagt: also preist er seine Welt. Seine Schlauheit ist es, die nicht redet:
so bekömmt er selten unrecht.

– Der Esel aber schrie dazu I-A.

Unscheinbar geht er durch die Welt. Grau ist die Leib-Farbe, in
welche er seine Tugend hüllt. Hat er Geist, so verbirgt er ihn; Jedermann aber glaubt an seine langen Ohren.

– Der Esel aber schrie dazu I-A.

Welche verborgene Weisheit ist das, daß er lange Ohren trägt und
allein Ja und nimmer Nein sagt! Hat er nicht die Welt erschaffen nach
seinem Bilde, nämlich so dumm als möglich?

– Der Esel aber schrie dazu I-A.

Du gehst gerade und krumme Wege, es kümmert dich wenig, was
uns Menschen gerade oder krumm dünkt. Jenseits von Gut und Böse
ist dein Reich. Es ist deine Unschuld, nicht zu wissen, was Unschuld ist.

– Der Esel aber schrie dazu I-A.

Siehe doch, wie du Niemanden von dir stößest, die Bettler nicht,
noch die Könige. Die Kindlein lässest du zu dir kommen, und wenn
dich die bösen Buben locken, so sprichst du einfältiglich I-A.

– Der Esel aber schrie dazu I-A.

Du liebst Eselinnen und frische Feigen, du bist kein Kostverächter.
Eine Distel kitzelt dir das Herz, wenn du gerade Hunger hast. Darin
liegt eines Gottes Weisheit.

– Der Esel aber schrie dazu I-A.

Das Eselsfest

1.

An dieser Stelle der Litanei aber konnte Zarathustra sich nicht länger
bemeistern, schrie selber I-A, lauter noch als der Esel, und sprang mit-

"Amen! And praise and honor and wisdom and thanks and laudation and strength be to our god from eternity to eternity!"

And the donkey responded: "Hee-haw!"

"He bears our burden, he has assumed the guise of a servant, he is long-suffering of heart and never says no; and whoever loves his god, chastises him."

And the donkey responded: "Hee-haw!"

"He speaks not, except that to the world he created he always says yea:[21] thus he praises his world. It is shrewdness in him not to speak: in that way he's seldom wrong.

And the donkey responded: "Hee-haw!"

"He goes through the world inconspicuously. Gray is the body color in which he envelops his virtue. If he has wit, he conceals it; but everyone believes in his long ears."

And the donkey responded: "Hee-haw!"

"What occult wisdom it is to have long ears and to say only yea and never no! Didn't he create the world in his own image: that is, as stupid as possible?"

And the donkey responded: "Hee-haw!"

"You travel straight and crooked ways; it matters little to you what we men consider straight or crooked. Your kingdom is beyond good and evil. Your innocence consists in ignorance of what innocence is."

And the donkey responded: "Hee-haw!"

"Just see how you drive no one away from you, not beggars, not kings! You suffer the little children to come to you, and if scoundrels inveigle you, you say hee-haw in your simplicity."

And the donkey responded: "Hee-haw!"

"You like female donkeys and fresh figs, you have an omnivorous appetite. A thistle tickles your heart whenever you're hungry. Therein lies the wisdom of a god."

And the donkey responded: "Hee-haw!"

The Festival of the Donkey

1.

But at this point in the litany Zarathustra could no longer control himself; he himself shouted hee-haw, even more loudly than the donkey, and

---

21. In the German, the *Ja* sounds a great deal like the donkey's *I-A*.

ten unter seine toll gewordenen Gäste. »Aber was treibt ihr da, ihr Menschenkinder?« rief er, indem er die Betenden vom Boden emporriß. »Wehe, wenn euch jemand Anderes zusähe als Zarathustra:

Jeder würde urteilen, ihr wäret mit eurem neuen Glauben die ärgsten Gotteslästerer oder die törichtsten aller alten Weiblein!

Und du selber, du alter Papst, wie stimmt Das mit dir selber zusammen, daß du solchergestalt einen Esel hier als Gott anbetest?« –

»Oh Zarathustra«, antwortete der Papst, »vergib mir, aber in Dingen Gottes bin ich aufgeklärter noch als du. Und so ist's billig.

Lieber Gott also anbeten, in dieser Gestalt, als in gar keiner Gestalt! Denke über diesen Spruch nach, mein hoher Freund: du errätst geschwind, in solchem Spruch steckt Weisheit.

Der, welcher sprach ›Gott ist ein Geist‹ – der machte bisher auf Erden den größten Schritt und Sprung zum Unglauben: solch Wort ist auf Erden nicht leicht wieder gutzumachen!

Mein altes Herz springt und hüpft darob, daß es auf Erden noch Etwas anzubeten gibt. Vergib das, oh Zarathustra, einem alten frommen Papst-Herzen! –«

– »Und du«, sagte Zarathustra zu dem Wandrer und Schatten, »du nennst und wähnst dich einen freien Geist? Und treibst hier solchen Götzen- und Pfaffendienst?

Schlimmer, wahrlich, treibst du's hier noch als bei deinen schlimmen braunen Mädchen, du schlimmer neuer Gläubiger!«

»Schlimm genug«, antwortete der Wandrer und Schatten, »du hast recht: aber was kann ich dafür! Der alte Gott lebt wieder, oh Zarathustra, du magst reden, was du willst.

Der häßlichste Mensch ist an Allem schuld: der hat ihn wieder auferweckt. Und wenn er sagt, daß er ihn einst getötet habe: *Tod* ist bei Göttern immer nur ein Vorurteil.«

– »Und du«, sprach Zarathustra, »du schlimmer alter Zauberer, was tatest du! Wer soll, in dieser freien Zeit, fürderhin an dich glauben, wenn *du* an solche Götter-Eseleien glaubst?

Es war eine Dummheit, was du tatest; wie konntest du, du Kluger, eine solche Dummheit tun!«

»Oh Zarathustra«, antwortete der kluge Zauberer, »du hast recht, es war eine Dummheit, – sie ist mir auch schwer genug geworden.«

– »Und du gar«, sagte Zarathustra zu dem Gewissenhaften des Geistes, »erwäge doch und lege den Finger an deine Nase! Geht hier denn Nichts wider dein Gewissen? Ist dein Geist nicht zu reinlich für dies Beten und den Dunst dieser Betbrüder?«

»Es ist Etwas daran«, antwortete der Gewissenhafte und legte den

dashed into the midst of his maddened guests. "What are you carrying on here, people?" he called, while pulling the worshippers up from the floor. "Woe, if anyone other than Zarathustra were watching you!

"Anyone would judge that, with your new faith, you were the worst blasphemers of God or the most foolish of all old females!

"And you yourself, you aged pope, how does it befit you to worship a donkey here as God in this way?"

"O Zarathustra," the pope replied, "forgive me, but in divine matters I'm even more enlightened than you are. And that's only reasonable.

"It's better to worship God in this shape than in no shape at all! Think over this maxim, my lofty friend; you'll soon discern that there's wisdom in such a maxim.

"The man who said 'God is a spirit' took the greatest step and leap toward disbelief so far on earth: such a saying can't easily be atoned for on earth!

"My old heart skips and hops because there's still something on earth to worship. O Zarathustra, forgive an old, pious papal heart for this!"

"And you," Zarathustra said to the wandering shadow, "you call and imagine yourself a freethinker? And you perform such idolatry and popery here?

"Truly, you're carrying on even worse here than with your nasty brown-skinned girls, you nasty new believer!"

"Nasty enough," said the wandering shadow; "you're right, but how can I help it? The old God is alive again, O Zarathustra, however much you may deny it.

"The ugliest man is to blame for it all: he woke him up again. And if he says he killed him once: with gods, death is always merely a pre-assumption."

"And you," said Zarathustra, "you nasty old sorcerer, what have you done? Who, in these liberated times, will believe in you any more if *you* believe in such donkey gods?

"What you did was stupid; how could you, so clever, do something that stupid?"

"O Zarathustra," replied the clever sorcerer, "you're right, it was stupid—and it has become quite hard on me."

"And you of all people," Zarathustra said to the intellectually conscientious man, "just consider, and lay your finger alongside your nose! Doesn't any of this go against your conscience? Isn't your intellect too wholesome for this praying and the incense of these bigots?"

"There's something to it," the conscientious man replied, laying his

Finger an die Nase, »es ist Etwas an diesem Schauspiele, das meinem Gewissen sogar wohltut.

Vielleicht, daß ich an Gott nicht glauben darf: gewiß aber ist, daß Gott mir in dieser Gestalt noch am glaubwürdigsten dünkt.

Gott soll ewig sein, nach dem Zeugnisse der Frömmsten: wer so viel Zeit hat, läßt sich Zeit. So langsam und so dumm als möglich: *damit* kann ein Solcher es doch sehr weit bringen.

Und wer des Geistes zu viel hat, der möchte sich wohl in die Dumm- und Narrheit selber vernarren. Denke über dich selber nach, oh Zarathustra!

Du selber – wahrlich! auch du könntest wohl aus Überfluß und Weisheit zu einem Esel werden.

Geht nicht ein vollkommner Weiser gern auf den krümmsten Wegen? Der Augenschein lehrt es, oh Zarathustra – *dein* Augenschein!«

– »Und du selber zuletzt«, sprach Zarathustra und wandte sich gegen den häßlichsten Menschen, der immer noch auf dem Boden lag, den Arm zu dem Esel emporhebend (er gab ihm nämlich Wein zu trinken). »Sprich, du Unaussprechlicher, was hast du da gemacht!

Du dünkst mich verwandelt, dein Auge glüht, der Mantel des Erhabenen liegt um deine Häßlichkeit: *was* tatest du?

Ist es denn wahr, was Jene sagen, daß du ihn wieder aufwecktest? Und wozu? War er nicht mit Grund abgetötet und abgetan?

Du selber dünkst mich aufgeweckt: was tatest du? Was kehrtest *du* um? Was bekehrtest *du dich?* Sprich, du Unaussprechlicher!«

»Oh Zarathustra«, antwortete der häßlichste Mensch, »du bist ein Schelm!

Ob *Der* noch lebt oder wieder lebt oder gründlich tot ist, – wer von uns Beiden weiß Das am besten? Ich frage dich.

Eins aber weiß ich, – von dir selber lernte ich's einst, oh Zarathustra: wer am gründlichsten töten will, der *lacht.*

›Nicht durch Zorn, sondern durch Lachen tötet man‹ – so sprachst du einst. Oh Zarathustra, du Verborgener, du Vernichter ohne Zorn, du gefährlicher Heiliger, – du bist ein Schelm!«

2.

Da aber geschah es, daß Zarathustra verwundert über lauter solche Schelmen-Antworten, zur Tür seiner Höhle zurücksprang und, gegen alle seine Gäste gewendet, mit starker Stimme schrie:

finger alongside his nose, "there's something to this spectacle which actually makes my conscience feel good.

"Maybe I shouldn't believe in God; but one thing is certain: that in this shape I find God most deserving of belief.

"God is supposed to be eternal, as the most pious testify: someone with that much time gives himself time. As slow and stupid as possible: *in that manner* someone like that can go a long way.

"And a man with too much intellect is liable to become foolishly enamored of stupidity and folly. Just think about yourself, O Zarathustra!

"Yes, yourself! You, too, from a surplus of wisdom, could become a donkey.

"Doesn't a perfect sage readily follow the crookedest paths? A careful inspection teaches us so, O Zarathustra—*your* inspection!"

"And, finally, you," said Zarathustra, turning toward the ugliest man, who was still on the floor raising his arms to the donkey (you see, he was giving it wine to drink). "Speak, you unspeakable one, what have you done here?

"You look transformed to me, your eyes are blazing, the mantle of the lofty one is cloaking your ugliness: *what* did you do?

"Is is true, then, what those people say, that you woke him up again? But what for? Wasn't he killed off and abolished for a good reason?

"You, too, look reawakened to me: what did you do? Why did you *revert?* Why did you *reconvert?* Speak, you unspeakable one!"

"O Zarathustra," the ugliest man replied, "you're a rascal!

"Whether *he* is still alive, or alive again, or absolutely dead—which of us two knows that best? I ask you.

"But I know one thing; I once learned it from you yourself, O Zarathustra: the man who wants to do the most thorough job of killing, *laughs.*

"'We kill, not through anger, but through laughter': that's what you said once. O Zarathustra, you concealed one, you annihilator without anger, you dangerous saint—you're a rascal!"

2.

But then it came about that Zarathustra, amazed at hearing nothing but such rascally answers, dashed back to the doorway of his cave and, facing all his guests, shouted in a loud voice:

»Oh ihr Schalks-Narren allesamt, ihr Possenreißer! Was verstellt und versteckt ihr euch vor mir!

Wie doch einem Jeden von euch das Herz zappelte vor Lust und Bosheit, darob, daß ihr endlich einmal wieder wurdet wie die Kindlein, nämlich fromm, –

– daß ihr endlich wieder tatet wie Kinder tun, nämlich betetet, hände-faltetet und ›lieber Gott‹ sagtet!

Aber nun laßt mir *diese* Kinderstube, meine eigne Höhle, wo heute alle Kinderei zu Hause ist. Kühlt hier draußen euren heißen Kinder-Übermut und Herzenslärm ab!

Freilich: so ihr nicht werdet wie die Kindlein, so kommt ihr nicht in das Himmelreich. (Und Zarathustra zeigte mit den Händen nach Oben.)

Aber wir wollen auch gar nicht ins Himmelreich: Männer sind wir worden, – *so wollen wir das Erdenreich*.«

3.

Und noch einmal hob Zarathustra an zu reden. »Oh meine neuen Freunde«, sprach er, – »ihr Wunderlichen, ihr höheren Menschen, wie gut gefallt ihr mir nun, –

– seit ihr wieder fröhlich wurdet! Ihr seid wahrlich Alle aufgeblüht: mich dünkt, solchen Blumen, wie ihr seid, tun *neue Feste* Not,

– ein kleiner tapferer Unsinn, irgendein Gottesdienst und Eselsfest, irgendein alter fröhlicher Zarathustra-Narr, ein Brause-wind, der euch die Seelen hell bläst.

Vergeßt diese Nacht und dieses Eselsfest nicht, ihr höheren Menschen! *Das* erfandet ihr bei mir, Das nehme ich als gutes Wahr-zeichen, – solcherlei erfinden nur Genesende!

Und feiert ihr es abermals, dieses Eselsfest, tut's euch zuliebe, tut's auch mir zuliebe! Und zu *meinem* Gedächtnis!«

Also sprach Zarathustra.

"Oh, you rogues and fools one and all, you clowns! Why are you disguising yourselves and hiding from me?

"How the heart of each one of you danced for joy and malice because you had finally become like little children again: namely, pious—

"Because you were finally doing what children do: namely, praying, folding your hands, and saying 'Dear God'!

"But now I want you to leave *this* nursery, my own cave, in which all childishness is at home today. Cool off your hot, childish boisterousness and cheerful noise outside there!

"Truly: unless you become as little children, you shall not enter the kingdom of heaven." (And Zarathustra pointed upward.)

"But we don't want to enter the kingdom of heaven: we've become adult men—*and we want the kingdom of earth.*"

3.

And once more Zarathustra began to speak. "O my new friends," he said, "you odd people, you higher men, how well I like you now—

"Now that you've become cheerful again! Truly, you have all blossomed out: I think that for such flowers as you are, *new festivals* are needed—

"A little brave nonsense, some sort of divine service and donkey festival, some jolly old Zarathustra fool, a roaring wind to blow your souls bright.

"Don't forget this night and this donkey festival, you higher men! You invented it in my home. I take that as a good omen—such things are invented only by men on their way to recovery!

"And if you celebrate this donkey festival again, do it for your sake, do it for my sake, too! And in *my* memory!"

Thus spoke Zarathustra.

Das trunkne Lied

1.

Inzwischen aber war Einer nach dem Andern hinausgetreten ins Freie und in die kühle nachdenkliche Nacht: Zarathustra selber aber führte den häßlichsten Menschen an der Hand, daß er ihm seine Nacht-Welt und den großen runden Mond und die silbernen Wasserstürze bei seiner Höhle zeige. Da standen sie endlich still beieinander, lauter alte Leute, aber mit einem getrösteten tapferen Herzen und verwundert bei sich, daß es ihnen auf Erden so wohl war; die Heimlichkeit der Nacht aber kam ihnen näher und näher ans Herz. Und von neuem dachte Zarathustra bei sich: »oh wie gut sie mir nun gefallen, diese höheren Menschen!« – aber er sprach es nicht aus, denn er ehrte ihr Glück und ihr Stillschweigen. –

Da aber geschah Das, was an jenem erstaunlichen langen Tage das Erstaunlichste war: der häßlichste Mensch begann noch einmal und zum letzten Mal zu gurgeln und zu schnauben, und als er es bis zu Worten gebracht hatte, siehe, da sprang eine Frage rund und reinlich aus seinem Munde, eine gute tiefe klare Frage, welche Allen, die ihm zuhörten, das Herz im Leibe bewegte.

»Meine Freunde insgesamt«, sprach der häßlichste Mensch, »was dünket euch? Um dieses Tags willen – *ich* bin's zum ersten Male zufrieden, daß ich das ganze Leben lebte.

Und daß ich so viel bezeuge, ist mir noch nicht genug. Es lohnt sich auf der Erde zu leben: Ein Tag, ein Fest mit Zarathustra lehrte mich die Erde lieben.

›War *Das* – das Leben?‹ will ich zum Tode sprechen. ›Wohlan! Noch Ein Mal!‹

Meine Freunde, was dünket euch? Wollt ihr nicht gleich mir zum Tode sprechen: *War Das* – das Leben? Um Zarathustra willen, wohlan! Noch Ein Mal!« – –

Also sprach der häßlichste Mensch; es war aber nicht lange vor Mitternacht. Und was glaubt ihr wohl, daß damals sich zutrug? Sobald die höheren Menschen seine Frage hörten, wurden sie sich mit Einem Male ihrer Verwandlung und Genesung bewußt, und wer ihnen dieselbe gegeben habe: da sprangen sie auf Zarathustra zu, dankend, verehrend, liebkosend, ihm die Hände küssend, so wie es der Art eines Jeden eigen war: also daß Einige lachten, Einige wein-

The Drunken Song[22]

1.

But in the meantime one after the other had stepped outdoors into the cool, contemplative night; and Zarathustra himself led the ugliest man by the hand so he could show him his nocturnal world and the big round moon and the silvery waterfalls near his cave. There they finally stood together in silence, nothing but elderly people but with a comforted, brave heart and secretly amazed that they felt so good in the world; and the mystery of night came closer and closer to their heart. And once again Zarathustra thought to himself: "Oh, how well I like them now, these higher men!" But he didn't say it aloud, because he respected their happiness and their silence.

But then something occurred which was the most astonishing event in that long, astonishing day: once again, and for the last time, the ugliest man began to gurgle and snort, and when he had finally formulated it in words, behold: a question leaped from his mouth, round and clean, a good, profound, clear question that stirred the heart in the bosom of all who were listening to him.

"My friends one and all," said the ugliest man, "what's your opinion? For the sake of this day—*I* for the first time am contented that I've lived my whole life.

"And testifying to this is still not enough for me. Life on earth is worthwhile: one day, one holiday with Zarathustra has taught me to love the earth.

"'Was *that* life?' I feel like saying to Death. 'All right! Let's start over!'

"My friends, what's your opinion? Don't you, like me, feel like saying to Death: 'Was *that* life? For Zarathustra's sake, all right! Let's start over!'"

Thus spoke the ugliest man; but it was not long before midnight. And what do you think happened next? As soon as the higher men heard his question, all at once they became aware of their transformation and recovery, and of who had bestowed those things on them; then they dashed over to Zarathustra, thanking him, revering him, caressing him, or kissing his hand, as each one's nature dictated: so that some laughed and some cried. But the old soothsayer danced with

---

22. In some editions, called "Das Nachtwandler-Lied" (Song of the Man Strolling at Night).

ten. Der alte Wahrsager aber tanzte vor Vergnügen; und wenn er auch, wie manche Erzähler meinen, damals voll süßen Weines war, so war er gewißlich noch voller des süßen Lebens und hatte aller Müdigkeit abgesagt. Es gibt sogar Solche, die erzählen, daß damals der Esel getanzt habe: nicht umsonst nämlich habe ihm der häßlichste Mensch vorher Wein zu trinken gegeben. Dies mag sich nun so verhalten oder auch anders; und wenn in Wahrheit an jenem Abende der Esel nicht getanzt hat, so geschahen doch damals größere und seltsamere Wunderdinge, als es das Tanzen eines Esels wäre. Kurz, wie das Sprichwort Zarathustras lautet: »was liegt daran!«

2.

Zarathustra aber, als sich dies mit dem häßlichsten Menschen zutrug, stand da wie ein Trunkener: sein Blick erlosch, seine Zunge lallte, seine Füße schwankten. Und wer möchte auch erraten, welche Gedanken dabei über Zarathustras Seele liefen? Ersichtlich aber wich sein Geist zurück und floh voraus und war in weiten Fernen und gleichsam »auf hohem Joche, wie geschrieben steht, zwischen zwei Meeren,

– zwischen Vergangenem und Zukünftigem als schwere Wolke wandelnd«. Allgemach aber, während ihn die höheren Menschen in den Armen hielten, kam er ein Wenig zu sich selber zurück und wehrte mit den Händen dem Gedränge der Verehrenden und Besorgten; doch sprach er nicht. Mit Einem Male aber wandte er schnell den Kopf, denn er schien Etwas zu hören: da legte er den Finger an den Mund und sprach: »*Kommt!*«

Und alsbald wurde es rings still und heimlich; aus der Tiefe aber kam langsam der Klang einer Glocke herauf. Zarathustra horchte darnach, gleich den höheren Menschen; dann aber legte er zum andern Male den Finger an den Mund und sprach wiederum: »*Kommt! Kommt! Es geht gen Mitternacht!*« – und seine Stimme hatte sich verwandelt. Aber immer noch rührte er sich nicht von der Stelle: da wurde es noch stiller und heimlicher, und Alles horchte, auch der Esel, und Zarathustras Ehrentiere, der Adler und die Schlange, insgleichen die Höhle Zarathustras und der große kühle Mond und die Nacht selber. Zarathustra aber legte zum dritten Male die Hand an den Mund und sprach:

Kommt! Kommt! Kommt! Laßt uns jetzo wandeln! Es ist die Stunde! Laßt uns in die Nacht wandeln!

contentment; and even if, as many narrators think, he was full of sweet wine at the time, he was surely even fuller of sweeter life and had renounced all weariness. There are even some who report that the donkey danced at that time: for it wasn't for nothing that the ugliest man had given him wine to drink previously. That may be so or not; and if the donkey didn't really dance that evening, greater and more unusual miracles then took place than a donkey's dancing. In short, as Zarathustra's saying goes: "What does it matter?"

2.

But when this incident with the ugliest man occurred, Zarathustra stood there like a drunken man: his eyes grew dull, his speech was slurred, his legs wavered. And who could guess what thoughts were passing through Zarathustra's soul at the time? But his spirit visibly lost ground and fled before him and was in remote distances and as if "on a high mountain pass," as it is written, "between two seas—

"Roaming between past and future as a heavy cloud." But gradually, while the higher men held him in their arms, he came to somewhat and waved off the reverent, concerned men who had been crowding him too closely; but he didn't speak. Then, all at once, he quickly turned his head, because he seemed to hear something; next, he put a finger to his lips and said: *"Come!"*

And immediately there was a mysterious silence all around; but from the depths the slow pealing of a bell ascended. Zarathustra listened to it, as did the higher men; but then he put a finger to his lips a second time and said again: *"Come! Come! It's nearly midnight!"* And his voice was different. But he still didn't budge from the spot; then it became ever more quiet and mysterious, and everyone listened, even the donkey, and Zarathustra's beasts of honor, the eagle and the serpent, as well as Zarathustra's cave and the big cool moon and the night itself. But Zarathustra put his hand to his lips for the third time and said:

"Come! Come! Come! Let us now stroll! It's the right time! Let us stroll into the night!"

3.

Ihr höheren Menschen, es geht gen Mitternacht: da will ich euch
Etwas in die Ohren sagen, wie jene alte Glocke es mir ins Ohr sagt, –
– so heimlich, so schrecklich, so herzlich, wie jene Mitternachts-
Glocke zu mir es redet, die mehr erlebt hat als Ein Mensch:
– welche schon eurer Väter Herzens-Schmerzens-Schläge abzählte
– ach! ach! wie sie seufzt! wie sie im Traume lacht! die alte tiefe tiefe
Mitternacht!
    Still! Still! Da hört sich Manches, das am Tage nicht laut werden
darf; nun aber, bei kühler Luft, da auch aller Lärm eurer Herzen stille
ward, –
– nun redet es, nun hört es sich, nun schleicht es sich in nächtliche
überwache Seelen: ach! ach! wie sie seufzt! wie sie im Traume lacht!
– hörst du's nicht, wie sie heimlich, schrecklich, herzlich zu *dir*
redet, die alte tiefe tiefe Mitternacht?
Oh Mensch, gib acht!

4.

Wehe mir! Wo ist die Zeit hin? Sank ich nicht in tiefe Brunnen? Die
Welt schläft –
    Ach! Ach! Der Hund heult, der Mond scheint. Lieber will ich ster-
ben, sterben, als euch sagen, was mein Mitternachts-Herz eben denkt.
    Nun starb ich schon. Es ist dahin. Spinne, was spinnst du um mich?
Willst du Blut? Ach! Ach! Der Tau fällt, die Stunde kommt –
– die Stunde, wo mich fröstelt und friert, die fragt und fragt und
fragt: »wer hat Herz genug dazu?
– wer soll der Erde Herr sein? Wer will sagen: so sollt ihr laufen,
ihr großen und kleinen Ströme!«
– die Stunde naht: oh Mensch, du höherer Mensch, gib acht! Diese
Rede ist für feine Ohren, für deine Ohren – *was spricht die tiefe
Mitternacht?*

5.

Es trägt mich dahin, meine Seele tanzt. Tagewerk! Tagewerk! Wer soll
der Erde Herr sein?

3.

"You higher people, it is almost midnight: so I want to say something in your ear, just as that old bell says it in my ear—

"Just as mysteriously, as frightfully, as cordially, as it is told to me by that midnight bell, which has experienced more than any one person—

"Which was already counting off your fathers' painful heartbeats.— Alas, alas! How it sighs! How it laughs in its dream: the old, deep, deep midnight!

"Quiet! Quiet! Then many things are heard which are not allowed to be spoken during the day; but now, when the air is cool, when all the noise of your hearts has become quiet, also—

"Now it speaks, now it is audible, now it steals into nocturnal, tensely awake souls. Alas, alas! How it sighs! How it laughs in its dream!

"Can't you hear how it's speaking mysteriously, frightfully, cordially to *you*, that old, deep, deep midnight?

"*O man, pay heed!*

4.

"Woe is me! Where has the time gone? Didn't I sink into deep wells? The world is asleep—

"Alas, alas! The dog howls, the moon shines. I'd rather die, die than tell you what my midnight heart is thinking right now.

"Now I'm already dead. It's all over. Spider, why are you spinning around me? Do you want blood? Alas, alas! The dew falls, the hour comes—

"The hour when I am chilled and frozen, the hour that asks and asks and asks: 'Who has heart enough for it?

"'Who shall be lord of the earth? Who will say: "You must run *in this way*, you currents large and small!"'

"The hour is nigh: O man, O higher man, pay heed! This speech is for subtle ears, for your ears: *What does deep midnight say?*

5.

"I'm being carried away, my soul is dancing. Daily tasks! Daily tasks! Who shall be lord of the earth?

Der Mond ist kühl, der Wind schweigt. Ach! Ach! Flogt ihr schon hoch genug? Ihr tanztet: aber ein Bein ist doch kein Flügel.

Ihr guten Tänzer, nun ist alle Lust vorbei: Wein ward Hefe, jeder Becher ward mürbe, die Gräber stammeln.

Ihr flogt nicht noch genug: nun stammeln die Gräber »erlöst doch die Toten! Warum ist so lange Nacht? Macht uns nicht der Mond trunken?«

Ihr höheren Menschen, erlöst doch die Gräber, weckt die Leichname auf! Ach, was gräbt noch der Wurm? Es naht, es naht die Stunde, –

– es brummt die Glocke, es schnarrt noch das Herz, es gräbt noch der Holzwurm, der Herzenswurm. Ach! Ach! *Die Welt ist tief!*

6.

Süße Leier! Süße Leier! Ich liebe deinen Ton, deinen trunkenen Unken-Ton! – wie lang her, wie fern her kommt mir dein Ton, weit her, von den Teichen der Liebe!

Du alte Glocke, du süße Leier! Jeder Schmerz riß dir ins Herz, Vaterschmerz, Väterschmerz, Urväterschmerz; deine Rede wurde reif, –

– reif gleich goldenem Herbste und Nachmittage, gleich meinem Einsiedlerherzen – nun redest du: die Welt selber ward reif, die Traube bräunt,

– nun will sie sterben, vor Glück sterben. Ihr höheren Menschen, riecht ihr's nicht? Es quillt heimlich ein Geruch herauf,

– ein Duft und Geruch der Ewigkeit, ein rosenseliger brauner Gold-Wein-Geruch von altem Glücke,

– von trunkenem Mitternachts-Sterbeglücke, welches singt: die Welt ist tief, *und tiefer als der Tag gedacht!*

7.

Laß mich! Laß mich! Ich bin zu rein für dich. Rühre mich nicht an! Ward meine Welt nicht eben vollkommen?

Meine Haut ist zu rein für deine Hände. Laß mich, du dummer tölpischer dumpfer Tag! Ist die Mitternacht nicht heller?

Die Reinsten sollen der Erde Herrn sein, die Unerkanntesten, Stärksten, die Mitternachts-Seelen, die heller und tiefer sind als jeder Tag.

"The moon is cool, the wind is still. Alas, alas! Have you flown high enough by now? You were dancing: but a leg is still not a wing.

"You good dancers, now all pleasure is gone: wine has become dregs, every cup has rotted, the graves are stammering.

"You haven't flown high enough: now the graves are stammering: 'Do redeem the dead! Why has it been night for so long? Isn't the moon making us drunk?

"You higher men, do redeem the graves, awaken the corpses! Ah, why is the worm still digging? It's nigh, the hour is nigh—

"The bell is booming; the heart is still humming; the woodworm, the heartworm, is still digging. *Alas, alas! The world is deep!*

6.

"Sweet lyre! Sweet lyre! I love your sound, your drunken toad-sound! From how long ago, from how far away your sound reaches me, from afar, from the pools of love!

"You old bell, you sweet lyre! Every pain has torn into your heart, father's pain, fathers' pain, ancestral pain; your speech has become ripe—

"Ripe, like golden autumn and afternoon, like my hermit heart— now you speak: the world itself has become ripe, the grape is turning brown—

"Now it wants to die, to die of happiness. You higher men, can't you smell it? An aroma is secretly gushing upward—

"A fragrance and aroma of eternity, a rosily blissful brown golden-wine aroma of old happiness—

"Of drunken midnight happiness in dying; and it sings: 'The world is deep, *and deeper than the day had thought!*'

7.

"Let me alone! Let me alone! I'm too pure for you. Don't touch me! Hasn't my world just become perfect?

"My skin is too clean for your hands. Let me alone, you stupid, foolish, dull day! Isn't midnight brighter?

"The purest are to be the lords of the earth, those least recognized, the strongest, the midnight souls, which are brighter and deeper than all daylight.

Oh Tag, du tappst nach mir? Du tastest nach meinem Glücke? Ich bin dir reich, einsam, eine Schatzgrube, eine Goldkammer?

Oh Welt, du willst mich? Bin ich dir weltlich? Bin ich dir geistlich? Bin ich dir göttlich? Aber Tag und Welt, ihr seid zu plump, –

– habt klügere Hände, greift nach tieferem Glücke, nach tieferem Unglücke, greift nach irgendeinem Gotte, greift nicht nach mir:

– mein Unglück, mein Glück ist tief, du wunderlicher Tag, aber doch bin ich kein Gott, keine Gottes-Hölle: *tief ist ihr Weh.*

8.

Gottes Weh ist tiefer, du wunderliche Welt! Greife nach Gottes Weh, nicht nach mir! Was bin ich! Eine trunkene süße Leier, –

– eine Mitternachts-Leier, eine Glocken-Unke, die niemand versteht, aber welche reden *muß*, vor Tauben, ihr höheren Menschen! Denn ihr versteht mich nicht!

Dahin! Dahin! Oh Jugend! Oh Mittag! Oh Nachmittag! Nun kam Abend und Nacht und Mitternacht, – der Hund heult, der Wind:

– ist der Wind nicht ein Hund? Er winselt, er kläfft, er heult. Ach! Ach! wie sie seufzt! wie sie lacht, wie sie röchelt und keucht, die Mitternacht.

Wie sie eben nüchtern spricht, diese trunkene Dichterin! Sie übertrank wohl ihre Trunkenheit? Sie wurde überwacht? Sie käut zurück?

– Ihr Weh käut sie zurück, im Traume, die alte tiefe Mitternacht, und mehr noch ihre Lust. Lust nämlich, wenn schon Weh tief ist: *Lust ist tiefer noch als Herzeleid.*

9.

Du Weinstock! Was preisest du mich? Ich schnitt dich doch! Ich bin grausam, du blutest –: was will dein Lob meiner trunkenen Grausamkeit?

»Was vollkommen ward, alles Reife – will sterben!« so redest du. Gesegnet, gesegnet sei das Winzermesser! Aber alles Unreife will leben: wehe!

Weh spricht: »Vergeh! Weg, du Wehe!« Aber Alles, was leidet, will leben, daß es reif werde und lustig und sehnsüchtig,

"O day, are you groping out for me? Are your fingers reaching for my happiness? Am I wealthy to you, solitary, a treasure trove, a room filled with gold?

"O world, do you want me? Do you find me worldly? Do you find me spiritual? Do you find me godlike? But, day and world, you're too coarse—

"Get cleverer hands, reach for deeper happiness, for deeper unhappiness, reach for some god; don't reach for me:

"My unhappiness and my happiness are deep, you peculiar day, and yet I'm not a god, not a god's hell: *deep is its woe.*

8.

"God's woe is deeper, you peculiar world! Reach for God's woe, not for me! What am I? A drunken, sweet lyre—

"A midnight lyre, a churchbell toad which no one understands, but which *must* speak, to the deaf, you higher men! Because you don't understand me!

"Gone! Gone! O youth! O noon! O afternoon! Now evening has come, and night and midnight—the dog howls, the wind:

"Isn't the wind a dog? It whines, it yelps, it howls. Alas, alas! How midnight sighs! How it laughs, rattles in its throat, and gasps!

"How soberly she is speaking just now, that drunken poetess! Has she possibly drunk herself sober again? Has she become all too wide awake? Is she ruminating?

"She's ruminating on her woe, in a dream, the old, deep midnight, and, even more, on her joy. For joy, even if woe is deep: *Joy is even deeper than heart's sorrow.*

9.

"You grapevine! Why do you praise me? Didn't I cut you? I'm cruel, you're bleeding: what do you mean by praising my drunken cruelty?

"'That which has become perfect, everything that's ripe—wants to die,' you say. Blessed, blessed be the vintager's knife! But everything unripe wants to live: woe!

"Woe says: 'Perish! Away with you, woe!' But everything that suffers wants to live, so it can become ripe and merry, and experience longing:

– sehnsüchtig nach Fernerem, Höherem, Hellerem. »Ich will Erben«, so spricht Alles, was leidet, »ich will Kinder, ich will nicht *mich*«, –

Lust aber will nicht Erben, nicht Kinder, – Lust will sich selber, will Ewigkeit, will Wiederkunft, will Alles-sich-ewig-gleich.

Weh spricht: »Brich, blute, Herz! Wandle, Bein! Flügel, flieg! Hinan! Hinauf! Schmerz!« Wohlan! Wohlauf! Oh mein altes Herz: *Weh spricht: »Vergeh!«*

10.

Ihr höheren Menschen, was dünket euch? Bin ich ein Wahrsager? Ein Träumender? Trunkener? Ein Traumdeuter? Eine Mitternachtsglocke?

Ein Tropfen Taus? Ein Dunst und Duft der Ewigkeit? Hört ihr's nicht? Riecht ihr's nicht? Eben ward meine Welt vollkommen, Mitternacht ist auch Mittag, –

Schmerz ist auch eine Lust, Fluch ist auch ein Segen, Nacht ist auch eine Sonne, – geh davon! oder ihr lernt: ein Weiser ist auch ein Narr.

Sagtet ihr jemals Ja zu Einer Lust? Oh, meine Freunde, so sagtet ihr Ja auch zu *allem* Wehe. Alle Dinge sind verkettet, verfädelt, verliebt, –

– wolltet ihr jemals Ein Mal zweimal, spracht ihr jemals »du gefällst mir, Glück! Husch! Augenblick!« so wolltet ihr *Alles* zurück!

– Alles von neuem, Alles ewig, Alles verkettet, verfädelt, verliebt, oh so *liebtet* ihr die Welt, –

– ihr Ewigen, liebt sie ewig und allezeit: und auch zum Weh sprecht ihr: vergeh, aber komm zurück! *Denn alle Lust will – Ewigkeit!*

11.

Alle Lust will aller Dinge Ewigkeit, will Honig, will Hefe, will trunkene Mitternacht, will Gräber, will Gräber-Tränen-Trost, will vergüldetes Abendrot –

– *was* will nicht Lust! sie ist durstiger, herzlicher, hungriger, schrecklicher, heimlicher als alles Weh, sie will *sich*, sie beißt in *sich*, des Ringes Wille ringt in ihr, –

– sie will Liebe, sie will Haß, sie ist überreich, schenkt, wirft weg, bettelt, daß Einer sie nimmt, dankt dem Nehmenden, sie möchte gern gehaßt sein, –

"Longing for the distant, the higher, the brighter. 'I want heirs,' says everything that suffers, 'I want children, I don't want *myself*—

"But joy doesn't want heirs or children; joy wants itself, wants eternity, wants to return, wants everything to be eternally the same.

"Woe says: 'Break, bleed, heart! Walk, leg! Wing, fly! Upward! To the heights! Pain!' All right! Perk up, my old heart! *Woe says: 'Perish!'*

10.

"You higher men, what's your opinion? Am I a soothsayer? A dreamer? A drunk? An interpreter of dreams? A midnight bell?

"A drop of dew? A vapor and fragrance of eternity? Can't you hear it? Can't you smell it? My world has just become perfect, midnight is also midday—

"Pains is also a joy. Curse is also a blessing, night is also a sun—go away! Or you'll learn: a wise man is also a fool.

"Have you ever said yea to one joy? O my friends, if so, you also said yea to *all* woe. All things are linked together, threaded together, in love with one another—

"If you have ever wanted once to be twice, if you have ever said: 'I like you, happiness! Wait! A moment!,' then you wanted *everything* back again!

"Everything anew, everything eternally, everything interlinked, threaded together, in shared love: oh, then you *loved* the world—

"You eternal ones, love it eternally and at all times; and even to woe say: 'Perish, but come back!' *For all joy wants—eternity!*

11.

"All joy wants the eternity of all things, wants honey, wants dregs, wants drunken midnight, wants graves, wants the consolation of tears at graves, wants the gilded sunset—

"What *doesn't* joy want!? It's thirstier, more cordial, hungrier, more frightful, more mysterious than all woe; it wants *itself*, it bites into *itself*, the will of the ring struggles within it—

"It wants love, it wants hatred, it's overabundant, it gives of itself, squanders itself, begs people to take it, thanks those who do—it would like to be hated—

– so reich ist Lust, daß sie nach Wehe durstet, nach Hölle, nach Haß, nach Schmach, nach dem Krüppel, nach *Welt*, – denn diese Welt, oh ihr kennt sie ja!

Ihr höheren Menschen, nach euch sehnt sie sich, die Lust, die unbändige, selige, – nach eurem Weh, ihr Mißratenen! Nach Mißratenem sehnt sich alle ewige Lust.

Denn alle Lust will sich selber, drum will sie auch Herzeleid! Oh Glück, oh Schmerz! Oh brich, Herz! Ihr höheren Menschen lernt es doch, Lust will Ewigkeit,

– Lust will *aller* Dinge Ewigkeit, *will tiefe, tiefe Ewigkeit!*

12.

Lerntet ihr nun mein Lied? Errietet ihr, was es will? Wohlan! Wohlauf! Ihr höheren Menschen, so singt mir nun meinen Rundgesang!

Singt mir nun selber das Lied, des Name ist »Noch einmal«, des Sinn ist »in alle Ewigkeit!« – singt, ihr höheren Menschen, Zarathustras Rundgesang!

> *Oh Mensch! Gib acht!*
> *Was spricht die tiefe Mitternacht?*
> *»Ich schlief, ich schlief –,*
> *Aus tiefem Traum bin ich erwacht: –*
> *Die Welt ist tief,*
> *Und tiefer als der Tag gedacht.*
> *Tief ist ihr Weh –,*
> *Lust – tiefer noch als Herzeleid:*
> *Weh spricht: Vergeh!*
> *Doch alle Lust will Ewigkeit –,*
> *– will tiefe, tiefe Ewigkeit!«*

Das Zeichen

Des Morgens aber nach dieser Nacht sprang Zarathustra von seinem Lager auf, gürtete sich die Lenden und kam heraus aus seiner Höhle, glühend und stark, wie eine Morgensonne, die aus dunklen Bergen kommt.

»Du großes Gestirn«, sprach er, wie er einstmals gesprochen hatte, »du tiefes Glücks-Auge, was wäre all dein Glück, wenn du nicht *Die* hättest, welchen du leuchtest!

"Joy is so rich that it thirsts for woe, for hell, for hatred, for disgrace, for the cripple, for *world*—because this world, oh, you're quite familiar with it!

"You higher men, joy, unruly, blissful joy longs for you—for your woe, you misbegotten! All eternal joy longs for that which is misbegotten.

"For all joy wants itself, therefore it also wants heart's sorrow! O happiness, O pain! Oh, break, heart! You higher men, learn this at least: joy wants eternity—

"Joy wants the eternity of *all* things, *wants deep, deep eternity!*

12.

"Have you learnt my song now? Have you guessed its intention? All right! Perk up! You higher men, now sing me my round!

"Now you yourselves sing me the song whose name is 'Once Again,' whose meaning is 'for all eternity!' You higher men, sing Zarathustra's round!

> *"O man, pay heed!*
> *What does deep midnight say?*
> *'I was asleep, I was asleep;*
> *I have awakened from a deep dream.*
> *The world is deep,*
> *and deeper than the day had thought.*
> *Deep is its woe;*
> *joy—even deeper than heart's sorrow.*
> *Woe says: "Perish!"*
> *But all joy wants eternity—*
> *wants deep, deep eternity!'"*

The Sign

But on the morning after that night Zarathustra leaped out of bed, girded his loins, and emerged from his cave, radiant and strong as a morning sun rising from dark mountains.

"You great star," he said, as he had once spoken, "you deep eye of happiness: how happy would you be if you didn't have beings to shine on?

Und wenn sie in ihren Kammern blieben, während du schon wach bist und kommst und schenkst und austeilst: wie würde darob deine stolze Scham zürnen!

Wohlan! Sie schlafen noch, diese höheren Menschen, während *ich* wach bin: *das* sind nicht meine rechten Gefährten! Nicht auf sie warte ich hier in meinen Bergen.

Zu meinem Werke will ich, zu meinem Tage: aber sie verstehen nicht, was die Zeichen meines Morgens sind, mein Schritt – ist für sie kein Weckruf.

Sie schlafen noch in meiner Höhle, ihr Traum trinkt noch an meinen trunknen Liedern. Das Ohr doch, das nach *mir* horcht, – das *gehorchende* Ohr fehlt in ihren Gliedern.«

– Dies hatte Zarathustra zu seinem Herzen gesprochen, als die Sonne aufging: da blickte er fragend in die Höhe, denn er hörte über sich den scharfen Ruf seines Adlers. »Wohlan!« rief er hinauf, »so gefällt und gebührt es mir. Meine Tiere sind wach, denn ich bin wach.

Mein Adler ist wach und ehrt gleich mir die Sonne. Mit Adlers-Klauen greift er nach dem neuen Lichte. Ihr seid meine rechten Tiere; ich liebe euch.

Aber noch fehlen mir meine rechten Menschen!« –

Also sprach Zarathustra; da aber geschah es, daß er sich plötzlich wie von unzähligen Vögeln umschwärmt und umflattert hörte, – das Geschwirr so vieler Flügel aber und das Gedräng um sein Haupt war so groß, daß er die Augen schloß. Und wahrlich, einer Wolke gleich fiel es über ihn her, einer Wolke von Pfeilen gleich, welche sich über einen neuen Feind ausschüttet. Aber siehe, hier war es eine Wolke der Liebe, und über einen neuen Freund.

»Was geschieht mir?« dachte Zarathustra in seinem erstaunten Herzen und ließ sich langsam auf dem großen Steine nieder, der neben dem Ausgange seiner Höhle lag. Aber, indem er mit den Händen um sich und über sich und unter sich griff und den zärtlichen Vögeln wehrte, siehe, da geschah ihm etwas noch Seltsameres: er griff nämlich dabei unvermerkt in ein dichtes warmes Haar-Gezottel hinein; zugleich aber erscholl vor ihm ein Gebrüll – ein sanftes langes Löwen-Brüllen.

»*Das Zeichen kommt*«, sprach Zarathustra, und sein Herz verwandelte sich. Und in Wahrheit, als es helle vor ihm wurde, da lag ihm ein gelbes mächtiges Getier zu Füßen und schmiegte das Haupt an seine Knie und wollte nicht von ihm lassen vor Liebe, und tat einem Hunde gleich, welcher seinen alten Herrn wiederfindet. Die Tauben aber waren mit ihrer Liebe nicht minder eifrig als der Löwe; und jedesmal,

"And if they stayed in their rooms while you're already awake, coming, giving and distributing gifts: how angry would your proud modesty be over it!

"Very well! They're still asleep, those higher people, while *I'm* awake: *they* aren't my proper companions! It's not them that I await here in my mountains.

"I want to set out to work, to my day; but they don't understand what the signs of my morning are; my footsteps aren't a wake-up call for them.

"They're still asleep in my cave; their dream is still absorbing my drunken songs. But the ear that listens to *me*—the obedient ear—is missing from their bodies."

Zarathustra had said that to his heart when the sun rose; then he looked upward inquiringly because he heard overhead the shrill cry of his eagle. "Good!" he shouted upward. "This is what pleases me and is due me. My animals are awake because I am awake.

"My eagle is awake and, like me, honoring the sun. With eagle's talons it reaches for the new light. You're my proper animals; I love you.

"But I still lack my proper people!"

Thus spoke Zarathustra; but it then befell that he suddenly heard a sound as if innumerable birds were flocking and fluttering around him; the whirring of so many wings and the throng around his head were so great that he shut his eyes. And, truly, they fell upon him like a cloud, like a cloud of arrows poured out over a new enemy. But behold, here it was a cloud of love, and over a new friend.

"What's happening to me?" Zarathustra thought in his astonished heart, and he sat down slowly on the big stone that lay beside the exit to his cave. But while he was reaching out around himself and overhead and below himself, warding off the affectionate birds, behold: something even stranger occurred: he unexpectedly reached into a thick, warm tuft of fur, and at the same time he heard a roar in front of him—the gentle, sustained roar of a lion.

"The sign is coming," said Zarathustra, and his heart was transformed. And indeed, when there was brightness before him once more, a powerful tawny animal was lying at his feet, cuddling its head against his knees. Out of love it refused to leave his side; it behaved like a dog that has found its former master again. But the doves were no less enthusiastic in their love than the lion; and each time a dove

wenn eine Taube über die Nase des Löwen huschte, schüttelte der Löwe das Haupt und wunderte sich und lachte dazu.

Zu dem Allen sprach Zarathustra nur Ein Wort: »*Meine Kinder sind nahe, meine Kinder*« –, dann wurde er ganz stumm. Sein Herz aber war gelöst, und aus seinen Augen tropften Tränen herab und fielen auf seine Hände. Und er achtete keines Dings mehr und saß da, unbeweglich und ohne daß er sich noch gegen die Tiere wehrte. Da flogen die Tauben ab und zu und setzten sich ihm auf die Schulter und liebkosten sein weißes Haar und wurden nicht müde mit Zärtlichkeit und Frohlocken. Der starke Löwe aber leckte immer die Tränen, welche auf die Hände Zarathustras herabfielen und brüllte und brummte schüchtern dazu. Also trieben es diese Tiere. –

Dies Alles dauerte eine lange Zeit, oder eine kurze Zeit: denn, recht gesprochen, gibt es für dergleichen Dinge auf Erden *keine Zeit* –. Inzwischen aber waren die höheren Menschen in der Höhle Zarathustras wach geworden und ordneten sich miteinander zu einem Zuge an, daß sie Zarathustra entgegengingen und ihm den Morgengruß böten: denn sie hatten gefunden, als sie erwachten, daß er schon nicht mehr unter ihnen weilte. Als sie aber zur Tür der Höhle gelangten und das Geräusch ihrer Schritte ihnen voranlief, da stutzte der Löwe gewaltig, kehrte sich mit Einem Male von Zarathustra ab und sprang, wild brüllend, auf die Höhle los; die höheren Menschen aber, als sie ihn brüllen hörten, schrien alle auf, wie mit Einem Munde, und flohen zurück und waren im Nu verschwunden.

Zarathustra selber aber, betäubt und fremd, erhob sich von seinem Sitze, sah um sich, stand staunend da, fragte sein Herz, besann sich und war allein. »Was hörte ich doch?« sprach er endlich langsam, »was geschah mir eben?«

Und schon kam ihm die Erinnerung, und er begriff mit Einem Blicke Alles, was zwischen Gestern und Heute sich begeben hatte. »Hier ist ja der Stein«, sprach er und strich sich den Bart, »auf *dem* saß ich gestern am Morgen; und hier trat der Wahrsager zu mir, und hier hörte ich zuerst den Schrei, den ich eben hörte, den großen Notschrei.

Oh ihr höheren Menschen, *von eurer Not* war's ja, daß gestern am Morgen jener alte Wahrsager mir wahrsagte, –

– zu eurer Not wollte er mich verführen und versuchen: oh Zarathustra, sprach er zu mir, ich komme, daß ich dich zu deiner letzten Sünde verführe.

Zu meiner letzten Sünde? rief Zarathustra und lachte zornig über sein eigenes Wort: *was* blieb mir doch aufgespart als meine letzte Sünde?«

– Und noch einmal versank Zarathustra in sich und setzte sich wieder auf den großen Stein nieder und sann nach. Plötzlich sprang er empor, –

whizzed over the lion's nose, the lion shook its head in surprise and laughed at it.

To all this, Zarathustra spoke only one sentence: *"My children are nigh, my children."* Then he fell altogether silent. But his heart was set free, and tears trickled down from his eyes and fell onto his hands. And he paid no further heed to anything, but sat there motionless, no longer warding off the animals. Then the doves flew to and fro and alighted on his shoulder and caressed his white hair, and their tenderness and rejoicing didn't grow weary. But the strong lion kept licking away the tears that fell onto Zarathustra's hands; as it did so it roared and growled coyly. That is how those animals behaved.

All this lasted a long while, or a short while: because, strictly speaking, for such things on earth there is *no time.* But meanwhile the higher men in Zarathustra's cave had awakened and were organizing themselves into a procession to meet Zarathustra and bid him good morning: for when they awoke they had found that he was already gone from their midst. But when they reached the cave door and the sound of their footsteps preceded them, the lion gave a violent start, suddenly turned away from Zarathustra, and, with a wild roar, dashed for the cave; and when the higher men heard him roar, they all cried out as if with one voice, fled back, and had vanished in a trice.

But Zarathustra himself, numbed and distant, arose from his seat, looked around, stood there in surprise, questioned his heart, thought things over, and was alone. "What *did* I hear?" he finally said slowly. "What just happened to me?"

And now his memory returned, and at one glance he comprehended all that had occurred between yesterday and today. "Yes, here's the stone," he said, patting his beard; "yesterday morning I was sitting on *it;* and here the soothsayer came up to me, and here I first heard the cry that I just heard, the great cry for help.

"O you higher men, it was *your distress* that that old soothsayer predicted to me yesterday morning—

"He wanted to lead me astray and into temptation with your distress. 'O Zarathustra,' he said to me, 'I've come to seduce you into your last sin.'

"To my last sin?" cried Zarathustra, and he laughed angrily at his own words. "*What* remained in store for me except my last sin?"

And once again Zarathustra became immersed in himself; again he sat down on the big stone and reflected. Suddenly he leaped up—

»*Mitleiden! Das Mitleiden mit dem höheren Menschen*!« schrie er auf, und sein Antlitz vewandelte sich in Erz. »Wohlan! *Das* – hatte seine Zeit!

Mein Leid und mein Mitleiden – was liegt daran! Trachte ich denn nach *Glücke?* Ich trachte nach meinem *Werke!*

Wohlan! Der Löwe kam, meine Kinder sind nahe, Zarathustra ward reif, meine Stunde kam: –

Dies ist *mein* Morgen, *mein* Tag hebt an: *herauf nun, herauf, du großer Mittag!*« – –

Also sprach Zarathustra und verließ seine Höhle, glühend und stark, wie eine Morgensonne, die aus dunklen Bergen kommt.

"*Compassion! Compassion for the higher man!*" he cried out, and his face turned to bronze. "Good! The time for *that* is over!

"My sorrow and my compassion—what do they count? Am I thinking about *happiness?* I'm thinking about my *task!*

"Good! The lion has come, my children are nigh, Zarathustra has grown ripe, my hour has come—

"This is *my* morning, *my* day is beginning: *arise now, arise, you great noonday!*"

Thus spoke Zarathustra, and he left his cave, radiant and strong as a morning sun rising from dark mountains.

A CATALOG OF SELECTED
DOVER BOOKS
IN ALL FIELDS OF INTEREST

A CATALOG OF SELECTED DOVER
BOOKS IN ALL FIELDS OF INTEREST

CONCERNING THE SPIRITUAL IN ART, Wassily Kandinsky. Pioneering work by father of abstract art. Thoughts on color theory, nature of art. Analysis of earlier masters. 12 illustrations. 80pp. of text. 5⅜ x 8½.   23411-8

ANIMALS: 1,419 Copyright-Free Illustrations of Mammals, Birds, Fish, Insects, etc., Jim Harter (ed.). Clear wood engravings present, in extremely lifelike poses, over 1,000 species of animals. One of the most extensive pictorial sourcebooks of its kind. Captions. Index. 284pp. 9 x 12.   23766-4

CELTIC ART: The Methods of Construction, George Bain. Simple geometric techniques for making Celtic interlacements, spirals, Kells-type initials, animals, humans, etc. Over 500 illustrations. 160pp. 9 x 12. (Available in U.S. only.)   22923-8

AN ATLAS OF ANATOMY FOR ARTISTS, Fritz Schider. Most thorough reference work on art anatomy in the world. Hundreds of illustrations, including selections from works by Vesalius, Leonardo, Goya, Ingres, Michelangelo, others. 593 illustrations. 192pp. 7⅛ x 10¼.   20241-0

CELTIC HAND STROKE-BY-STROKE (Irish Half-Uncial from "The Book of Kells"): An Arthur Baker Calligraphy Manual, Arthur Baker. Complete guide to creating each letter of the alphabet in distinctive Celtic manner. Covers hand position, strokes, pens, inks, paper, more. Illustrated. 48pp. 8¼ x 11.   24336-2

EASY ORIGAMI, John Montroll. Charming collection of 32 projects (hat, cup, pelican, piano, swan, many more) specially designed for the novice origami hobbyist. Clearly illustrated easy-to-follow instructions insure that even beginning papercrafters will achieve successful results. 48pp. 8¼ x 11.   27298-2

THE COMPLETE BOOK OF BIRDHOUSE CONSTRUCTION FOR WOODWORKERS, Scott D. Campbell. Detailed instructions, illustrations, tables. Also data on bird habitat and instinct patterns. Bibliography. 3 tables. 63 illustrations in 15 figures. 48pp. 5¼ x 8½.   24407-5

BLOOMINGDALE'S ILLUSTRATED 1886 CATALOG: Fashions, Dry Goods and Housewares, Bloomingdale Brothers. Famed merchants' extremely rare catalog depicting about 1,700 products: clothing, housewares, firearms, dry goods, jewelry, more. Invaluable for dating, identifying vintage items. Also, copyright-free graphics for artists, designers. Co-published with Henry Ford Museum & Greenfield Village. 160pp. 8¼ x 11.   25780-0

HISTORIC COSTUME IN PICTURES, Braun & Schneider. Over 1,450 costumed figures in clearly detailed engravings—from dawn of civilization to end of 19th century. Captions. Many folk costumes. 256pp. 8⅜ x 11¾.   23150-X

STICKLEY CRAFTSMAN FURNITURE CATALOGS, Gustav Stickley and L. & J. G. Stickley. Beautiful, functional furniture in two authentic catalogs from 1910. 594 illustrations, including 277 photos, show settles, rockers, armchairs, reclining chairs, bookcases, desks, tables. 183pp. 6½ x 9¼. 23838-5

AMERICAN LOCOMOTIVES IN HISTORIC PHOTOGRAPHS: 1858 to 1949, Ron Ziel (ed.). A rare collection of 126 meticulously detailed official photographs, called "builder portraits," of American locomotives that majestically chronicle the rise of steam locomotive power in America. Introduction. Detailed captions. xi+ 129pp. 9 x 12. 27393-8

AMERICA'S LIGHTHOUSES: An Illustrated History, Francis Ross Holland, Jr. Delightfully written, profusely illustrated fact-filled survey of over 200 American lighthouses since 1716. History, anecdotes, technological advances, more. 240pp. 8 x 10¾. 25576-X

TOWARDS A NEW ARCHITECTURE, Le Corbusier. Pioneering manifesto by founder of "International School." Technical and aesthetic theories, views of industry, economics, relation of form to function, "mass-production split" and much more. Profusely illustrated. 320pp. 6⅛ x 9¼. (Available in U.S. only.) 25023-7

HOW THE OTHER HALF LIVES, Jacob Riis. Famous journalistic record, exposing poverty and degradation of New York slums around 1900, by major social reformer. 100 striking and influential photographs. 233pp. 10 x 7⅞. 22012-5

FRUIT KEY AND TWIG KEY TO TREES AND SHRUBS, William M. Harlow. One of the handiest and most widely used identification aids. Fruit key covers 120 deciduous and evergreen species; twig key 160 deciduous species. Easily used. Over 300 photographs. 126pp. 5⅜ x 8½. 20511-8

COMMON BIRD SONGS, Dr. Donald J. Borror. Songs of 60 most common U.S. birds: robins, sparrows, cardinals, bluejays, finches, more–arranged in order of increasing complexity. Up to 9 variations of songs of each species.
Cassette and manual 99911-4

ORCHIDS AS HOUSE PLANTS, Rebecca Tyson Northen. Grow cattleyas and many other kinds of orchids–in a window, in a case, or under artificial light. 63 illustrations. 148pp. 5⅜ x 8½. 23261-1

MONSTER MAZES, Dave Phillips. Masterful mazes at four levels of difficulty. Avoid deadly perils and evil creatures to find magical treasures. Solutions for all 32 exciting illustrated puzzles. 48pp. 8¼ x 11. 26005-4

MOZART'S DON GIOVANNI (DOVER OPERA LIBRETTO SERIES), Wolfgang Amadeus Mozart. Introduced and translated by Ellen H. Bleiler. Standard Italian libretto, with complete English translation. Convenient and thoroughly portable–an ideal companion for reading along with a recording or the performance itself. Introduction. List of characters. Plot summary. 121pp. 5¼ x 8½. 24944-1

TECHNICAL MANUAL AND DICTIONARY OF CLASSICAL BALLET, Gail Grant. Defines, explains, comments on steps, movements, poses and concepts. 15-page pictorial section. Basic book for student, viewer. 127pp. 5⅜ x 8½. 21843-0

THE CLARINET AND CLARINET PLAYING, David Pino. Lively, comprehensive work features suggestions about technique, musicianship, and musical interpretation, as well as guidelines for teaching, making your own reeds, and preparing for public performance. Includes an intriguing look at clarinet history. "A godsend," *The Clarinet,* Journal of the International Clarinet Society. Appendixes. 7 illus. 320pp. 5⅜ x 8½. 40270-3

HOLLYWOOD GLAMOR PORTRAITS, John Kobal (ed.). 145 photos from 1926-49. Harlow, Gable, Bogart, Bacall; 94 stars in all. Full background on photographers, technical aspects. 160pp. 8⅜ x 11¼. 23352-9

THE ANNOTATED CASEY AT THE BAT: A Collection of Ballads about the Mighty Casey/Third, Revised Edition, Martin Gardner (ed.). Amusing sequels and parodies of one of America's best-loved poems: Casey's Revenge, Why Casey Whiffed, Casey's Sister at the Bat, others. 256pp. 5⅜ x 8½. 28598-7

THE RAVEN AND OTHER FAVORITE POEMS, Edgar Allan Poe. Over 40 of the author's most memorable poems: "The Bells," "Ulalume," "Israfel," "To Helen," "The Conqueror Worm," "Eldorado," "Annabel Lee," many more. Alphabetic lists of titles and first lines. 64pp. 5$\frac{3}{16}$ x 8¼. 26685-0

PERSONAL MEMOIRS OF U. S. GRANT, Ulysses Simpson Grant. Intelligent, deeply moving firsthand account of Civil War campaigns, considered by many the finest military memoirs ever written. Includes letters, historic photographs, maps and more. 528pp. 6⅛ x 9¼. 28587-1

ANCIENT EGYPTIAN MATERIALS AND INDUSTRIES, A. Lucas and J. Harris. Fascinating, comprehensive, thoroughly documented text describes this ancient civilization's vast resources and the processes that incorporated them in daily life, including the use of animal products, building materials, cosmetics, perfumes and incense, fibers, glazed ware, glass and its manufacture, materials used in the mummification process, and much more. 544pp. 6⅛ x 9¼. (Available in U.S. only.) 40446-3

RUSSIAN STORIES/RUSSKIE RASSKAZY: A Dual-Language Book, edited by Gleb Struve. Twelve tales by such masters as Chekhov, Tolstoy, Dostoevsky, Pushkin, others. Excellent word-for-word English translations on facing pages, plus teaching and study aids, Russian/English vocabulary, biographical/critical introductions, more. 416pp. 5⅜ x 8½. 26244-8

PHILADELPHIA THEN AND NOW: 60 Sites Photographed in the Past and Present, Kenneth Finkel and Susan Oyama. Rare photographs of City Hall, Logan Square, Independence Hall, Betsy Ross House, other landmarks juxtaposed with contemporary views. Captures changing face of historic city. Introduction. Captions. 128pp. 8¼ x 11. 25790-8

AIA ARCHITECTURAL GUIDE TO NASSAU AND SUFFOLK COUNTIES, LONG ISLAND, The American Institute of Architects, Long Island Chapter, and the Society for the Preservation of Long Island Antiquities. Comprehensive, well-researched and generously illustrated volume brings to life over three centuries of Long Island's great architectural heritage. More than 240 photographs with authoritative, extensively detailed captions. 176pp. 8¼ x 11. 26946-9

NORTH AMERICAN INDIAN LIFE: Customs and Traditions of 23 Tribes, Elsie Clews Parsons (ed.). 27 fictionalized essays by noted anthropologists examine religion, customs, government, additional facets of life among the Winnebago, Crow, Zuni, Eskimo, other tribes. 480pp. 6⅛ x 9¼. 27377-6

CATALOG OF DOVER BOOKS

FRANK LLOYD WRIGHT'S DANA HOUSE, Donald Hoffmann. Pictorial essay of residential masterpiece with over 160 interior and exterior photos, plans, elevations, sketches and studies. 128pp. 9¼ x 10¾. 29120-0

THE MALE AND FEMALE FIGURE IN MOTION: 60 Classic Photographic Sequences, Eadweard Muybridge. 60 true-action photographs of men and women walking, running, climbing, bending, turning, etc., reproduced from rare 19th-century masterpiece. vi + 121pp. 9 x 12. 24745-7

1001 QUESTIONS ANSWERED ABOUT THE SEASHORE, N. J. Berrill and Jacquelyn Berrill. Queries answered about dolphins, sea snails, sponges, starfish, fishes, shore birds, many others. Covers appearance, breeding, growth, feeding, much more. 305pp. 5¼ x 8¼. 23366-9

ATTRACTING BIRDS TO YOUR YARD, William J. Weber. Easy-to-follow guide offers advice on how to attract the greatest diversity of birds: birdhouses, feeders, water and waterers, much more. 96pp. 5³⁄₁₆ x 8¼. 28927-3

MEDICINAL AND OTHER USES OF NORTH AMERICAN PLANTS: A Historical Survey with Special Reference to the Eastern Indian Tribes, Charlotte Erichsen-Brown. Chronological historical citations document 500 years of usage of plants, trees, shrubs native to eastern Canada, northeastern U.S. Also complete identifying information. 343 illustrations. 544pp. 6½ x 9¼. 25951-X

STORYBOOK MAZES, Dave Phillips. 23 stories and mazes on two-page spreads: Wizard of Oz, Treasure Island, Robin Hood, etc. Solutions. 64pp. 8¼ x 11. 23628-5

AMERICAN NEGRO SONGS: 230 Folk Songs and Spirituals, Religious and Secular, John W. Work. This authoritative study traces the African influences of songs sung and played by black Americans at work, in church, and as entertainment. The author discusses the lyric significance of such songs as "Swing Low, Sweet Chariot," "John Henry," and others and offers the words and music for 230 songs. Bibliography. Index of Song Titles. 272pp. 6½ x 9¼. 40271-1

MOVIE-STAR PORTRAITS OF THE FORTIES, John Kobal (ed.). 163 glamor, studio photos of 106 stars of the 1940s: Rita Hayworth, Ava Gardner, Marlon Brando, Clark Gable, many more. 176pp. 8⅜ x 11¼. 23546-7

BENCHLEY LOST AND FOUND, Robert Benchley. Finest humor from early 30s, about pet peeves, child psychologists, post office and others. Mostly unavailable elsewhere. 73 illustrations by Peter Arno and others. 183pp. 5⅜ x 8½. 22410-4

YEKL and THE IMPORTED BRIDEGROOM AND OTHER STORIES OF YIDDISH NEW YORK, Abraham Cahan. Film Hester Street based on Yekl (1896). Novel, other stories among first about Jewish immigrants on N.Y.'s East Side. 240pp. 5⅜ x 8½. 22427-9

SELECTED POEMS, Walt Whitman. Generous sampling from Leaves of Grass. Twenty-four poems include "I Hear America Singing," "Song of the Open Road," "I Sing the Body Electric," "When Lilacs Last in the Dooryard Bloom'd," "O Captain! My Captain!"–all reprinted from an authoritative edition. Lists of titles and first lines. 128pp. 5³⁄₁₆ x 8¼. 26878-0

CATALOG OF DOVER BOOKS

THE BEST TALES OF HOFFMANN, E. T. A. Hoffmann. 10 of Hoffmann's most important stories: "Nutcracker and the King of Mice," "The Golden Flowerpot," etc. 458pp. 5⅜ x 8½.   21793-0

FROM FETISH TO GOD IN ANCIENT EGYPT, E. A. Wallis Budge. Rich detailed survey of Egyptian conception of "God" and gods, magic, cult of animals, Osiris, more. Also, superb English translations of hymns and legends. 240 illustrations. 545pp. 5⅜ x 8½.   25803-3

FRENCH STORIES/CONTES FRANÇAIS: A Dual-Language Book, Wallace Fowlie. Ten stories by French masters, Voltaire to Camus: "Micromegas" by Voltaire; "The Atheist's Mass" by Balzac; "Minuet" by de Maupassant; "The Guest" by Camus, six more. Excellent English translations on facing pages. Also French-English vocabulary list, exercises, more. 352pp. 5⅜ x 8½.   26443-2

CHICAGO AT THE TURN OF THE CENTURY IN PHOTOGRAPHS: 122 Historic Views from the Collections of the Chicago Historical Society, Larry A. Viskochil. Rare large-format prints offer detailed views of City Hall, State Street, the Loop, Hull House, Union Station, many other landmarks, circa 1904-1913. Introduction. Captions. Maps. 144pp. 9⅜ x 12¼.   24656-6

OLD BROOKLYN IN EARLY PHOTOGRAPHS, 1865-1929, William Lee Younger. Luna Park, Gravesend race track, construction of Grand Army Plaza, moving of Hotel Brighton, etc. 157 previously unpublished photographs. 165pp. 8⅞ x 11¾.   23587-4

THE MYTHS OF THE NORTH AMERICAN INDIANS, Lewis Spence. Rich anthology of the myths and legends of the Algonquins, Iroquois, Pawnees and Sioux, prefaced by an extensive historical and ethnological commentary. 36 illustrations. 480pp. 5⅜ x 8½.   25967-6

AN ENCYCLOPEDIA OF BATTLES: Accounts of Over 1,560 Battles from 1479 B.C. to the Present, David Eggenberger. Essential details of every major battle in recorded history from the first battle of Megiddo in 1479 B.C. to Grenada in 1984. List of Battle Maps. New Appendix covering the years 1967-1984. Index. 99 illustrations. 544pp. 6½ x 9¼.   24913-1

SAILING ALONE AROUND THE WORLD, Captain Joshua Slocum. First man to sail around the world, alone, in small boat. One of great feats of seamanship told in delightful manner. 67 illustrations. 294pp. 5⅜ x 8½.   20326-3

ANARCHISM AND OTHER ESSAYS, Emma Goldman. Powerful, penetrating, prophetic essays on direct action, role of minorities, prison reform, puritan hypocrisy, violence, etc. 271pp. 5⅜ x 8½.   22484-8

MYTHS OF THE HINDUS AND BUDDHISTS, Ananda K. Coomaraswamy and Sister Nivedita. Great stories of the epics; deeds of Krishna, Shiva, taken from puranas, Vedas, folk tales; etc. 32 illustrations. 400pp. 5⅜ x 8½.   21759-0

THE TRAUMA OF BIRTH, Otto Rank. Rank's controversial thesis that anxiety neurosis is caused by profound psychological trauma which occurs at birth. 256pp. 5⅜ x 8½.   27974-X

A THEOLOGICO-POLITICAL TREATISE, Benedict Spinoza. Also contains unfinished Political Treatise. Great classic on religious liberty, theory of government on common consent. R. Elwes translation. Total of 421pp. 5⅜ x 8½.   20249-6

MY BONDAGE AND MY FREEDOM, Frederick Douglass. Born a slave, Douglass became outspoken force in antislavery movement. The best of Douglass' autobiographies. Graphic description of slave life. 464pp. 5⅜ x 8½.   22457-0

FOLLOWING THE EQUATOR: A Journey Around the World, Mark Twain. Fascinating humorous account of 1897 voyage to Hawaii, Australia, India, New Zealand, etc. Ironic, bemused reports on peoples, customs, climate, flora and fauna, politics, much more. 197 illustrations. 720pp. 5⅜ x 8½.   26113-1

THE PEOPLE CALLED SHAKERS, Edward D. Andrews. Definitive study of Shakers: origins, beliefs, practices, dances, social organization, furniture and crafts, etc. 33 illustrations. 351pp. 5⅜ x 8½.   21081-2

THE MYTHS OF GREECE AND ROME, H. A. Guerber. A classic of mythology, generously illustrated, long prized for its simple, graphic, accurate retelling of the principal myths of Greece and Rome, and for its commentary on their origins and significance. With 64 illustrations by Michelangelo, Raphael, Titian, Rubens, Canova, Bernini and others. 480pp. 5⅜ x 8½.   27584-1

PSYCHOLOGY OF MUSIC, Carl E. Seashore. Classic work discusses music as a medium from psychological viewpoint. Clear treatment of physical acoustics, auditory apparatus, sound perception, development of musical skills, nature of musical feeling, host of other topics. 88 figures. 408pp. 5⅜ x 8½.   21851-1

THE PHILOSOPHY OF HISTORY, Georg W. Hegel. Great classic of Western thought develops concept that history is not chance but rational process, the evolution of freedom. 457pp. 5⅜ x 8½.   20112-0

THE BOOK OF TEA, Kakuzo Okakura. Minor classic of the Orient: entertaining, charming explanation, interpretation of traditional Japanese culture in terms of tea ceremony. 94pp. 5⅜ x 8½.   20070-1

LIFE IN ANCIENT EGYPT, Adolf Erman. Fullest, most thorough, detailed older account with much not in more recent books, domestic life, religion, magic, medicine, commerce, much more. Many illustrations reproduce tomb paintings, carvings, hieroglyphs, etc. 597pp. 5⅜ x 8½.   22632-8

SUNDIALS, Their Theory and Construction, Albert Waugh. Far and away the best, most thorough coverage of ideas, mathematics concerned, types, construction, adjusting anywhere. Simple, nontechnical treatment allows even children to build several of these dials. Over 100 illustrations. 230pp. 5⅜ x 8½.   22947-5

THEORETICAL HYDRODYNAMICS, L. M. Milne-Thomson. Classic exposition of the mathematical theory of fluid motion, applicable to both hydrodynamics and aerodynamics. Over 600 exercises. 768pp. 6⅛ x 9¼.   68970-0

SONGS OF EXPERIENCE: Facsimile Reproduction with 26 Plates in Full Color, William Blake. 26 full-color plates from a rare 1826 edition. Includes "The Tyger," "London," "Holy Thursday," and other poems. Printed text of poems. 48pp. 5¼ x 7.   24636-1

OLD-TIME VIGNETTES IN FULL COLOR, Carol Belanger Grafton (ed.). Over 390 charming, often sentimental illustrations, selected from archives of Victorian graphics–pretty women posing, children playing, food, flowers, kittens and puppies, smiling cherubs, birds and butterflies, much more. All copyright-free. 48pp. 9¼ x 12¼.   27269-9

PERSPECTIVE FOR ARTISTS, Rex Vicat Cole. Depth, perspective of sky and sea, shadows, much more, not usually covered. 391 diagrams, 81 reproductions of drawings and paintings. 279pp. 5⅜ x 8½.   22487-2

DRAWING THE LIVING FIGURE, Joseph Sheppard. Innovative approach to artistic anatomy focuses on specifics of surface anatomy, rather than muscles and bones. Over 170 drawings of live models in front, back and side views, and in widely varying poses. Accompanying diagrams. 177 illustrations. Introduction. Index. 144pp. 8⅜ x11¼.   26723-7

GOTHIC AND OLD ENGLISH ALPHABETS: 100 Complete Fonts, Dan X. Solo. Add power, elegance to posters, signs, other graphics with 100 stunning copyright-free alphabets: Blackstone, Dolbey, Germania, 97 more—including many lower-case, numerals, punctuation marks. 104pp. 8⅛ x 11.   24695-7

HOW TO DO BEADWORK, Mary White. Fundamental book on craft from simple projects to five-bead chains and woven works. 106 illustrations. 142pp. 5⅜ x 8.
                                                                            20697-1

THE BOOK OF WOOD CARVING, Charles Marshall Sayers. Finest book for beginners discusses fundamentals and offers 34 designs. "Absolutely first rate . . . well thought out and well executed."—E. J. Tangerman. 118pp. 7¾ x 10⅝.   23654-4

ILLUSTRATED CATALOG OF CIVIL WAR MILITARY GOODS: Union Army Weapons, Insignia, Uniform Accessories, and Other Equipment, Schuyler, Hartley, and Graham. Rare, profusely illustrated 1846 catalog includes Union Army uniform and dress regulations, arms and ammunition, coats, insignia, flags, swords, rifles, etc. 226 illustrations. 160pp. 9 x 12.   24939-5

WOMEN'S FASHIONS OF THE EARLY 1900s: An Unabridged Republication of "New York Fashions, 1909," National Cloak & Suit Co. Rare catalog of mail-order fashions documents women's and children's clothing styles shortly after the turn of the century. Captions offer full descriptions, prices. Invaluable resource for fashion, costume historians. Approximately 725 illustrations. 128pp. 8⅜ x 11¼.   27276-1

THE 1912 AND 1915 GUSTAV STICKLEY FURNITURE CATALOGS, Gustav Stickley. With over 200 detailed illustrations and descriptions, these two catalogs are essential reading and reference materials and identification guides for Stickley furniture. Captions cite materials, dimensions and prices. 112pp. 6½ x 9¼.   26676-1

EARLY AMERICAN LOCOMOTIVES, John H. White, Jr. Finest locomotive engravings from early 19th century: historical (1804–74), main-line (after 1870), special, foreign, etc. 147 plates. 142pp. 11⅜ x 8¼.   22772-3

THE TALL SHIPS OF TODAY IN PHOTOGRAPHS, Frank O. Braynard. Lavishly illustrated tribute to nearly 100 majestic contemporary sailing vessels: Amerigo Vespucci, Clearwater, Constitution, Eagle, Mayflower, Sea Cloud, Victory, many more. Authoritative captions provide statistics, background on each ship. 190 black-and-white photographs and illustrations. Introduction. 128pp. 8⅞ x 11¾.
                                                                            27163-3

LITTLE BOOK OF EARLY AMERICAN CRAFTS AND TRADES, Peter Stockham (ed.). 1807 children's book explains crafts and trades: baker, hatter, cooper, potter, and many others. 23 copperplate illustrations. 140pp. 4⅝ x 6.   23336-7

VICTORIAN FASHIONS AND COSTUMES FROM HARPER'S BAZAR, 1867–1898, Stella Blum (ed.). Day costumes, evening wear, sports clothes, shoes, hats, other accessories in over 1,000 detailed engravings. 320pp. 9⅜ x 12¼. 22990-4

GUSTAV STICKLEY, THE CRAFTSMAN, Mary Ann Smith. Superb study surveys broad scope of Stickley's achievement, especially in architecture. Design philosophy, rise and fall of the Craftsman empire, descriptions and floor plans for many Craftsman houses, more. 86 black-and-white halftones. 31 line illustrations. Introduction 208pp. 6½ x 9¼.   27210-9

THE LONG ISLAND RAIL ROAD IN EARLY PHOTOGRAPHS, Ron Ziel. Over 220 rare photos, informative text document origin (1844) and development of rail service on Long Island. Vintage views of early trains, locomotives, stations, passengers, crews, much more. Captions. 8⅞ x 11¾.   26301-0

VOYAGE OF THE LIBERDADE, Joshua Slocum. Great 19th-century mariner's thrilling, first-hand account of the wreck of his ship off South America, the 35-foot boat he built from the wreckage, and its remarkable voyage home. 128pp. 5⅜ x 8½.
40022-0

TEN BOOKS ON ARCHITECTURE, Vitruvius. The most important book ever written on architecture. Early Roman aesthetics, technology, classical orders, site selection, all other aspects. Morgan translation. 331pp. 5⅜ x 8½.   20645-9

THE HUMAN FIGURE IN MOTION, Eadweard Muybridge. More than 4,500 stopped-action photos, in action series, showing undraped men, women, children jumping, lying down, throwing, sitting, wrestling, carrying, etc. 390pp. 7⅞ x 10⅝.
20204-6 Clothbd.

TREES OF THE EASTERN AND CENTRAL UNITED STATES AND CANADA, William M. Harlow. Best one-volume guide to 140 trees. Full descriptions, woodlore, range, etc. Over 600 illustrations. Handy size. 288pp. 4½ x 6⅜.   20395-6

SONGS OF WESTERN BIRDS, Dr. Donald J. Borror. Complete song and call repertoire of 60 western species, including flycatchers, juncoes, cactus wrens, many more–includes fully illustrated booklet.   Cassette and manual 99913-0

GROWING AND USING HERBS AND SPICES, Milo Miloradovich. Versatile handbook provides all the information needed for cultivation and use of all the herbs and spices available in North America. 4 illustrations. Index. Glossary. 236pp. 5⅜ x 8½.
25058-X

BIG BOOK OF MAZES AND LABYRINTHS, Walter Shepherd. 50 mazes and labyrinths in all–classical, solid, ripple, and more–in one great volume. Perfect inexpensive puzzler for clever youngsters. Full solutions. 112pp. 8⅛ x 11.   22951-3

PIANO TUNING, J. Cree Fischer. Clearest, best book for beginner, amateur. Simple repairs, raising dropped notes, tuning by easy method of flattened fifths. No previous skills needed. 4 illustrations. 201pp. 5⅜ x 8½. 23267-0

HINTS TO SINGERS, Lillian Nordica. Selecting the right teacher, developing confidence, overcoming stage fright, and many other important skills receive thoughtful discussion in this indispensible guide, written by a world-famous diva of four decades' experience. 96pp. 5⅜ x 8½. 40094-8

THE COMPLETE NONSENSE OF EDWARD LEAR, Edward Lear. All nonsense limericks, zany alphabets, Owl and Pussycat, songs, nonsense botany, etc., illustrated by Lear. Total of 320pp. 5⅜ x 8½. (Available in U.S. only.) 20167-8

VICTORIAN PARLOUR POETRY: An Annotated Anthology, Michael R. Turner. 117 gems by Longfellow, Tennyson, Browning, many lesser-known poets. "The Village Blacksmith," "Curfew Must Not Ring Tonight," "Only a Baby Small," dozens more, often difficult to find elsewhere. Index of poets, titles, first lines. xxiii + 325pp. 5⅝ x 8¼. 27044-0

DUBLINERS, James Joyce. Fifteen stories offer vivid, tightly focused observations of the lives of Dublin's poorer classes. At least one, "The Dead," is considered a masterpiece. Reprinted complete and unabridged from standard edition. 160pp. 5$\frac{3}{16}$ x 8¼. 26870-5

GREAT WEIRD TALES: 14 Stories by Lovecraft, Blackwood, Machen and Others, S. T. Joshi (ed.). 14 spellbinding tales, including "The Sin Eater," by Fiona McLeod, "The Eye Above the Mantel," by Frank Belknap Long, as well as renowned works by R. H. Barlow, Lord Dunsany, Arthur Machen, W. C. Morrow and eight other masters of the genre. 256pp. 5⅜ x 8½. (Available in U.S. only.) 40436-6

THE BOOK OF THE SACRED MAGIC OF ABRAMELIN THE MAGE, translated by S. MacGregor Mathers. Medieval manuscript of ceremonial magic. Basic document in Aleister Crowley, Golden Dawn groups. 268pp. 5⅜ x 8½. 23211-5

NEW RUSSIAN-ENGLISH AND ENGLISH-RUSSIAN DICTIONARY, M. A. O'Brien. This is a remarkably handy Russian dictionary, containing a surprising amount of information, including over 70,000 entries. 366pp. 4½ x 6⅛. 20208-9

HISTORIC HOMES OF THE AMERICAN PRESIDENTS, Second, Revised Edition, Irvin Haas. A traveler's guide to American Presidential homes, most open to the public, depicting and describing homes occupied by every American President from George Washington to George Bush. With visiting hours, admission charges, travel routes. 175 photographs. Index. 160pp. 8¼ x 11. 26751-2

NEW YORK IN THE FORTIES, Andreas Feininger. 162 brilliant photographs by the well-known photographer, formerly with *Life* magazine. Commuters, shoppers, Times Square at night, much else from city at its peak. Captions by John von Hartz. 181pp. 9¼ x 10¾. 23585-8

INDIAN SIGN LANGUAGE, William Tomkins. Over 525 signs developed by Sioux and other tribes. Written instructions and diagrams. Also 290 pictographs. 111pp. 6⅛ x 9¼. 22029-X

ANATOMY: A Complete Guide for Artists, Joseph Sheppard. A master of figure drawing shows artists how to render human anatomy convincingly. Over 460 illustrations. 224pp. 8⅜ x 11¼. 27279-6

MEDIEVAL CALLIGRAPHY: Its History and Technique, Marc Drogin. Spirited history, comprehensive instruction manual covers 13 styles (ca. 4th century through 15th). Excellent photographs; directions for duplicating medieval techniques with modern tools. 224pp. 8⅜ x 11¼. 26142-5

DRIED FLOWERS: How to Prepare Them, Sarah Whitlock and Martha Rankin. Complete instructions on how to use silica gel, meal and borax, perlite aggregate, sand and borax, glycerine and water to create attractive permanent flower arrangements. 12 illustrations. 32pp. 5⅜ x 8½. 21802-3

EASY-TO-MAKE BIRD FEEDERS FOR WOODWORKERS, Scott D. Campbell. Detailed, simple-to-use guide for designing, constructing, caring for and using feeders. Text, illustrations for 12 classic and contemporary designs. 96pp. 5⅜ x 8½. 25847-5

SCOTTISH WONDER TALES FROM MYTH AND LEGEND, Donald A. Mackenzie. 16 lively tales tell of giants rumbling down mountainsides, of a magic wand that turns stone pillars into warriors, of gods and goddesses, evil hags, powerful forces and more. 240pp. 5⅜ x 8½. 29677-6

THE HISTORY OF UNDERCLOTHES, C. Willett Cunnington and Phyllis Cunnington. Fascinating, well-documented survey covering six centuries of English undergarments, enhanced with over 100 illustrations: 12th-century laced-up bodice, footed long drawers (1795), 19th-century bustles, 19th-century corsets for men, Victorian "bust improvers," much more. 272pp. 5⅜ x 8¼. 27124-2

ARTS AND CRAFTS FURNITURE: The Complete Brooks Catalog of 1912, Brooks Manufacturing Co. Photos and detailed descriptions of more than 150 now very collectible furniture designs from the Arts and Crafts movement depict davenports, settees, buffets, desks, tables, chairs, bedsteads, dressers and more, all built of solid, quarter-sawed oak. Invaluable for students and enthusiasts of antiques, Americana and the decorative arts. 80pp. 6½ x 9¼. 27471-3

WILBUR AND ORVILLE: A Biography of the Wright Brothers, Fred Howard. Definitive, crisply written study tells the full story of the brothers' lives and work. A vividly written biography, unparalleled in scope and color, that also captures the spirit of an extraordinary era. 560pp. 6⅛ x 9¼. 40297-5

THE ARTS OF THE SAILOR: Knotting, Splicing and Ropework, Hervey Garrett Smith. Indispensable shipboard reference covers tools, basic knots and useful hitches; handsewing and canvas work, more. Over 100 illustrations. Delightful reading for sea lovers. 256pp. 5⅜ x 8½. 26440-8

FRANK LLOYD WRIGHT'S FALLINGWATER: The House and Its History, Second, Revised Edition, Donald Hoffmann. A total revision–both in text and illustrations–of the standard document on Fallingwater, the boldest, most personal architectural statement of Wright's mature years, updated with valuable new material from the recently opened Frank Lloyd Wright Archives. "Fascinating"–*The New York Times*. 116 illustrations. 128pp. 9¼ x 10¾. 27430-6

PHOTOGRAPHIC SKETCHBOOK OF THE CIVIL WAR, Alexander Gardner. 100 photos taken on field during the Civil War. Famous shots of Manassas Harper's Ferry, Lincoln, Richmond, slave pens, etc. 244pp. 10⅝ x 8¼.   22731-6

FIVE ACRES AND INDEPENDENCE, Maurice G. Kains. Great back-to-the-land classic explains basics of self-sufficient farming. The one book to get. 95 illustrations. 397pp. 5⅜ x 8½.   20974-1

SONGS OF EASTERN BIRDS, Dr. Donald J. Borror. Songs and calls of 60 species most common to eastern U.S.: warblers, woodpeckers, flycatchers, thrushes, larks, many more in high-quality recording.   Cassette and manual 99912-2

A MODERN HERBAL, Margaret Grieve. Much the fullest, most exact, most useful compilation of herbal material. Gigantic alphabetical encyclopedia, from aconite to zedoary, gives botanical information, medical properties, folklore, economic uses, much else. Indispensable to serious reader. 161 illustrations. 888pp. 6½ x 9¼. 2-vol. set. (Available in U.S. only.)   Vol. I: 22798-7
Vol. II: 22799-5

HIDDEN TREASURE MAZE BOOK, Dave Phillips. Solve 34 challenging mazes accompanied by heroic tales of adventure. Evil dragons, people-eating plants, blood-thirsty giants, many more dangerous adversaries lurk at every twist and turn. 34 mazes, stories, solutions. 48pp. 8¼ x 11.   24566-7

LETTERS OF W. A. MOZART, Wolfgang A. Mozart. Remarkable letters show bawdy wit, humor, imagination, musical insights, contemporary musical world; includes some letters from Leopold Mozart. 276pp. 5⅜ x 8½.   22859-2

BASIC PRINCIPLES OF CLASSICAL BALLET, Agrippina Vaganova. Great Russian theoretician, teacher explains methods for teaching classical ballet. 118 illustrations. 175pp. 5⅜ x 8½.   22036-2

THE JUMPING FROG, Mark Twain. Revenge edition. The original story of The Celebrated Jumping Frog of Calaveras County, a hapless French translation, and Twain's hilarious "retranslation" from the French. 12 illustrations. 66pp. 5⅜ x 8½.
22686-7

BEST REMEMBERED POEMS, Martin Gardner (ed.). The 126 poems in this superb collection of 19th- and 20th-century British and American verse range from Shelley's "To a Skylark" to the impassioned "Renascence" of Edna St. Vincent Millay and to Edward Lear's whimsical "The Owl and the Pussycat." 224pp. 5⅜ x 8½.
27165-X

COMPLETE SONNETS, William Shakespeare. Over 150 exquisite poems deal with love, friendship, the tyranny of time, beauty's evanescence, death and other themes in language of remarkable power, precision and beauty. Glossary of archaic terms. 80pp. 5⁵⁄₁₆ x 8¼.   26686-9

THE BATTLES THAT CHANGED HISTORY, Fletcher Pratt. Eminent historian profiles 16 crucial conflicts, ancient to modern, that changed the course of civilization. 352pp. 5⅜ x 8½.   41129-X

THE WIT AND HUMOR OF OSCAR WILDE, Alvin Redman (ed.). More than 1,000 ripostes, paradoxes, wisecracks: Work is the curse of the drinking classes; I can resist everything except temptation; etc. 258pp. 5⅜ x 8½. 20602-5

SHAKESPEARE LEXICON AND QUOTATION DICTIONARY, Alexander Schmidt. Full definitions, locations, shades of meaning in every word in plays and poems. More than 50,000 exact quotations. 1,485pp. 6½ x 9¼. 2-vol. set.
Vol. 1: 22726-X
Vol. 2: 22727-8

SELECTED POEMS, Emily Dickinson. Over 100 best-known, best-loved poems by one of America's foremost poets, reprinted from authoritative early editions. No comparable edition at this price. Index of first lines. 64pp. 5³⁄₁₆ x 8¼. 26466-1

THE INSIDIOUS DR. FU-MANCHU, Sax Rohmer. The first of the popular mystery series introduces a pair of English detectives to their archnemesis, the diabolical Dr. Fu-Manchu. Flavorful atmosphere, fast-paced action, and colorful characters enliven this classic of the genre. 208pp. 5³⁄₁₆ x 8¼. 29898-1

THE MALLEUS MALEFICARUM OF KRAMER AND SPRENGER, translated by Montague Summers. Full text of most important witchhunter's "bible," used by both Catholics and Protestants. 278pp. 6⅝ x 10. 22802-9

SPANISH STORIES/CUENTOS ESPAÑOLES: A Dual-Language Book, Angel Flores (ed.). Unique format offers 13 great stories in Spanish by Cervantes, Borges, others. Faithful English translations on facing pages. 352pp. 5⅜ x 8½. 25399-6

GARDEN CITY, LONG ISLAND, IN EARLY PHOTOGRAPHS, 1869–1919, Mildred H. Smith. Handsome treasury of 118 vintage pictures, accompanied by carefully researched captions, document the Garden City Hotel fire (1899), the Vanderbilt Cup Race (1908), the first airmail flight departing from the Nassau Boulevard Aerodrome (1911), and much more. 96pp. 8⅞ x 11¾. 40669-5

OLD QUEENS, N.Y., IN EARLY PHOTOGRAPHS, Vincent F. Seyfried and William Asadorian. Over 160 rare photographs of Maspeth, Jamaica, Jackson Heights, and other areas. Vintage views of DeWitt Clinton mansion, 1939 World's Fair and more. Captions. 192pp. 8⅞ x 11. 26358-4

CAPTURED BY THE INDIANS: 15 Firsthand Accounts, 1750-1870, Frederick Drimmer. Astounding true historical accounts of grisly torture, bloody conflicts, relentless pursuits, miraculous escapes and more, by people who lived to tell the tale. 384pp. 5⅜ x 8½. 24901-8

THE WORLD'S GREAT SPEECHES (Fourth Enlarged Edition), Lewis Copeland, Lawrence W. Lamm, and Stephen J. McKenna. Nearly 300 speeches provide public speakers with a wealth of updated quotes and inspiration–from Pericles' funeral oration and William Jennings Bryan's "Cross of Gold Speech" to Malcolm X's powerful words on the Black Revolution and Earl of Spenser's tribute to his sister, Diana, Princess of Wales. 944pp. 5⅜ x 8⅜. 40903-1

THE BOOK OF THE SWORD, Sir Richard F. Burton. Great Victorian scholar/adventurer's eloquent, erudite history of the "queen of weapons"–from prehistory to early Roman Empire. Evolution and development of early swords, variations (sabre, broadsword, cutlass, scimitar, etc.), much more. 336pp. 6⅛ x 9¼. 25434-8

AUTOBIOGRAPHY: The Story of My Experiments with Truth, Mohandas K. Gandhi. Boyhood, legal studies, purification, the growth of the Satyagraha (nonviolent protest) movement. Critical, inspiring work of the man responsible for the freedom of India. 480pp. 5⅜ x 8½. (Available in U.S. only.) 24593-4

CELTIC MYTHS AND LEGENDS, T. W. Rolleston. Masterful retelling of Irish and Welsh stories and tales. Cuchulain, King Arthur, Deirdre, the Grail, many more. First paperback edition. 58 full-page illustrations. 512pp. 5⅜ x 8½. 26507-2

THE PRINCIPLES OF PSYCHOLOGY, William James. Famous long course complete, unabridged. Stream of thought, time perception, memory, experimental methods; great work decades ahead of its time. 94 figures. 1,391pp. 5⅜ x 8½. 2-vol. set. Vol. I: 20381-6 Vol. II: 20382-4

THE WORLD AS WILL AND REPRESENTATION, Arthur Schopenhauer. Definitive English translation of Schopenhauer's life work, correcting more than 1,000 errors, omissions in earlier translations. Translated by E. F. J. Payne. Total of 1,269pp. 5⅜ x 8½. 2-vol. set. Vol. 1: 21761-2 Vol. 2: 21762-0

MAGIC AND MYSTERY IN TIBET, Madame Alexandra David-Neel. Experiences among lamas, magicians, sages, sorcerers, Bonpa wizards. A true psychic discovery. 32 illustrations. 321pp. 5⅜ x 8½. (Available in U.S. only.) 22682-4

THE EGYPTIAN BOOK OF THE DEAD, E. A. Wallis Budge. Complete reproduction of Ani's papyrus, finest ever found. Full hieroglyphic text, interlinear transliteration, word-for-word translation, smooth translation. 533pp. 6½ x 9¼. 21866-X

MATHEMATICS FOR THE NONMATHEMATICIAN, Morris Kline. Detailed, college-level treatment of mathematics in cultural and historical context, with numerous exercises. Recommended Reading Lists. Tables. Numerous figures. 641pp. 5⅜ x 8½. 24823-2

PROBABILISTIC METHODS IN THE THEORY OF STRUCTURES, Isaac Elishakoff. Well-written introduction covers the elements of the theory of probability from two or more random variables, the reliability of such multivariable structures, the theory of random function, Monte Carlo methods of treating problems incapable of exact solution, and more. Examples. 502pp. 5⅜ x 8½. 40691-1

THE RIME OF THE ANCIENT MARINER, Gustave Doré, S. T. Coleridge. Doré's finest work; 34 plates capture moods, subtleties of poem. Flawless full-size reproductions printed on facing pages with authoritative text of poem. "Beautiful. Simply beautiful."–*Publisher's Weekly*. 77pp. 9¼ x 12. 22305-1

NORTH AMERICAN INDIAN DESIGNS FOR ARTISTS AND CRAFTSPEOPLE, Eva Wilson. Over 360 authentic copyright-free designs adapted from Navajo blankets, Hopi pottery, Sioux buffalo hides, more. Geometrics, symbolic figures, plant and animal motifs, etc. 128pp. 8⅜ x 11. (Not for sale in the United Kingdom.) 25341-4

SCULPTURE: Principles and Practice, Louis Slobodkin. Step-by-step approach to clay, plaster, metals, stone; classical and modern. 253 drawings, photos. 255pp. 8⅛ x 11. 22960-2

THE INFLUENCE OF SEA POWER UPON HISTORY, 1660–1783, A. T. Mahan. Influential classic of naval history and tactics still used as text in war colleges. First paperback edition. 4 maps. 24 battle plans. 640pp. 5⅜ x 8½. 25509-3

CATALOG OF DOVER BOOKS

THE STORY OF THE TITANIC AS TOLD BY ITS SURVIVORS, Jack Winocour (ed.). What it was really like. Panic, despair, shocking inefficiency, and a little hero-ism. More thrilling than any fictional account. 26 illustrations. 320pp. 5⅜ x 8½.
20610-6

FAIRY AND FOLK TALES OF THE IRISH PEASANTRY, William Butler Yeats (ed.). Treasury of 64 tales from the twilight world of Celtic myth and legend: "The Soul Cages," "The Kildare Pooka," "King O'Toole and his Goose," many more. Introduction and Notes by W. B. Yeats. 352pp. 5⅜ x 8½.
26941-8

BUDDHIST MAHAYANA TEXTS, E. B. Cowell and others (eds.). Superb, accu-rate translations of basic documents in Mahayana Buddhism, highly important in his-tory of religions. The Buddha-karita of Asvaghosha, Larger Sukhavativyuha, more. 448pp. 5⅜ x 8½.
25552-2

ONE TWO THREE . . . INFINITY: Facts and Speculations of Science, George Gamow. Great physicist's fascinating, readable overview of contemporary science: number theory, relativity, fourth dimension, entropy, genes, atomic structure, much more. 128 illustrations. Index. 352pp. 5⅜ x 8½.
25664-2

EXPERIMENTATION AND MEASUREMENT, W. J. Youden. Introductory man-ual explains laws of measurement in simple terms and offers tips for achieving accu-racy and minimizing errors. Mathematics of measurement, use of instruments, exper-imenting with machines. 1994 edition. Foreword. Preface. Introduction. Epilogue. Selected Readings. Glossary. Index. Tables and figures. 128pp. 5⅜ x 8½.   40451-X

DALÍ ON MODERN ART: The Cuckolds of Antiquated Modern Art, Salvador Dalí. Influential painter skewers modern art and its practitioners. Outrageous evaluations of Picasso, Cézanne, Turner, more. 15 renderings of paintings discussed. 44 calligraphic decorations by Dalí. 96pp. 5⅜ x 8½. (Available in U.S. only.)   29220-7

ANTIQUE PLAYING CARDS: A Pictorial History, Henry René D'Allemagne. Over 900 elaborate, decorative images from rare playing cards (14th–20th centuries): Bacchus, death, dancing dogs, hunting scenes, royal coats of arms, players cheating, much more. 96pp. 9¼ x 12¼.   29265-7

MAKING FURNITURE MASTERPIECES: 30 Projects with Measured Drawings, Franklin H. Gottshall. Step-by-step instructions, illustrations for constructing hand-some, useful pieces, among them a Sheraton desk, Chippendale chair, Spanish desk, Queen Anne table and a William and Mary dressing mirror. 224pp. 8⅛ x 11¼.
29338-6

THE FOSSIL BOOK: A Record of Prehistoric Life, Patricia V. Rich et al. Profusely illustrated definitive guide covers everything from single-celled organisms and dinosaurs to birds and mammals and the interplay between climate and man. Over 1,500 illustrations. 760pp. 7½ x 10⅛.   29371-8

Paperbound unless otherwise indicated. Available at your book dealer, online at **www.doverpublications.com**, or by writing to Dept. GI, Dover Publications, Inc., 31 East 2nd Street, Mineola, NY 11501. For current price information or for free catalogues (please indicate field of interest), write to Dover Publications or log on to **www.doverpublications.com** and see every Dover book in print. Dover publishes more than 500 books each year on science, elementary and advanced mathematics, biology, music, art, literary history, social sciences, and other areas.